How to Research

FOURTH EDITION

How to Research

FOURTH EDITION

Loraine Blaxter, Christina Hughes and Malcolm Tight

Open University Press

Open University Press
McGraw-Hill Education
McGraw-Hill House
Shoppenhangers Road
Maidenhead
Berkshire
England
SL6 2QL

email: enquiries@openup.co.uk
world wide web: www.openup.co.uk

and Two Penn Plaza, New York, NY 10121-2289, USA

First edition published 2006
First published in this fourth edition 2010

Copyright © Loraine Blaxter, Christina Hughes and Malcolm Tight
2010

A catalogue record of this book is available from the British Library

ISBN-13: 978 0 335 23867 5 (pbk)   978 0 335 23868 2 (hbk)
ISBN-10: 0 335 23867 X (pbk)   0 335 23868 8 (hbk)

Library of Congress Cataloging-in-Publication Data
CIP data applied for

Typeset by RefineCatch Limited, Bungay, Suffolk
Printed in the UK by Bell and Bain Ltd, Glasgow

Fictitious names of companies, products, people, characters and/or
data that may be used herein (in case studies or in examples) are not
intended to represent any real individual, company, product or event.

Mixed Sources
Product group from well-managed
forests and other controlled sources
www.fsc.org Cert no. TT-COC-002769
© 1996 Forest Stewardship Council

The McGraw·Hill Companies

Contents

List of boxes

1

All at sea but learning to swim

*Introduction • The first time researcher • Getting a flavour of possibilities
• Why am I doing this research? • Will I have anything new to say? • In
whose interests is this research? • At last, writing up • How to use this
book • What's different about this edition? • Summary • Exercises •
Further reading*

Introduction

This book focuses on the processes of research as well as research methods. It
aims to demystify research, recognizing the everyday skills and techniques
involved. It encourages you to think of research as a kind of spiral through
which you revisit the various stages of the process, but always with different
and developed insights. The book is multidisciplinary in scope. It is designed
to be suitable for those undertaking research in the social sciences, as well as in
related subjects such as education, business studies and health and social care.

Are you currently feeling *all at sea* and not knowing in which direction to
turn with your research project? Or is your research *going swimmingly* and you
are *steaming ahead* sure in the knowledge that you are doing a good job? Perhaps you are fluctuating between the ends of this spectrum. You have a sense
of *drowning* at one moment in the size of the task ahead, and then *floating*
serenely along at the next moment content with the work you have produced
so far. Maybe you are *treading water* and feeling your work has come to a stand-
still. Or perhaps you are at the stage of *dipping your feet* into icy cold waters for a
short *paddle* in order to test the water before you *take the plunge* and begin your

research. Or, maybe, if you are engaged in a piece of small-group research, you have yet to *synchronize your swimming*.

As a new, or not so new, researcher, such feelings are common. Indeed, we could say that they go with the territory of research. There is excitement at the prospect of discovering new insights into a topic of interest. There is a sense of confusion over what you are meant to be doing and when. You are aware that you have the ability to build on your current skills and aptitudes to complete the task ahead successfully. But this can be undermined by a hint of fear that maybe you are not really up to the mark of undertaking what is, after all, a major form of independent study.

Surviving and feeling that you are thriving across the period of your study is, therefore, an important goal, as this will enable you to maintain motivation when things get tough, and to develop a sense of competence and expertise in the conduct of your work. This book is about the practice and experience of doing research, and is designed to ensure that you survive and thrive. It is aimed at those, particularly the less experienced, who are involved in small-scale research projects. It is intended to be useful to both those doing research, whether for academic credit or not, and those responsible for teaching, supervising or managing new researchers.

However, to survive and thrive does not simply mean staying in *familiar seas*. As a person involved in learning, surviving as a research student is about accumulating knowledge and extending skills. Thriving as a research student can be helped by anticipating the sorts of skills, the different forms of knowledge and the resources that you will need. This involves looking ahead and doing some preparation. It means that you need to simulate *stormy seas* in order to begin to develop the *swimming* skills that you need to thrive.

With this in mind, this opening chapter is designed to encourage you to look ahead in several senses. Through a series of case studies, this chapter takes you through key aspects of the research process. These range from getting started to writing up. In addition, this chapter introduces you to a number of common dilemmas and concerns facing research students. These include maintaining motivation, understanding the meanings of originality, and exploring issues of truth, power and values. Overall, this chapter is designed to encourage you to gain a sense of the route you are taking, because if you don't know the destination, how are you going to get there? Happy swimming!

The chapter is organized into the following sections:

- **The first time researcher.** Undertaking an audit of the skills, knowledge and resources you already possess, and developing a Personal Development Plan for the successful completion of your research.
- **Getting a flavour of possibilities.** Introducing some elements of research design and developing understandings of the varied nature of research.
- **Why am I doing this research?** Exploring your motivations for undertaking research.
- **Will I have anything new to say?** Debunking the idea of originality.

- **In whose interests is this research?** Issues of truth, power and values and the context of your research.
- **At last, writing up.** Planning ahead means ensuring you know the rules, regulations and audiences for your research.
- **How to use this book.** What you will find in it, and how to make your way through it.
- **What is different about this edition?** What has changed and what has been added since the third edition.

The chapter ends with a summary.

The first time researcher

John has an appointment to see his dissertation supervisor. He is worried. He has no idea what topic he might research or even a clear idea about the different kinds of methodological techniques available to him. His assumption is that it is only great men, who have far more superior skills and knowledge than he might ever possess, who actually do 'real' research. But his intellectual anxieties are only one of his concerns. He also has doubts about whether he will be organized enough to complete a piece of work that he will have to design and execute himself. To date, his only experiences of education have been on courses with set tasks and readings. This dissertation is really going to test him. 'Am I up to it?' he thinks, as he knocks on the supervisor's door.

In our experience, it doesn't really matter what level you are studying at, doing research usually provokes a series of anxieties. You might be asked to undertake research for an 'A' level module or as part of your undergraduate degree. You may be writing a dissertation for an MA or a PhD thesis. At the outset you may, therefore, be feeling all at sea, wondering what is expected and how you are going to cope. Indeed, it is often the case that these anxieties and worries occur *despite* other positive experiences of research. For example, you might be embarking on your undergraduate dissertation having already written methodological essays for a research methods module. Or you might be beginning your PhD having recently completed a 15,000 word MA dissertation. Whatever your situation, as a first time researcher or a not-quite-first-time researcher, you are likely to experience various concerns and worries. In such a situation it is easy to forget that by the time you are required to undertake first-hand research you already have a wide knowledge and sets of skills that have been developed to enable you to be successful.

Our intention in this book is to give you the skills and confidence that will take you successfully from the initial idea to a completed piece of research. With this in mind, there is no better time to start than now. Whatever your level, you will be beginning this particular research project with a host of skills, resources and knowledge derived from your education and life experiences to date. These skills will be technical (e.g. use of information retrieval systems such as libraries and the internet) and social (e.g. working collaboratively with fellow students, getting on with others). Resources will include social resources (e.g. family, friends, teachers), emotional resources (e.g. resilience) and material resources (e.g. time and money). And of course, you will have knowledge about your subject area (e.g. sociology, psychology, education, business studies, health, etc.).

One way of gaining a sense of the skills, resources and knowledge you already possess is to undertake an audit. You can do this by completing Exercise 1.1 at the end of this chapter. Exercise 1.1 should provide you with the baseline you are working from. However, there is no doubt that undertaking first-hand research will require you – and indeed will enable you – to increase your skill and knowledge levels, to work more independently and to have a greater sense of self-direction.

The gap between the level you are working at now and the level required for successful completion of your research project represents your personal learning needs. In order to produce a development plan that will enable you to meet these learning needs, you will need to assess the adequacy of your current skills, resources and knowledge for the task you are now facing. Do you, for example, need to have a higher level of skill in searching for existing research relating to your topic using, for example, internet search engines or specialist journal sources? Or are there specific knowledge areas relating to your topic that you need to be more familiar with? For example, if your research is concerned with the role of professionalism in nursing, are you required to have an understanding of the changing nature of professionalism in a range of employment fields? Moreover, do you need to have a better appreciation of the financial resources you will need for your research?

Some of the resources, skills and knowledge you possess will, though, be more than adequate for the task ahead. Exercise 1.2 is designed to help you work out where the gaps are, and to identify your specific learning needs. Exercise 1.2 should highlight four issues:

1 That you already possess some of the main elements that will contribute to your successfully completing your dissertation or project. When things get tough, don't forget this.
2 That, in terms of skills and knowledge, you have some learning needs that need addressing in either the short or the long term.
3 That you have resource needs that need addressing.
4 That there are some areas of skill, knowledge and resources that you are unsure or unclear about and, in consequence, need to explore further.

In terms of your learning needs, it is at this point that you should consider creating a Personal Development Plan. Such a plan can be relatively simple in that it records three aspects which will be central for the successful completion of your project: your identified learning needs; how they are going to be met; and the planned timescale for meeting these. An example is provided in Box 1.1.

Box 1.1 An example of a Personal Development Plan

Identified learning need	How will I achieve this need?	What is my timescale?
Settle on a topic	Talk to friends and other students Work through Chapter 2 of this book	In the next week
Review existing research on my topic	Conduct a range of literature reviews	In the next 6 weeks
Questionnaire design	Consult textbooks and supervisor	In the next 2 weeks
	Look at examples in other research	In the next 3 weeks
Qualitative data analysis	Attend a course	In the next 4 months

---

For resource needs and areas where you are unclear or do not yet have sufficient information (points 3 and 4 in the list on p. 4), it is worthwhile identifying the sources of help that will address these. Box 1.2 provides a list of some of the potential ones that we have identified.

Box 1.2 Some potential sources of help

- Your supervisor
- Your fellow students
- The departmental secretary
- University or college services (counselling, information technology, careers, library)
- Specialist departments (e.g. computing, English language support)
- Student union
- Your manager
- Other work colleagues, particularly those who have undertaken similar research projects recently
- Family
- Friends
- Lecturers/supervisors/teachers from previous courses of study
- The various handbooks that your department or school provides
- The various textbooks that have been written for research students (including, of course, this one)

So far, our aim has been to encourage you to recognize that you bring valuable skills, knowledge and resources to your research. You already possess many of the requirements that are necessary for success at this stage. We have also encouraged you to recognize that you can contribute to the likelihood of your being successful through developing an understanding of your learning and resource needs, both for the immediate future and in the longer term. This means that, as well as looking back at what you have learnt and understood, you also need to look forward to what will be required. Now is the time, therefore, to draft your Personal Development Plan (see Exercise 1.3).

Getting a flavour of possibilities

'Well, that wasn't too bad,' Samia thought, as she left her supervisor's office. 'I now know that all that reading I did on Malthusian economics might pay off for me. And my IT skills are in pretty good shape. I still don't really have a handle on the variety of different kinds of research though. My supervisor said I might think about what kinds of methodological approaches I prefer. Do I want to do numbers or do I want to talk to people? The only research I really know about is surveys and questionnaires. I hadn't given any thought to something like spending long periods of time with a small group of people and doing participant observation. But she said it was a possibility. And I never even knew that I could base the whole of the design of my project on library research. I had always thought that was just the literature review part of it. I will have to give some thought to the different types of research and see which appeal or are possible.'

It is often not fully appreciated that, at the very earliest stages of thinking about research, there are many ways in which this might proceed. For example, say your general topic is 'Asylum Seekers in the UK'. You might research this in any, and indeed all, of the following ways:

- By gathering together existing statistics.
- By looking at policy at local and national levels.
- By exploring the responses of relevant charitable organizations.
- By devising a questionnaire for various 'stakeholders' in this field.
- By conducting interviews with asylum seekers.
- By living among asylum seekers over a period of time.
- By undertaking an analysis of media representations of asylum seekers.

Your decision on how you might proceed clearly depends upon a number of factors. The most significant of these is what you are interested in finding out. For example, if your research questions whether the numbers of asylum seekers coming to the UK are increasing or decreasing, which countries they are travelling from, and what sex and age they are, then an analysis of existing statistics would be a very useful place to start. You would then be in a position to use percentages and bar charts to demonstrate your findings. Alternatively, if you are more interested in the experiences of asylum seekers once they have arrived in the UK, then you might consider interviews or even try to spend some time living among them as a form of participant observation. Your project or dissertation would then present the words of your research participants or extracts from your research diary detailing, for example, something of daily life for a particular group of asylum seekers.

> The section on **Focusing** in Chapter 2, particularly Box 2.8, considers the issues involved in drafting a research proposal.

In addition, your methodological decisions will depend upon how much time you have available, the expected word length of your project or dissertation, your research skills, the regulations and preferences of your department, school, examination board, manager and/or supervisor, what and whom you are able to access, the ethical parameters of your proposal, and your own preferences. These represent some very practical concerns, and you would be well advised to consult with your supervisor or manager at the very outset.

For example, if you are thinking of conducting an interview-based study and you are completing a 10,000 word MA dissertation conducted over a three-month period (full-time; or six months or more part-time), you might plan to interview between six and eight people once only. By comparison, for a PhD of 80,000 words conducted over a three-year period (or five to six years part-time), and using a qualitative research approach, you might be expected to have an in-depth knowledge of the lives of your research respondents, and be planning to spend an equivalent of twelve months conducting fieldwork. If you are planning to take a more quantitative approach and you are an undergraduate student undertaking a dissertation, you are unlikely to have the resources, in terms of time and money, to conduct a large-scale survey. Secondary data analysis may, therefore, be a more fruitful strategy. Conversely, if you are conducting a quantitatively based PhD, then you should expect to have already, and to acquire further, a high level of statistical ability.

The ways in which your research questions and interests shape the possible design of your research combine with practical issues such as time, resources and abilities. Accordingly, they each contribute to the ways in which your project will proceed. With this in mind, take a look at the representations of research shown in Box 1.3. These diagrams give alternative views of the research process. The most common understanding of research is the upper diagram, showing a linear design, where the research begins with a problem and proceeds through data collection and analysis to the written report. The lower diagram shows a far more iterative approach. This design seeks to convey the interrelationship between data collection, analysis and report

Box 1.3 Representations of the research process

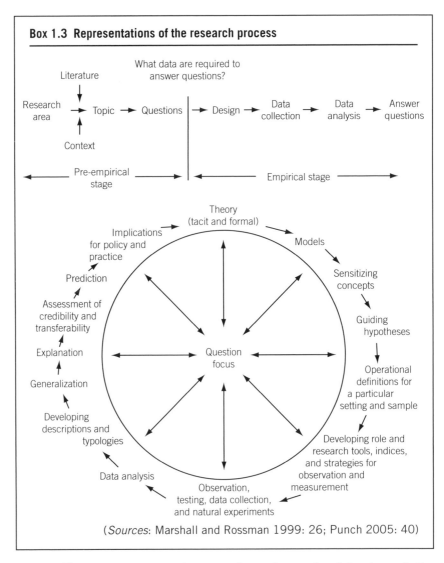

(*Sources*: Marshall and Rossman 1999: 26; Punch 2005: 40)

writing. These two representations may be understood as lying towards the polar ends of a continuum where, between these points, there are many variations.

Indeed, there are at least four common viewpoints when it comes to conveying and understanding the various processes of research:

- Research is often presented as a fixed, linear series of stages, with a clear start and end. This is the most common view, and reflects the way in which research is normally written up.

- There are also somewhat more complicated representations of this linear view that allow for slightly different routes to be taken through the process at particular stages.
- Another common representation portrays research as a circular process, analogous to the more general process of learning. Much the same set of stages is included, and in much the same order as in the linear view, but there is an implication both that the process might be entered at a number of points, and that the experience of later stages might lead to a reinterpretation or revisiting of earlier stages.
- There are also variants, often associated with action research, that see the research process as cyclical. Here, the process is shown as going through a number of cycles, the effects of each one impacting upon the way in which successive cycles are approached.

Our preferred view builds on these representations, seeing the research process as a spiral (see Box 1.4). Seen from this perspective, research: is cyclical; can be

Box 1.4 The research spiral

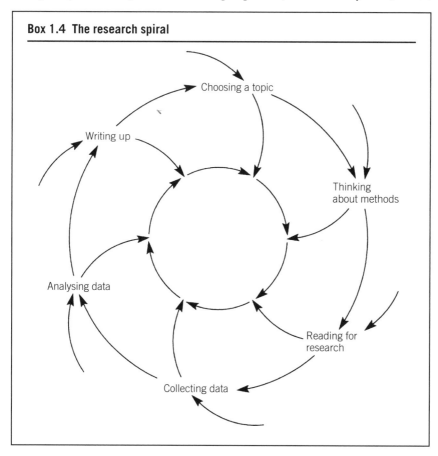

entered at almost any point; is a never ending process; will cause you to reconsider your practice; and will return you to a different starting place.

The nature of the cycle varies between research designs. For example, in most quantitative research projects, decisions about analysis have to be taken before any fieldwork or data collection is undertaken. This is because the types of statistical techniques that are possible vary with the types of data collected. In the case of qualitative research, by contrast, data collection, sorting, analysis and reading can take place simultaneously. Getting a flavour of each of the possible – even ideal – ways your project might proceed is an important part of the initial stage. This will enable you to select the most appropriate research process for your needs and interests, and to develop a sense of the limitations of the one you do select. This will also enable you to develop an understanding of the implications of your research approach, in terms of when the different elements are staged and accomplished, and in terms of what you might expect about the process and your associated experiences.

Why am I doing this research?

Helen is sitting in the library. She has several books on the desk in front of her. One is open but unread. The others are stacked in short piles giving the look of a stockade around her. Her notepad is open, the page already containing her first embryonic notes and several doodles. She has spent the best part of the morning searching for these texts, and counts herself lucky that at least some of those on her list were actually still on the shelves. And she had a breakthrough the other day as she decided that her research design would be based on qualitative approaches. Yet now she's got herself organized to this stage, she is wondering why she's doing this research. Is it really going to be that interesting a topic? Isn't there too much (i.e. boring) preparatory work to do before she can really get going? She would much rather get out there talking to and interviewing people. But, actually, even that seems too much effort now. Maybe it's best to pack up. Start another day. Not do it at all . . .

While there are many highs when doing research, it also has to be acknowledged that there will be many moments when the task ahead appears daunting or tedious, or simply not worth the effort. It is important, therefore, to remind yourself from time to time of why you are undertaking, or interested in undertaking, research. Quite often, researchers are initially motivated by hopes that their work will change the world in some, albeit probably small, way. There are also many researchers who reflect upon how their initial choice of topic was motivated by their personal circumstances or something that is close to their personal interests. For example, stepmothers may study stepfamilies, or non-traditional students may study the experiences of other non-traditional students. Of course, research is a job like any other. Researchers, therefore, often undertake studies on topics that are not of their personal choosing but because they pay the rent or may take them on to the next stage of their career. Think about your reasons for doing your project and try to complete Exercise 1.4.

As a researcher, you will find it useful to understand why you are involved in research. This will affect how you go about your research, and what you get out of it. If you are in doubt about your motivation, or reach a low spot when you feel that you want to give up, you might ask yourself the following questions:

• What are the personal rewards from completing this study? For example, how will the award of the qualification associated with your research enhance your career and employment prospects? What new skills will you have acquired? Will your research have enabled you to develop new contacts or visit new places? Will it have enabled you to demonstrate hitherto hidden competences to significant others? What kinds of satisfaction will you experience once the last word is written on the last page?
• How will the knowledge you produce contribute to furthering understandings or changing lives? Most often this question is understood in terms of large-scale change through, for example, finding the solution to a perennial problem. However, most contributions from research tend to be smaller in scale, though no less significant in terms of their importance to the individuals involved. For example, your research respondents may feel that this is the first time anyone has ever taken a real interest in their concerns. After all, it is quite rare – outside of therapeutic encounters – for anyone to sit down, listen intently and record everything you say for an hour or so. Research can, therefore, be an important validating experience for research respondents. The enthusiasm you garner from being involved in research can also be very persuasive for others who may develop insights from, or become more interested in, the issues arising from your research. This can create incremental and cascading changes that, while they may not rock the world immediately, nonetheless become significant in themselves.

But what might you do if you really feel you have no motivation at all? After all, if you aren't motivated, or are not motivated very strongly, this will affect your drive to finish the research project successfully. The obvious answer to the researcher with no motivation is to get some quickly or do something else! If the latter is not possible, you might seek motivation in one of the following ways:

• By changing your research project to something you are more interested in.
• By focusing on the skills you will develop through undertaking the research.
• By incorporating within the research some knowledge acquisition of relevance to you.

- By seeing the research project as part of a larger activity, which will have knock-on benefits for your work, your career, your social life or your life in general.
- By finding someone who will support you and push you through until you finish.
- By promising yourself a reward when it is successfully completed.

> If you are still troubled by your lack of motivation, have a look at the section in Chapter 2 on **What to do if you can't think of a topic**.

Will I have anything new to say?

It's all been done before. Everything I was planning to do I can now see that other researchers have done before. What's the point, then, of carrying on? Hussain felt a strong sense of rising panic as the deadline for handing in his dissertation was fast approaching. He had completed all the data collection and had also completed quite a lot of the analysis. He realized that his findings were not terribly new to anyone who knew his research field. They also confirmed much of what he had previously thought was the case.

For many research projects, particularly those carried out for a university degree, there is often a need for some kind or level of originality. This will typically be expressed in regulations or guidance in very general terms, for example 'an original project', 'making a contribution to the field' or 'evidence of original thinking'.

But what is originality? And where can you get some? If you are unsure, and it matters to you in your research, take a look at Box 1.5. Here you will find fifteen definitions of originality, collected together by others. Have a look at them and consider if your research meets any of the criteria listed. As the definitions quoted indicate, it is possible to be original in terms of topic, approach or presentation. The element of originality in your own research is, realistically, likely to be very small. Highly original research is very unusual, and you are probably setting your sights far too high if you try aiming for it.

The corollary of this is that your research is almost certainly original in some way, always provided, that is, that you are not slavishly copying someone else's earlier research. So be reassured. Indeed, it is quite common for researchers to become so familiar with their topic that they forget that it was all new to them when they started. While good researchers need to be over-familiar with the relevant literature, their data and their findings, this can lead to a mistaken assumption that everyone else is as knowledgeable as they are.

Box 1.5 Fifteen definitions of originality

Here are 15 definitions of originality, as put together by Phillips and Pugh. The first six are derived from a previous author, Francis, while the other nine derive from interviews with Australian students, supervisors and examiners.

1   Setting down a major piece of new information in writing for the first time.
2   Continuing a previously original piece of work.
3   Carrying out original work designed by the supervisor.
4   Providing a single original technique, observation or result in an otherwise unoriginal but competent piece of research.
5   Having many original ideas, methods and interpretations all performed by others under the direction of the postgraduate.
6   Showing originality in testing somebody else's idea.
7   Carrying out empirical work that hasn't been done before.
8   Making a synthesis that hasn't been made before.
9   Using already known material but with a new interpretation.
10 Trying out something in this country that has previously only been done in other countries.
11 Taking a particular technique and applying it in a new area.
12 Bringing new evidence to bear on an old issue.
13 Being cross-disciplinary and using different methodologies.
14 Looking at areas that people in the discipline haven't looked at before.
15 Adding to knowledge in a way that hasn't been done before.

(*Sources*: Phillips and Pugh 2005: 62; also Francis 1976)

Researchers can forget their initial excitement and interest in gaining new knowledge and, in consequence, that what they have to say may well be novel and new to other audiences. But if you are in doubt, check it out as early as possible with those who will judge the originality of your research. This advice also applies if you fear that you may be being too original for comfort. If you want to complete a useful piece of research in a particular context, it would not be sensible, for example, to present it in a way which is unacceptable.

In whose interests is this research?

Rishi thought his research was telling the facts of the case. He was very pleased that he had proven how poor the management was at Britwell and Company. He was shocked when his supervisor told him that all he could say was that 'such and such' was someone's perspective. Actually he said that Rishi needed to con-sider how much his values and experiences had impacted upon the selection of data and the analysis. 'It wasn't a perspective;' Rishi raged, 'it was the truth.' The management was lazy and inept. All of his research respondents told him so.

Many people coming to research for the first time have a tendency to think that they are in the business of establishing 'the truth' about a particular issue or subject. They want to find out 'the facts' or want to 'prove' (or perhaps disprove) a particular argument. They believe that they can be 'objective' in their research and that others will sit up and take notice when they present their findings. We shouldn't be surprised that this is the case because the 'standard' view of research is that of a detached scientist examining the facts of the case coolly and unemotionally. However, this standard view of research belies the extent to which, as we have suggested, research is a social activity that can be powerfully affected by the researcher's own motivations and values. It also takes place within a broader social context, within which politics and power relations influence what research is undertaken, how it is carried out, and whether and how it is reported and acted upon. To examine how this affects the different forms of data that can be collected, its subsequent analysis and findings, try Exercise 1.5.

Exercise 1.5 suggests that politics, power and values may be important con-siderations for your research, especially if you carry it out within your own or another organization. Your contacts will affect your access to the subjects of your research, may require you to submit your research proposals for scrutiny, and to revise them, and may exercise some veto over what you can actually write up or publish. If your research requires ethical approval prior to proceed-ing, which is increasingly likely to be the case, you will be required to adhere to a broader set of values and ways of proceeding, regardless of whether your research is organizationally based or not. And if you are unlucky, misread the organizational politics or irritate the researched, you may find cooperation withdrawn part-way through your project.

It is important, therefore, to understand the perspectives and motivations of those who facilitate your access, or take part in, or who may be stakeholders in, your research. Preparatory time spent in learning about this is always time well spent as it constitutes valuable contextual research in its own right. Rather than expecting to 'find the truth', therefore, it is better to think of research work in terms of words like rigour, reliability, professionalism and systematiza-tion. No one research project can realistically aspire to do more than advance our understanding in some way. Most researchers have to compromise their practices to fit into the time and other resources available for their studies. Doing research is, therefore, about producing something that is 'good enough' rather than providing the final word of truth on a particular topic.

This does not mean, of course, that such research cannot be pursued with drive, passion and commitment. These are important qualities that help main-tain momentum and interest, and can impact beyond the research into dissemination. However, all researchers need to take care that their passion does not take the form of dogma or an uncritical acceptance of the views of research participants. Rather, researchers need to maintain their levels of critical reflection, and so ensure their research is conducted in as open and transparent a way as possible in terms of its intentions, methodology, analysis and findings.

At last, writing up

The data had all been collected. The analysis was virtually complete. Now is the time to open the Word file and begin to write it all up. 'But hang on,' thought Becky. 'How do I do this? What is the format? I've never written a dissertation before. Do I need an index and chapters? Or do I just set it all down like an essay? How many references should I use? Do I have enough? Or maybe, lucky me, I have too many? Then again, I promised to give a copy to the manager of the call centre where I conducted the research. She was really keen to see it because she's hoping it will help her improve productivity. Will she want to read all this literature review stuff? Also, how is she going to take some of the things the staff had to say about her? Oh dear . . .'

It may seem that the writing-up stage is a long way off, but it is important to consider the rules, regulations and expectations of the various audiences for your research early on. For example, if you are researching for a university degree or another type of formal qualification, you will have to produce a dissertation or a thesis that will be assessed according to academic criteria. It may be, however, that you are carrying out a research project for your employer, who will expect a concise report emphasizing the implications of your findings and recommending action. You may be balancing both of these roles. However, while the processes may be broadly similar, the outputs are likely to look very different.

> For more advice here, look at the section in Chapter 10 on **Who am I writing for?**

Your audience may also include those you are researching, whether at work or within a community organization. If the latter, your approach may be to work from the bottom up, gaining consensus and support from all involved throughout the process; and the research may be as much about the change and development engendered in your audience as about any written output.

The important theme which runs through this discussion is your need, as a researcher, to be aware of the context in which you are researching. This manifests itself in rules, whether written or unwritten. You need to be aware of these rules and to follow them if you wish to succeed. You cannot hope just to muddle along and not run into problems.

Hint: Open a file on 'Regulations and Expectations'. Include copies of all the written regulations that apply to your research project and add notes on any unwritten expectations which you may find out about during your work.

How to use this book

Organization of the book

If you have already leafed through this book, or looked at the contents page, you will probably have noticed that it is organized in the kind of sequential, linear fashion which we criticized earlier in this chapter when discussing different representations of the research process. It is difficult to organize a book in any other way.

Thus, there are eleven chapters, as follows:

Chapter 1 **All at sea but learning to swim**, which considers the knowledge, skills, resources required, and the associated processes and concerns of research.

Chapter 2 **Getting started**, which discusses how to focus your research project.

Chapter 3 **Thinking about methods**, which examines the most common approaches and techniques used in research.

Chapter 4 **Reading for research**, which discusses how and what to read, and reading as a source of data.

Chapter 5 **Managing your project**, which deals with the planning and progressing of the work.

Chapter 6 **Preparing to collect data**, which considers the issues involved in data collection.

Chapter 7 **Collecting data**, which reviews the techniques which can be used for data collection.

Chapter 8 **Preparing to analyse data**, which considers the nature of data and how it might be handled.

Chapter 9 **Analysing your data**, which examines how you can analyse and interpret different kinds of data.

Chapter 10 **Writing up**, which deals with the organization and drafting of your report or thesis.

Chapter 11 **Finishing off**, which looks at how to complete your project and what you might do afterwards.

The elements of the book

In looking at this book, you will probably have noticed that it does not consist of straightforward text, but is composed of a number of elements. These are:

- The **text** itself, which is designed to offer guidance and lead you through the book.
- A series of over one hundred **boxes** which provide summaries, illustrations, examples and lists relevant to the issues discussed in the text.
- A range of **exercises**, located at the end of each chapter, which are designed to get you thinking about some of the issues raised in the context of your own research plans and experiences.
- Dozens of **quotations**, either in the text or in boxes, exemplifying and illustrating both the experience of other researchers and their insights into researching.
- Up-to-date and extensive **bibliographies** at the end of each chapter, listing relevant books on the topics covered.
- At the end of the book, a complete list of the **references** mentioned in the text.
- Within the text, **cross-references** to guide you between parts of the book.
- And finally, occasional **hints**, tips and health warnings, designed to keep you on track.

We have adopted this varied presentational form to help you to engage with what are rich and complex issues and debates, but without using complicated language. It is also intended to encourage different ways of using the book and its contents.

As social scientists trained in three different disciplines – anthropology, sociology and geography respectively – we have tried to include examples and illustrations from across the range of the social sciences. You will, however, find traces of our biographies throughout the book.

How to find your way through the book

There are many possible ways of using this book. The approach you adopt will depend upon your experience and preferences, the other support you are receiving and the kind of research project you are engaged in. You may, for example, already be well into your research by the time you pick up this book, and be looking for guidance on specific issues; or you may not have started yet and be scouting around for general advice.

Among the different ways in which you might use this book we may identify the following:

- You could start at the beginning and read through to the end. Although this is commonly perceived as the normal way to read a book, and to conduct research, we do not imagine that many of you will be doing this.
- You could start by reading Chapter 4, **Reading for research**, and then work both backwards and forwards from there.
- You could scan the contents page, read this introductory chapter, flick through the other chapters and sections, and then focus your attention on the pages that are of current interest to you.
- You could use the index to find references to topics that concern you.
- You could use the book as a basis for discussion, dialogue or exchange of ideas between yourself and others engaged in similar research projects.
- If you are involved in teaching or supervising those undertaking research, you might use the book as a source for exercises or ideas.

These are just some of the possibilities. We do not wish to restrict the ways in which you might use the book. Indeed, we would see your use of it as in many ways paralleling the research process itself: starting at any point, jumping from place to place, doing several things simultaneously, returning with renewed understanding to places you have already visited. To help you in this process, we have built in lots of cross-references between the different sections.

> We would welcome your ideas on and responses to the book. If you would like to make a suggestion, please contact the authors through the publishers.

What's different about this edition?

In producing this fourth edition, we have drawn on the many helpful suggestions made by readers, and our own experiences, since the first edition was published in 1996. In particular, we have:

- thoroughly updated the bibliographies and references, to reflect contemporary concerns and issues in social research;
- added new examples and illustrations;
- split two existing chapters into four chapters, so as to give greater attention to the issues involved in collecting and analysing data.

We hope that you find this edition even more useful than the last one!

Summary

Having read this chapter, you should:

- have an awareness of the skills, knowledge and resources you already possess that will enable you to survive stormy waters ahead;
- have an awareness of the skills, knowledge and resources that you need to enhance or acquire to enable you to thrive through your research work;
- now recognize the need to produce a Personal Development Plan;
- have some understanding of the variety of activities which may be considered to be 'research';
- appreciate that the research process is not straightforward, predictable or linear;
- have a clearer idea of your own motivations for engaging in research and of the context for your research;
- be more confident about your own ability to carry out a small-scale research project.

Exercises

1.1 *What skills, resources and knowledge do you already have?* Identify as many of the following as you can that have contributed to your success in academic work in the past: skills (e.g. information technology, reading, writing, managing time); resources (e.g. time, money, support networks); knowledge (e.g. subject knowledge, research knowledge, knowledge of systems, processes); your personality/temperament.

1.2 *Expanding on past successes.* Using the list of skills, resources and knowledge that you have produced in Exercise 1.1, identify those areas: that you know are adequate for your current needs; that you know need developing for your future needs; or where you are unsure whether you have a high enough level of a particular skill, resource or knowledge.

1.3 *My Personal Development Plan.* To produce a Personal Development Plan, you should enter at least one item under each of the following three headings:

Identified learning need
How will I achieve this need?
What is my timescale?

Review your plan periodically as your research progresses.

1.4 *Reasons for undertaking research.* List your reasons for your current or anticipated involvement in research. List as many as you can think of.

1.5 *The context of your research.* Imagine you are doing research on experiences of training at work, whether within your own company or another. Would your findings be different if you approached your interviewees through: the managing director, the personnel manager, the shop stewards' committee, the unemployment centre? How might they differ? How might this affect your conclusions? What if you had to write a report of your conclusions for each of these audiences? You can think about this as an exercise in finding out what is safe and what is risky in terms of expectations, theory, styles of writing, etc.

Further reading

As this is the first chapter in the book, and designed to be introductory, no specific suggestions for further reading are given here. If you are keen to read more at this stage, however, you might look at the suggestions in the next chapter, or any of the other chapters. In many cases, of course, the items referred to could have been listed in more than one chapter, and contain sections that are relevant to a number of chapters.

We have designed the bibliographies, included in the further reading sections at the end of each of the following chapters, to enable you to:

- browse through and identify texts which are likely to be of particular interest to you;
- identify books which focus on social science research in general, and those which are specific to particular disciplines or subject areas;
- quickly access deeper, more detailed or more theoretical treatments of the social research process.

The bibliographies have been restricted to books in print. You will find that they vary considerably in length. The list of further reading included in the final chapter is particularly extensive as it includes more theoretical and extended treatments for those who wish, or need, to probe the literature in more detail.

Please note that, if a book isn't listed, this doesn't mean that we think it's not very good – it's probably that we just haven't got round to reading it yet!

2

Getting started

Introduction • Choosing a topic • What to do if you can't think of a topic •
Focusing • Finding and choosing your supervisor • Individual and group
research • Researching in your workplace • Keeping your research diary •
Summary • Exercises • Further reading

Introduction

The purpose of this chapter is to help you move from the position of
having decided to do a piece of research to having a good idea of what you are
going to do.
   The chapter looks at seven closely related issues:

- **Choosing a topic**. The issues to bear in mind in deciding what you are
  going to research.
- **What to do if you can't think of a topic**. Some hints and tips on how to
  develop one.
- **Focusing**. How to get from your initial idea to something that is feasible
  and relevant.
- **Finding and choosing your supervisor**. How to go about selecting your
  most important research contact.
- **Individual and group research**. The different factors to bear in mind if
  you are going to be researching with others.
- **Researching in your workplace**. The advantages and disadvantages, and
  how to cope.
- **Keeping your research diary**. Make up your mind now to record your
  feelings, experience, decisions and ideas as you undertake your research
  project.

> **Remember**: The minute you've decided to do something, you've started your research project. By reading this, you've started.

Choosing a topic

> Being selfish is something few adults would, openly at least, admit to. Yet it is central to the sanity of the hard-pressed researcher. At the start of your project you are about to take on a considerable commitment which is probably in addition to many continuing demands on your time . . . So be selfish, focus on what interests you, think about your curriculum vitae and your future professional development as well as the impact your study might have on the workplace, and then step forward with confidence.
>
> (Edwards and Talbot 1999: 3)

Choosing your research topic is probably the single most important decision you have to make in doing research. In this section, we discuss twelve points you might bear in mind in making that choice.

How much choice you have

You may not, of course, have much choice in what you do. The general area for your research, and perhaps the detailed specification, may be determined by your employer or funder. But even in these cases, you will likely have some scope for making the project more interesting or relevant to your own concerns. If, for example, you have to do a piece of research which you are not particularly interested in, you might make it more palatable by adding something to it or by focusing on a part of the project which does interest you.

It is quite common for part-time students or researchers, who are registered for degrees which require them to undertake a piece of small-scale research, and who are receiving some support from their employers, to have their choice of research topic at least partly determined by their boss. Their employer will usually then expect to receive a report on the research project, and may also be seeking a more practical result in terms, for example, of improved working practices. In such cases, it is important to be aware of the different expectations of employers and educational institutions, and to plan ahead accordingly.

> More guidance on this is given in the section in Chapter 10 on **Who am I writing for?**

Your motivation

> If you have not already read it, you might usefully read the section in Chapter 1 on **Why am I doing this research?**

If you are in doubt about whether you have the necessary motivation to carry through the piece of research you have in mind, ask yourself:

Will it get me out of bed early on a wet Monday morning?

Or, if you are an early morning person:

Will I want to work on it on Friday evening?

If your answer is no, you may well have problems ahead, and you might be best advised to change or modify your research topic, if you can, to something which rouses your passion or drive rather more strongly.

Regulations and expectations

As we noted in Chapter 1, understanding any and all written regulations and unwritten expectations which apply to your research is of critical importance. If you are undertaking a research project for, or as part of, a university degree, then you should be provided with a copy of the relevant rules and regulations. If you do not have a copy, ask for one or look them up online. Read these regulations, question any you are not clear about, and follow them.

If you don't follow the regulations – and produce a dissertation or thesis which is too long or too short, in the wrong format or inappropriately written – you are laying yourself open to problems. It may still get through if the infringements are relatively minor, but don't count on it. You may have to substantially revise and resubmit your work. At best, you are likely to irritate your examiners, whereas, by following the rules, you should immediately create a good impression.

> Further advice on the processes of writing up and presentation is given in Chapters 10 and 11.

Whatever documentation you are given about rules and regulations, however, it is unlikely to deal with 'unwritten rules' or expectations. These you may need to tease out by pertinent questioning of your supervisor, manager, colleagues or fellow researchers.

If you are undertaking research not for a degree, but for your employer, funder or somebody else, or just perhaps for personal interest, there will likely still be rules and regulations which you have to follow, both written and unwritten. Funders may provide quite precise specifications for the work, often requiring regular updates or reports on your progress. Your employer may not be so clear, but will still have expectations which you will need to uncover and address if the process is to be successfully carried through. And, if you wish to publish the results of your research, the publisher will have another set of expectations for you to satisfy.

Your subject or field of study

Many of the unwritten rules and expectations associated with your research will have to do with the particular discipline or subject area you are working in. It may have preferred styles or conventions for writing, and preferred methodologies for undertaking research. There will certainly be established traditions, and work by 'key thinkers', which you will need to be aware of and perhaps refer to. Your supervisor or department may also have their own preferences or specialisms.

You should check on all of these by:

- talking to your supervisor, their colleagues or other researchers in the area;
- looking at other examples of recent research projects carried out in your subject area;
- looking at the research literature for your subject area (books, journals and reports).

Previous examples of research projects

Whatever subject you are studying, there are likely to be previous examples of similarly sized research projects on similar kinds of topic to which you can get access. If you can't find any in the libraries you have access to, or on the internet, ask a librarian, your supervisor, manager, colleagues or fellow researchers for help.

If you can get hold of some previous examples, don't turn down the chance to do so, because you can learn a lot. This learning will be not so much about the particular subject you are going to research as about what a completed piece of research looks like, the way it is put together, its scope and its limitations. When you see a completed thesis, dissertation or research report for the first time, you may feel daunted and unable to produce something of that scale. As you become more familiar with your topic, however, you should begin to feel that you could write something at least as good.

If you can, get some advice from your supervisor or someone else on which are considered to be better examples of previous research projects, and why. But make your own judgement as well.

The size of your topic

One of the key skills involved in choosing a topic is to be able to pick one of the right size: not too big, not too small, but doable within the time, space and resources available.

> **Hint**: Think of choosing your research topic in terms of the Goldilocks strategy. You want to select a topic which is not too big, and not too small, but just right (and one which will not break).

If you are new to research you will probably not have developed this skill. Indeed, it is a very common failing, but not necessarily that serious a one, for new researchers to choose topics which are far too big for them to carry out. Hence the need to focus down your study – the theme of another section in this chapter.

If you are carrying out a research project for a university degree, there will almost certainly be restrictions on both the size and the format of your final dissertation or report. In most cases a typewritten or word-processed submission will be required. There will commonly be a maximum number of words allowed, and possibly also a minimum. Appendices or references may be within these totals, or additional to them.

If you don't already know, find out what these restrictions on size are, and keep within them. You may think that the quality of what you write should be more important than its quantity, but think of your readers. Another of the key skills associated with doing research is being able to deliver a 'good enough' product within the time and space allowed. You should be able to write your research up within any reasonable word limit. Overwriting is really just self-indulgence.

> Further advice on this is given in the section on **Drafting and redrafting** in Chapter 10.

If you are undertaking research for professional or employment reasons, rather than for a degree, there will almost certainly still be restrictions on the size and format of your report. In business, for example, where you may be writing for very busy people, the need for brevity is paramount. Lengthy and tedious reports will not be read, even by enthusiasts. You need to make your report as to the point and interesting as possible; so keep it short and punchy.

The time you have available

Similar considerations relate to the time you have available for your research study. For a small-scale research study, this will typically be of the order of a few hundred hours in total. You need to make the best use possible of this time. It is unlikely, therefore, that you will be able to do empirical research a long way from your home, university or work (though a surprising amount can be done using the internet, email and the telephone). You will also have to limit the extent of any data collection you undertake: there are, for example, only so many interviews or questionnaires you can get completed, or, more importantly, usefully analysed, within a given amount of time.

Of course, time issues vary for different groups of people and different research approaches. For example, if you are a busy professional researching your own practice, you may have a strong temptation to focus on completing your interviews or questionnaire survey, and then hurriedly get on with the job of analysis and writing. Even though you cannot see the 'products' immediately, it cannot be said too loudly that it is imperative that time and space are given to reflecting on your methods and your data, and to reading around the relevant literatures. For those of you who are considering action research approaches, for example, you need to allow sufficient time to progress through the varied cycles involved.

The limitations on your time highlight the importance of planning ahead, scheduling and piloting your work.

> See also the sections in Chapter 5 on **Managing time** and **Piloting**.

The cost of research

Don't forget the cost factor. Unless you have an employer, funder or sponsor who is going to meet absolutely *all* of the costs of your research project, you should be aware of the different costs associated with alternative kinds of research. You will find a list of the kinds of expenses most commonly associated with social science research projects in Box 2.1.

Box 2.1 The costs of research

- Fees for degree registration or examination.
- Travel costs to and from your university or college, and/or your research sites.
- The costs of consumables such as paper, tapes, ink cartridges and batteries.
- Charges for access to certain institutions or individuals, or the internet.
- Equipment purchase or hire costs (e.g. computer, tape recorder, software).
- Book, report and journal purchases.
- Photocopying, printing and publication costs.
- Postage and telephone costs.
- Library fines!

For even a relatively modest project, the costs which you may have to bear will very easily amount to hundreds of pounds; or, if you have to pay registration fees, thousands of pounds. Draw up a budget now, and then check whether you are going to be able to afford it. Try Exercise 2.1.

> **Hint**: You may be able to cut your costs in very simple ways. For example, keep your interviews short to cut down on transcription costs. Buy your tape recorder second-hand. You can reduce the costs of photocopying by copying two pages on to one. Buy or borrow key texts from previous researchers. Never use first class post. Do your own typing, word processing and transcribing. Print drafts on recycled paper.

The resources you have available

If you have colleagues or friends to help you with your research, this will clearly allow you to do rather more than if you are on your own: but make sure you are aware of any regulations or restrictions relating to this. The particular case of group research is considered later in this chapter.

Most people undertaking small-scale research projects will, however, probably be working largely on their own. But this does not mean that you have no resources. Your resources may include, for example, a personal computer, access to some administrative support, and, perhaps most importantly, a good library and access to the internet. Against these you need to set the resources you will probably need in order to undertake your research project successfully. Doing Exercise 2.2 should help you to address these questions.

Once you've completed this exercise, focus on the differences between your two lists. If there is a huge difference between the resources you have available and the resources you think you will need, you might be best advised to start thinking of a research topic or approach which requires fewer resources. If the difference between the two lists is not so great, you could usefully think about how you are going to get access to any additional resources you need.

Your need for support

One of the key resources you may have identified in Exercise 2.2 is your need for support. Here we are talking about personal and emotional support, rather than the academic kind. In other words, who will ask you 'how's it going', who will make you cups of tea, who will give you permission not to do things, and who will you be able to 'earbash' about your research?

> **Health warning**: Undertaking research, or any kind of education, can threaten your personal, family, work or social life. Be aware of the demands which your research project may put on your loved ones, friends and colleagues. See also the discussion of acknowledgements in the section on **Added extras** in Chapter 11.

If you don't have people to fill these kinds of support roles, you may need to find them or develop them unless, that is, you are an unusually confident, organized and self-aware kind of person. You may think you can go it alone, that you can successfully complete a demanding research project without anybody's support; indeed, even with their active opposition. But what if you are mistaken?

Access issues

Virtually any research project involves questions of access to people, places and/or documents. These are discussed in rather more detail later in this book.

> See the section in Chapter 6 on **Access and ethical issues**, which also considers the issue of consent.

Here we are primarily concerned with the influence of access on your choice of topic. Access can be seen as relating as much to the resources you have available (e.g. a good library), as discussed in a previous subsection, as to the subjects of your research.

Obviously, from this point of view, it may make sense to choose a topic for which you believe access will be less problematic. This may suggest doing your research project within your own institution, though that does not guarantee there will be no problems. Your own institution or employer is likely, for example, to try to exert influence upon, or control, your research strategy and the dissemination of your findings. However, when time is limited, such ready access will be easier than getting permission to research in an organization where you know no one and no one knows you.

More generally, it is a good idea if you check out the access issues you may run into before you become completely committed to one particular research topic.

Methods for researching

In choosing a research topic, it makes sense to think about the methods you will use to collect and analyse data as soon as possible. If you have a choice, consider the methods you will enjoy using and those you will not. For example, if you like talking to people, you might be well advised to make use of interview methods. If, on the other hand, you don't like talking to people, you might think about undertaking library, internet or document-based research. And if you like carrying out statistical or multivariate analyses, you might consider a more quantitative methodology.

The methods you use are a key part of your research, so you need to understand something of the alternatives available to you, and their strengths and weaknesses.

See Chapter 3, **Thinking about methods**, for a discussion of the main kinds of research methods which you might use.

If you enjoy or have a flair for a particular method, this can make your research project more interesting, and help to motivate you to carry it through. Or you might like to use your research project to learn about, or develop your skills in, methods you are not familiar with.

What to do if you can't think of a topic

It may be, of course, that you are committed to doing a piece of research, but you just can't think of what to do. This is quite a common problem, and may be associated with your confidence, or lack of it, in undertaking a research project. This section is designed to help you address this problem. It may also help you if you have already thought of a topic but wish to refine it a bit or consider some alternatives to it; or if you've got too many ideas as to what you might research. It considers ten suggestions for helping you develop your ideas for a research project. You should then be in a better position to make a selection and begin to refine your choice down to a workable project.

Ask your supervisor, manager, friends, colleagues, customers, clients or mother

You could usefully ask almost anybody for ideas; non-specialists and those who aren't involved, as well as experts and those who are. Your supervisor may have a good deal of advice to offer, and might welcome your researching a topic of interest to them. Or they may put you in touch with a colleague in a similar position. Similarly, your manager and colleagues at work may have ideas for research which would be of value to your organization. Or your friends and neighbours might have suggestions for research which could help your local community in some way. Talking about your ideas to people who aren't involved with research can be very revealing and helpful.

Look at previous research work

This is another obvious suggestion, and one which we have already made.

> I was desperate for an idea, any idea, so I began by asking around. Surely someone out there in practice would have an exciting question that they felt must be asked but not the knowledge or resources to pursue? . . . When it became obvious that no one was going to present a research question to me on a plate I began my search in earnest. I read a lot and went through back copies of journals. I particularly chose the *Journal of Advanced Nursing* and the *International Journal of Nursing Studies* to look through because these were very general in their content, were academic in nature and very often researchers would mention 'implications for further research' at the end of their paper. After leafing through several journals I came across an article about creativity and nursing.
>
> (Miles 1994: 18–19)

There are almost certainly many examples of similar kinds of research projects which you could look at, whether these are presented in the form of published articles or as research reports or theses. You might consider replicating one of these: using the same methods to analyse the same problem, but in a different area or institution. This can be very useful and illuminating, whether you confirm, add to or cast doubt upon the earlier findings.

See the section in Chapter 1 on **Will I have anything new to say?** if you are worried that developing your project from previous research work is insufficiently original.

Develop some of your previous research, or your practice at work

You may already have done a piece of small-scale research, or perhaps just researched a particular field of study for an essay or shorter paper. Think about whether it would be possible and interesting to develop this line of thought further. Or, alternatively, you might choose to research a topic which was engaging your attention, and demanding your time, at work. Your own *curiosity* and *desire to learn* are excellent places to start.

Relate it to your other interests

You will probably have a range of interests outside of your work or course of study. These might include, for example, family, social, voluntary, community or sporting activities. It is quite possible, depending upon the limitations on the subject area for your research, that you could link your research to one of these interests. Thus, if you are carrying out management research, you might base it, at least partly, on a voluntary or community group you work with.

Think of a title

You may find that thinking of possible titles for research suggests topics of interest to you. After all, a lot of the initial attraction in a book, television programme or film resides in the title. They may be punning, alliterative and/or pithy. They might pose a key research question in a succinct fashion, or suggest a new area for research. For example:

Chaos of Disciplines
The Empire Strikes Back
Women's Ways of Knowing
Images of Organization

Titles need to be as short as possible. Try to think of some you like that will motivate you. A good title should help you focus your subsequent work. However, don't feel that you have to keep to the title you originally thought of: the time may come when you need to change it.

Start from a quote that engages you

Another approach is to extract from the literature you have read one or more quotations which really engage your attention. We are talking here about the kind of statement which draws a strong positive or negative reaction; which makes you think that the author really knows their stuff, or, alternatively, doesn't know what they are talking about. These quotations may be comments, interpretations of research data, questions or assertions. They may even directly identify areas needing further research.

Follow your hunches

You may have a strong instinctive feeling that a particular area or issue needs researching, or will raise interesting questions. This may be because of a critical incident you have experienced. Or it may be that something about it surprises or puzzles you, or just doesn't seem quite right. Don't be afraid to follow such hunches and see where they lead. But, as with all the suggestions given here, don't expend too much time and energy on them if it appears they are not getting you anywhere.

Draw yourself a picture or diagram

Producing a spider diagram of issues, interests, questions and their possible interconnections is a standard technique. It can be undertaken individually or in a group. It may help you to identify or isolate particular areas for research, and suggest how these are related to your general subject area. You might then wish to share your diagram with others, to get their responses and suggestions. An example of such a diagram is given in Box 2.2.

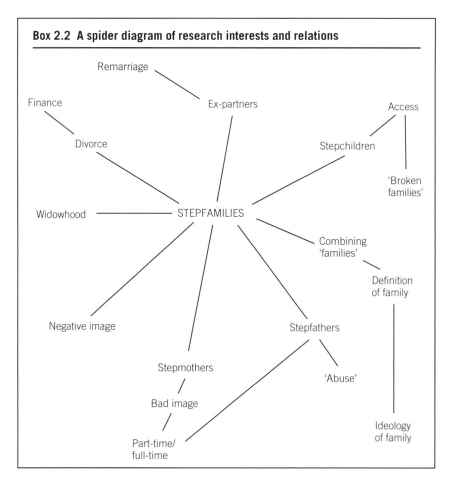

Box 2.2 A spider diagram of research interests and relations

As an alternative to the spider diagram, depending on your interests and skills, you might draw a picture or a map. The choice really is up to you. The idea is simply to get you thinking about possible areas or questions for research, their relationships and relevance.

Just start anywhere

Finally, if none of the above engages or appeals to you, you could just start anywhere. Go away and read something, or talk to somebody, about some of the issues relevant to your general subject area. Sketch out and begin a research project, any research project of about the right size, even if it feels dull and routine at first. Something better is likely to come out of this activity, perhaps something completely different.

Be prepared to change direction

Changing direction may become necessary if you are denied access to important people or documents, if insufficient people respond to your questions, if you cannot find the data you thought was there, if you change job or move house, if you get bored, or for other reasons. Having some in-built flexibility in your research plans, a Plan B – thoughts about alternative approaches to the same question, or about different directions away from your starting point – is a very good idea.

Remember:

- Change can be positive.
- It's OK to change.
- Lots of people change their research project or focus.
- You always end up at a different place from where you thought you were going anyway.

Focusing

Once you have chosen a topic, or perhaps a number of possible alternative topics, you will almost certainly need to refine it and focus it. Focusing is not an instantaneous process, but takes place over time. During this period you will likely be doing a lot of background reading, thinking about the methods you will use in your research, and refining your research design. Indeed, many research projects are not finally focused until the data collection and analysis process is well advanced.

> You may find that working through some of the ideas in Chapter 4, **Reading for research**, helps you to focus your research topic.

You will need to focus your project to ensure that it is relevant to your needs, and to any regulations or expectations you are operating under. Above all, focusing is almost invariably necessary to produce a project that is feasible within the time, space, costs and other practical constraints affecting you. Whatever your chosen research method, this section suggests that you would find it useful to address the questions set out by Mason (2002) to help you focus down from your initial idea or ideas to an achievable project (see Box 2.3).

For further help in developing your research framework see the section on **Which method is best?** in Chapter 3.

Box 2.3   Five important focusing questions

Working from a qualitative research perspective, Mason (2002: 13–22) suggests there are five sets of difficult questions that you need to work through in order to find out what is the essence of your inquiry. These are:

1   What is the nature of the phenomena, or entities, or social 'reality' that you wish to investigate? For example, are you interested in social actors or behaviours, in feelings, in memories, in policy, in organizational practices?
2   What might represent knowledge or evidence of the entities or social 'reality' that you wish to investigate? For example, what would count as evidence of organizational practices?
3   What topic or broad substantive area is the research concerned with? What would be the generic label for your research?
4   What is the intellectual puzzle? What do you wish to explain or explore? What type of puzzle is it? For example, are you interested in how something works or how and why something has developed? Mason suggests three common intellectual puzzles: (a) developmental puzzles, i.e. how and why did X come about; (b) mechanical puzzles, i.e. how does X work; (c) causal puzzles, i.e. what influence does X have on Y.
5   What is the purpose of your research? What are you doing it for? Mason indicates that this question requires us to consider the political and ethical issues of our research.

Identifying your research questions or hypotheses

An obvious starting point for focusing is to try to set out, loosely at first and then more precisely, the questions you want to answer in your research project. If it suits you, you might express these as hypotheses which you will then seek either to prove or to disprove. But, for most people, straightforward questions will probably be fine. You might like to try Exercise 2.3 at this point, to see how well you can identify your research questions.

In a small-scale research project you are unlikely to be able to handle more than two or three main research questions. You may only have one, and it may actually be defined for you already. If you have four or more, you should probably be thinking of cutting them down in number and focusing on just a few.

If, or when, you get your research questions right, they should suggest not just the field for study but also the methods for carrying out the research and the kind of analysis required. If they don't, they are probably pitched at too general a level. Research questions are like objectives rather than aims: they should contain within themselves the means for assessing their achievement. Box 2.4 uses two examples to illustrate what is involved in refining your research questions.

Box 2.4 Refining research questions

In one case, a student stated that they wanted to do 'something on vocational qualifications'. In the second, the researcher was interested in the 'politics of development'.

Both of these cases, particularly the second, are clearly unfocused and unmanageable subjects for small-scale research. They are the stuff of lifetimes of scholarship or extensive team research. To focus them down to something manageable, issues like the following need to be addressed:

• What vocational areas might I examine? Will I focus on particular institutions or classes? Am I concerned with a given time period? From whose perspective might I examine them: that of the policy-maker, educator, student or funder?
• Am I interested in development in a particular country or area? Over what period of time? Am I talking about economic, political, social or techno-logical development? What level of political analysis am I concerned with: local, regional, national, international or what?

By addressing these kinds of issues, the proposed research project can be refined down in size and appropriate research questions developed. Thus, in the case of 'something on vocational qualifications', the basic question might be 'How successfully has a new diploma in accounting been introduced within two colleges in Somerset?' Or, in the case of the 'politics of development', the main research question might be 'What public subsidies have been attracted to a village in rural France over a ten year period, and how have these been used?'

Defining the key concepts, issues and contexts

Defining the key concepts, issues and contexts of your research project should also assist you in focusing your work, as well as being of great help to you later on in your project. These concepts, issues and contexts establish the territory for your research, indicate the literature you need to consult and suggest the methods and theories you might apply. The nature and meaning of concepts, issues and contexts are explored in Box 2.5.

Box 2.5   Concepts, issues and contexts

Concepts. Dey (1993: 275) defines the term 'concept' as 'a general idea which stands for a class of objects'. Concepts are 'umbrella' terms and, in research, are often associated with a particular theory or theories. For example, the concept of class refers both to the classification of people according to, say, income or employment, and to judgements that we might make about others (or of course ourselves). Examples of concepts include truth, beauty, time, ethnicity, gender, class and space. In quantitative research it is very important to define the meanings of your key concepts in advance in order to be able to systematically measure them. This requires you to be clear about the *indicators* that you are going to use that will stand in for the concept. For example, if your research is concerned with poverty you might define poverty in terms of income, receipt of state benefit, house size and so forth. For some qualitative researchers, generating conceptual categories at the analysis stage will be much more common, because such researchers are interested in the perceptions of their respondents. This does not, however, mean that if you are planning to conduct qualitative research you need give no initial thought to defining concepts. You still need to be explicit and aware of how you are defining concepts in the research questions that you formulate, and in the observations and interviews you conduct. The way you define concepts will shape the data you collect.

Issues. These refer to the broad questions that underlie and direct disciplines, sub-disciplines or subject areas, as well as public affairs. They are the subject of continuing debate and study from a range of perspectives. Examples of issues include the links between educational participation and economic development, the effects of television programmes on people's behaviour, and the relationship between road building and traffic congestion. It is often the case in small-scale research that the focus on a particular issue leads to a neglect of the wider disciplinary concerns and theories.

Context. This relates to the background of existing research, knowledge and understanding that informs new and ongoing research projects. Research seldom, if ever, breaks wholly new ground. It builds on an extensive history of other people's work. You will need to have some familiarity with this if you are to make the most of your own research work. Your work might, for example, ask similar questions, replicate a study in another area or seek to modify existing findings. Your research context will include many studies that are not specifically relevant to your particular research questions but are illustrative of broader issues in your disciplinary field, applications of your methodological approach or comparative studies in other countries.

Do you already know what the concepts, issues and contexts relating to your research project are? Try Exercise 2.4.

Using the doughnut and jam roly-poly models of research

Researchers, particularly those with limited experience, often approach their chosen research topic with considerable enthusiasm, reading widely, checking sources and contacting experts as appropriate. But their focus can be almost exclusively upon the topic itself, rather narrowly defined, with little reference to how it relates to the broader field of research and study within which it is set. Their desire to thoroughly explore their growing interests in specific areas has to be reconciled with the need for each research project to be focused and contextualized within a more general framework. Some examples of this tendency are discussed in Box 2.6.

Box 2.6 All focus and no context

Edward wanted to examine the impact that fitness training might have on his colleagues. He believed that if they all undertook such training, their performance on the job would be improved, there would be less absenteeism, long-term sickness and early retirement, with consequent improvements in cost-effectiveness for the organization.

Juanita wanted to look at the incidence of post-traumatic stress among her colleagues, the consequences for their work and the implications for their training. As her organization was an emergency service, her expectation was that most of those questioned would have suffered such stress, though they might feel under pressure to minimize or deny it. She believed that pre-training was necessary to help people cope with the stresses they would have to face in their work.

Tessa wanted to understand the processes involved in decision making within organizations. Her concern was with learning how employees could be kept sufficiently up to date with developments in their job area. She believed that new practices should be introduced to facilitate this.

In each of these three cases, the students initially chose far too big a field to successfully research and write up in a year of spare-time commitment. Their ambitions had to be gradually pared down during the research study period. In each case, the students' focus was almost exclusively upon the topic itself, rather narrowly defined, with little reference to how it related to the broader field of human resource development which they were studying.

Thus, Edward became very concerned with measures of human fitness, alternative fitness regimes and the practices of comparable professional organizations in other countries. Juanita concentrated on measures of stress, critical incidents and their effects, and alternative counselling approaches. And Tessa focused on different organizational models and systems, and the psychology of decision making.

We would argue that a balanced research project should consist of a detailed study set within, and linked to, an understanding of the broader context of the subject field. It is possible to put rough proportions on this balance. Thus, while the bulk of the time available for the research, say 70–80 per cent, will usually be devoted to the specific research question or questions, a substantial chunk, 20–30 per cent, would be spent on the contextual issues and connections. A similar proportioning would probably apply in writing up the research.

> The allocation and organization of space in writing up your research is discussed in the section on **How to argue** in Chapter 10.

We have called this balance of context and focus the doughnut model of research (we are referring here to the English jam doughnut rather than the American ring doughnut: see Hughes and Tight 1996). It is illustrated in Box 2.7.

Box 2.7 Doughnuts and jam roly-polys

The doughnut   The inverted doughnut   The jam surprise

The jam roly-poly

In practice, however, novice and small-scale researchers often tend towards two other patterns. Both of these over-focus on the details of the particular research project being undertaken. In one pattern, the positions of the study and its context are reversed, so that limited reference to the wider field is found embedded within the details of the research. In the other pattern, often presented as an initial response to criticism, the detailed study is placed within its context, but the latter is far too thinly presented. We call these two patterns the inverted doughnut, clearly a structure which could not sustain itself, and the jam surprise, something rather sickly and only to be eaten if lots of tissues are available.

There is a danger, of course, in overextending the use of any metaphor; and the image of the doughnut may also seem rather too simplistic. We have already argued that it is more realistic to present the research process as a spiral; which is cyclical, can be entered at almost any point, is a never-ending process, will cause you to reconsider your practice, and will return you to a different starting place.

> See the section in Chapter 1 on **Getting a flavour of possibilities**.

The doughnut provides a static image, a beginning or end point, and does not convey much about the process of research. As such, while it offers a good starting point for using metaphors in this context, it needs further development. Hence the jam roly-poly or Swiss roll.

This alternative image expresses the continual interleaving of context and specifics, as well as the multiple possibilities for interconnections between them. Thus, the jam roly-poly can be sliced at any point to give a stratified mixture of jam and pastry, or, by analogy, research data and theory or context. These relationships hold throughout the length of the jam roly-poly, suggesting a thematic approach to research, running from beginning to end. And the image allows for different conceptualizations: there could be different proportions of jam and roly-poly, different flavours of jam and different colourings used.

Sketching a research outline or project proposal

Another technique which should help you to focus your research ideas is to try to sketch out a proposal or outline of your research project and plans. This may well be required of you if you are studying for a degree, or if you need to get the approval of your manager for your project. It will be essential if you are trying to get some funding from somewhere to support your research. Box 2.8 summarizes the key questions a research proposal would be expected to address and answer.

You may already have drafted your research questions, and have a good idea of the key concepts, issues and contexts involved, but do you have a clear notion of what the whole project might look like? Can you sketch out a summary of how your eventual research report, dissertation or thesis might be organized? This is the theme of Exercise 2.5.

A parallel approach is to draft a schedule for the research work itself. Knowing you will have only so much time in which to do the work, sketch out what you will be doing, month by month or week by week, in order to achieve your ends. Remember to leave yourself some flexibility and some 'free time', to allow for when things don't go exactly as planned.

Box 2.8 Questions a research proposal should answer

At the most general level:

1 What:
   • What is my research about?
   • What is its purpose?
   • What is it trying to find out or achieve?
   especially:
   • What questions is it trying to answer?
2 How:
   • How will my research answer its questions?
3 Why:
   • Why is this research worth doing?
   More specifically:
4 What is my research area? Have I clearly identified it?
5 What is my topic? Have I clearly identified it and shown how it fits within the research area?
6 What are my general research questions?
7 What are my specific research questions?
8 Does each specific research question meet the empirical criterion? Is it clear what data are required to answer each question?

(*Source*: Punch 2000: 32)

This approach is discussed in more detail in Chapter 5, in the section on **Mapping your project**.

These exercises should help you to highlight just how realistic your proposals actually are. Look at your proposed chapter or section contents, and at your monthly or weekly plans. Do you really think you will be able to squeeze that much into the time and space available?

Trying it out on a non-specialist: explaining your topic in simple language

It is important that you are able to explain your research project in simple, everyday terms. You need to be able to render the strange familiar, as well as, at other times, the familiar strange.

There will not be many people who will understand, or want to understand, the details of your theoretical framework, methodology, sampling strategy or analytical approach. This may be the case even if you are carrying out your research within a university department or research institute, if only because research outside the sciences tends to be both a specialized and individualized activity.

Yet you may have to deal with many people in the course of your research, to whom you will need to give some explanation of just what it is you are doing. These may include people in organizations you are researching, and contacts who may enable you to access sources or information. They will also likely be fellow researchers or colleagues with whom you wish to share or exchange experiences, and all your other day-to-day social and family contacts who are interested in what you are up to.

You will need, therefore, to be able to summarize what you are doing both briefly and in non-technical language. In doing so, you may clarify your thoughts and avoid some of the jargon and humbug within which researchers can find themselves immersed. And the non-specialists you talk to may also have useful suggestions to make.

So try explaining your research plans to your grandma, or your neighbour, or the person standing next to you in the bar, or your babysitter. They could be invaluable in helping you to focus your work.

Informal piloting

One final suggestion in this section is to actually start your research project with some 'informal' pilot activity. We are using the term 'informal' here to distinguish this from the pilot surveys which are commonly built into research projects. An informal pilot could turn into a pilot, but is meant as an early initial try-out through which you can judge the feasibility of your overall research plans and then make modifications as necessary. By doing an informal pilot you are not committing yourself but checking and focusing your ideas.

See also the section on **Piloting** in Chapter 5.

If you like the idea of informal piloting, try to carry out a couple of interviews, or get some friends to fill in a few questionnaires, or go and observe some organizational activities – or whatever else it was that you had in mind. You will almost certainly learn a great deal from the activity, not least an idea of the amount of time that collecting data can take. If you do it early, it should enable you to alter your strategy, if necessary, to something more effective and feasible.

Finding and choosing your supervisor

Much has been written, and a lot more spoken, about the varied relationships between researchers and their supervisors. If you doubt this, talk to some more experienced researchers: they will likely all have horror stories, even if only second- or third-hand, to relate. If you are a novice or small-scale researcher, the sort of person whom this book is aimed at, you will most likely have or need a supervisor, though you may not use that term.

Your relationship with your supervisor is of critical importance for you and your research. This is not to say that you can't get through the job without having a good supervisor and a wonderful supervisory relationship, but you will probably find it a lot easier, more stimulating and more rewarding if you do.

What is a supervisor?

'Supervisor' is the term most commonly used within universities and colleges for academics who have personal responsibility for overseeing the progress of individual students' research projects. The term 'tutor' is sometimes used in a similar way. Ideally, such supervisors should have some knowledge of the specialist areas in which their students are researching, plus a general understanding of the research process and the various strategies possible. They should have an inside knowledge of the rules and regulations, both written and unwritten, affecting your research project. They should have some skill in conducting the kind of in-depth, but partial and discontinuous, relationships required for successful supervision. And they should help to keep you focused on your research.

There are, however, significant differences in the ways in which supervision is organized in different universities and subjects. While many students in the social sciences are supervised on an individual basis by a single supervisor, other patterns are also common. You may have two supervisors, who meet with you separately or together, or may be supervised by a small committee of academics. You may find yourself as part of a small research group that has shared supervisions. Each of these arrangements has different implications for power, attention and dynamics.

You may, of course, not be doing your research in a university or as part of a degree, but it is still probable you will have or need a supervisor. If you are carrying out research within and/or for your own organization, your supervisor might be called your mentor, or perhaps just your manager or boss. If you are researching outside an organization, or within the community, your supervisor might be a colleague.

Whatever they are called, there is little doubt that the great majority of researchers can benefit from having a supervisor of some kind. So if you haven't got one, or think you can do well enough without one, think again. Maybe you could at least ask a friend or colleague, or a fellow student or researcher, to be your informal mentor or supporter, because you will need someone to talk to about your research from time to time. You should, however, be prepared to negotiate the terms of the relationship. Supervisors, like researchers, need to have some idea of what they are getting themselves into.

These issues are discussed further in the section on **Dealing with key figures and institutions** in Chapter 5.

What to look for in your supervisor

Whatever the nature of, or context for, your research, you may have little or no choice in who is your supervisor. They may come with the job, or they may be chosen for you by someone else, or they may appear to be the only one with the specialist knowledge who is available. Nevertheless, you should still see yourself as having some say in this most important matter. If you think there is someone more suitable who might be available, or you would prefer a different kind of arrangement, do what you can to arrange for this either formally or informally. Even if this is not possible, you should be able to affect the nature of the supervisory relationship.

Before you get this far, however, it might be as well to ask yourself just what you want, and by implication what you don't want, from your supervisor. Try Exercise 2.6.

In Box 2.9 you will find two lists:

• Nine qualities which research students expect from their supervisors
• Six qualities which supervisors expect from their students.

It does seem significant that the supervisors appear to have fewer expectations than the students. You might like to compare these lists with your answers to Exercise 2.6.

On reflection, do you think any of the qualities which you listed, or which were identified in Box 2.9, were unrealistic? You would be very lucky indeed to find all of these qualities in one person. In practice, you will probably have to settle for someone who has some of the qualities identified – perhaps those which you regard as the most essential – or use a number of people to address your different expectations. In our judgement, there is only one quality which is essential for a successful supervisor–researcher relationship: that

---

Box 2.9 Students' and supervisors' expectations

What students expect of their supervisors

- To be supervised
- To read their work well in advance
- To be available when needed
- To be friendly, open and supportive
- To be constructively critical
- To have a good knowledge of their research area
- To structure the tutorial so that it is relatively easy to exchange ideas
- To have sufficient interest in their research to put more information in the student's path
- To be sufficiently involved in their success to help them get a good job at the end of it all!

What supervisors expect of their students

- To be independent
- To produce written work that is not just a first draft
- To have regular meetings
- To be honest when reporting upon their progress
- To follow the advice that they give, when it has been given at their request
- To be excited about their work, able to surprise them and fun to be with!

(*Source*: Phillips and Pugh 2005: chs 8 and 11)

---

both you and your supervisor are committed to your successfully completing your research.

Individual and group research

As Totter once said: when you are swinging helplessly at the end of a hundred-foot rope it is important to know that the man at the other end is a *friend*.

(Bowman 1992: 21)

The small-scale research exercise which you are engaged in may be a group effort rather than your responsibility alone. This may be a matter of choice, may be dictated to some extent by the nature of the research itself, or may be a formal requirement of your degree programme or employment. While many of the issues affecting the processes of group research are in essence the same as those for individual research, there are some key differences. These are the subject of this section.

> **Hint:** If group processes are important to your learning programme, you may want to ask your supervisor or manager for references, guidance or training on group dynamics.

Individual versus group research

What are the advantages and disadvantages of doing group research? Our assessment of the strengths of group and individual research is summarized in Box 2.10.

Box 2.10 Individual or group research?

Group research

- Enables you to share responsibility
- Lets you specialize in those aspects of the work to which you are best suited
- Provides you with useful experience of team working
- Allows you to take on larger-scale topics than you could otherwise manage
- Provides you with a ready-made support network
- May be essential for certain kinds of research.

Individual research

- Gives you sole ownership of the research
- Means that you are wholly responsible for its progress and success
- May result in a more focused project
- Is of an overall quality determined by you alone
- Means that you have to carry out all elements of the research process.

Like many aspects of researching, your choice of whether to do individual or group research should be informed by your awareness of yourself. What are your strengths and weaknesses, preferences and hates? Would they be better accommodated within the support network of a group, or would you be better advised to work largely on your own?

If you have no choice about engaging in group research, you will have to make the best of it. If you do have a choice, however, it should be informed.

Managing the group

If you are involved in a small-scale group research activity, much depends, of course, on the size and composition of the group undertaking the research, and on the existing power relationships among these people. Unless you are all of much the same age, from the same kind of background, on the same wavelengths, and with similar motivations, you will need to work out ways of resolving differences, planning ahead and implementing the research project. This will almost certainly involve some division of responsibilities, regular discussion of progress and probably also some leadership.

Box 2.11 summarizes the key issues for those involved in group research projects. If you cannot satisfactorily answer the questions it poses, you should address them at your next group meeting. If you do not, individually and collectively, know who is doing what and how the research will be progressed, you are heading for problems. If your group is lacking in individuals with key skills, you will either need to develop them quickly or recruit additional members.

Box 2.11 Key issues for group researchers

1   Does the group need and have a leader?
2   Who is responsible for:
    • organizing meetings?
    • keeping records?
    • chasing progress?
3   What are the strengths and weaknesses of the group for carrying out the research project?
4   How are the different roles and tasks required for the successful completion of the research project shared among the group?
5   Will everyone in the group have a role in each phase of the research, or will some specialize in particular phases?
6   Does every member of the group have a clear idea of their tasks and responsibilities?
7   Do you each feel able to respect differences between group members?
8   Are there individuals or subgroups within the group who are not happy with the task or organization of the group?
9   How will the group deal with emotions?
10 Will the results of the research be reported on and written up individually, collectively, or both?

See also the section in Chapter 5 on **Sharing responsibility**.

Producing the finished product

When undertaking any piece of research, it is always a good idea to have an idea of what the finished product might look like. This is particularly true for group research. Here, as indicated in Box 2.11, the issue arises whether the final report or dissertation (and its assessment) is going to be a truly joint effort, or whether separate reports are going to be produced by the different individuals involved in the group.

You may formally need not only to produce a separate individual product, but also to demonstrate clearly what your own contribution has been and how you have carved out something of your own from the overall group research. If this is the case, you should plan your work within the group accordingly so that you are not disadvantaged.

Researching in your workplace

You may have noticed that, throughout this chapter, we have regularly referred to some of the issues involved in undertaking research in your own workplace. Like group research, this has both advantages and disadvantages. We have identified some of the more significant in Box 2.12. If you are considering undertaking a research project in your workplace, or even if you have no choice in the matter, you might care to reflect on how these issues may impact upon you at this point.

If you do have a choice, then there are many good reasons for opting to research your own workplace, and many others for not doing so. In the end, like all research projects, it will probably come down to which topics or methods most engage you. And how well it works out may not be down to you, but to events over which you have no control.

Keeping your research diary

The research indicated that writing learning journals had the potential significantly to enhance and develop the depth and range of student learning . . . First, journals gave students an opportunity to write regularly and at length, allowing them to develop their ideas and writing fluency . . . Second, writing journals enabled students to construct a 'map' of the complex structures and relationships in a course or range of material . . . Third, writing journals encouraged the students to think differently.

(Crème 2000: 98–9)

Box 2.12 The pros and cons of researching your own workplace

Advantages

- Ease of access
- You may be able to do some research in work time
- You may receive financial and other support from your employer
- Insider knowledge
- You can get down a lot deeper quicker
- Your colleagues may provide you with lots of useful contacts
- You may know the answers already
- It may help your promotion.

Disadvantages

- Pressure from your employer to research what they want, how they want and to reach the conclusions they want
- Problems with researching those you also manage, or are managed by
- Difficulties in maintaining anonymity
- Knowing where the bodies are buried
- It can feel like you're always at work
- You may be expected to do your research and your job
- Your conclusions may be rejected or ignored
- What happens if you change your job?
- You may think that you know the answers already
- You may overlook the significance of things that seem obvious
- You could learn a lot more by researching the unfamiliar.

A journal also allows one to grapple with the deep and lasting effect that fieldwork produces . . . which is often more evident when analysing the data than when collecting it. During the months I spent transcribing 27 lengthy taped life-history interviews of members of Jews for Jesus, I was forced to continually examine my own relationship to Judaism and religion in general. While I could put off my informants' questions about my 'position with God' by saying 'I'm not ready to consider this commitment', alone with my typewriter and those convincing tapes I asked this kind of question many times: 'Why not me? Sarah is so like me in background and abilities. She has found such peace, purpose, growth, and understanding in life because of her commitment. What am I afraid of?'

(Lipson 1991: 85)

Whatever kind of research project you are engaged in, regardless of the methodology you are using, and whether it is focused on your workplace or not, you may find it a good idea to keep a research diary. In this diary, you might record your progress, feelings, thoughts, insecurities and insights, day by day, as your research continues. A variety of formats are possible. While most diaries will probably be kept on paper, there is no reason why you shouldn't keep one on tape or on a computer (perhaps as a blog).

One school of thought recommends that you organize your research diary in terms of observational notes, methodological notes, theoretical notes and analytical memos (see Schatzman and Strauss 1973). This is just one strategy, however, and you might opt to use a different format, perhaps more akin to the literary notion of the diary.

> See also the section in Chapter 6 on **Recording your progress.**

Your research diary should prove to be an invaluable resource in filling in the context for your research, and reminding you of critical incidents and particular aspects of data collection or fieldwork. It will also give you regular practice in distilling your ideas in writing. It could be a support, in which you can confide and work out your concerns and fears. And, as it builds up during the project, it will serve as a trigger for reflection and a physical (but hopefully not too embarrassing) reminder of just how far you have progressed.

Summary

Having read this chapter, you should:

- be better able to choose a research topic which is feasible and motivates you;
- have an understanding of how you may focus your original ideas into something more achievable;
- be aware of the issues involved in choosing a supervisor;
- have a clearer idea of the advantages and disadvantages of group research, and of researching your own organization;
- be ready to get on with the actual research work!

Exercises

2.1   Make as complete a list as you can of all the costs you are likely to incur during your research project. Add an additional figure for unexpected costs. Can you afford it?

2.2   Make a list of all the (financial and non-financial) resources you have access to, and of those you believe you will need access to in order to carry out your research project. How will you access those resources you don't already have access to?

2.3   Write down up to four key questions which your research project seeks to address. Begin each one with a questioning word such as how, who, what, when or why. Which of these questions is the most important or central to your research?

2.4   Make a list of the key concepts, issues and contexts of importance to your research (see Box 2.5 for explanations of these terms).

2.5   Note down the prospective contents of your planned dissertation, thesis or report. You can do this chapter by chapter, or section by section, but include subheadings and details. Try to set yourself realistic word limits for the various chapters or sections.

2.6   Identify and list the qualities you are looking for in your supervisor(s). Once you have done this, arrange them in order of priority.

Further reading

In this section we list a selection of books that are of particular relevance to the topics discussed in this chapter. We would stress two points about this listing. First, that a particular book is not included does not mean that we don't rate it: social research is a vast field, and we simply have not read everything. Second, we have deliberately kept the list to recently published books that are still in print. There are many older texts that you may come across, perhaps earlier editions of some of those we mention, in the library or second-hand, and which are also valuable.

Andrews, R. (2003) *Research Questions*. London: Continuum.
    Discusses how to formulate research questions, subsidiary and contributory questions, and the relationship between research questions and methodology.
Bell, J. (2005) *Doing Your Research Project: A guide to first-time researchers in education and social science*, 4th edition. Maidenhead: Open University Press.
    This introductory text reviews the stages of implementing a research project.
Biggam, J. (2008) *Succeeding with your Master's Dissertation: A practical step-by-step handbook*. Maidenhead: Open University Press.
    Takes the student through the stages of planning, researching and writing a dissertation.
Boynton, P. (2005) *The Research Companion: A practical guide for the social and health sciences*. London: Routledge.

Offers advice on all the main elements of the research process, including safety issues and ethics.

Brause, R. (2000) *Writing Your Doctoral Dissertation: Invisible rules for success.* London: Falmer Press.
Covering more than just writing, this book is organized in three main sections: getting a sense of the terrain, preparing for your study, and doing your study.

Burton, D. (ed.) (2000) *Research Training for Social Scientists: A handbook for postgraduate researchers.* London: Sage.
Eight main sections consider philosophical issues; ethical and legal issues; getting started; qualitative research design, data collection and analysis; qualitative software; survey research design and data collection; quantitative data analysis; and finishing off.

Burton, N., Brundrett, M. and Jones, M. (2008) *Doing Your Education Research Project.* London: Sage.
Considers planning, practice, gathering evidence, analysis and presentation.

Cryer, P. (2006) *The Research Student's Guide to Success*, 3rd edition. Buckingham: Open University Press.
From registering and settling in, through interacting with your supervisor, managing yourself and cooperating with others, to dealing with flagging, producing your thesis and conducting yourself in the examination.

Denscombe, M. (2002) *Ground Rules for Good Research: A 10 point guide for social researchers.* Buckingham: Open University Press.
This book is organized in terms of the ten points identified: purpose, relevance, resources, originality, accuracy, accountability, generalizations, objectivity, ethics and proof.

Denscombe, M. (2007) *The Good Research Guide for Small-Scale Social Research Projects*, 3rd edition. Maidenhead: Open University Press.
The three parts of the book focus on strategies (surveys, case studies, experiments, action research, ethnography), methods (questionnaires, interviews, observation, documents) and analysis (quantitative, qualitative, writing up).

Gray, D. (2004) *Doing Research in the Real World.* London: Sage.
A clear and accessible guide, particularly for those undertaking research projects in the workplace.

Grix, J. (2001) *Demystifying Postgraduate Research: From MA to PhD.* Birmingham: University of Birmingham Press.
An introductory guide, with summaries, suggestions for further reading and a useful glossary of research terms. Covers the nature of doctoral research, nuts and bolts issues, getting started, the process of research, supervision and the viva.

Hunt, A. (2005) *Your Research Project: How to manage it.* London: Routledge.
Focuses on the process, covering management, the literature survey, communication, report writing and the viva.

Knight, P. (2002) *Small-Scale Research: Pragmatic inquiry in social science and the caring professions.* London: Sage.

A systematic guide to the process and methods of small-scale research, aimed at improving research practice.

Leonard, D. (2001) *A Woman's Guide to Doctoral Studies*. Buckingham: Open University Press.
A process-based guide written from the perspective of a woman for other women.

Levin, P. (2005) *Excellent Dissertations!* Maidenhead: Open University Press.
Designed as a brief, 'student-friendly' guide.

Meloy, J. (2002) *Writing the Qualitative Dissertation: Understanding by doing*. Mahwah, NJ: Lawrence Erlbaum.
Slightly misleadingly titled, this book covers much more than just writing, and is informed by quotations from 40 recent doctoral students.

Murray, L. and Lawrence, B. (2000) *Practitioner-Based Enquiry: Principles and practices for postgraduate research*. London: Falmer.
Designed for postgraduate students undertaking small-scale research projects in or around their work environments and/or as part of a higher education programme.

O'Leary, Z. (2004) *The Essential Guide to Doing Research*. London: Sage.
Designed to get students to reflect on every stage in the research process.

Phillips, E. and Pugh, D. (2005) *How to Get a PhD*, 4th edition. Maidenhead: Open University Press.
A classic, full of useful guidance.

Potter, S. (ed.) (2002) *Doing Postgraduate Research*. London: Sage.
An Open University reader, its eight chapters examine topics such as getting going, planning and organizing, writing, using computers, responsibilities and the examination process.

Punch, K. (2000) *Developing Effective Research Proposals*. London: Sage.
Accessible guide, with examples, to the processes involved in drawing up a research proposal.

Robson, C. (2002) *Real World Research: A resource for social scientists and practitioner researchers*, 2nd edition. Oxford: Blackwell.
Comprehensive in scope, the text includes discussion of surveys, case studies, experimental design outside the laboratory, observation, interviews, questionnaires, analysis of quantitative and qualitative data, dissemination and the practitioner-researcher.

Rugg, G. and Petre, M. (2004) *The Unwritten Rules of PhD Research*. Maidenhead: Open University Press.
Aims to tell you the things that former PhD students wish they had known before they started.

Thomas, G. (2009) *How to do your Research Project: A guide for students in education and applied social sciences*. London: Sage.
Aims to take the reader through all of the stages involved in doing a research project.

Walliman, N. (2005) *Your Research Project: A step-by-step guide for the first-time researcher*, 2nd edition. London: Sage.

Includes new material on ethics, critical reading skills and literature reviews.
Wisker, G. (2001) *The Postgraduate Research Handbook: Succeed with your MA, MPhil, EdD or PhD*. Basingstoke: Palgrave.
Organized in four parts, focusing on starting research, getting going, maintaining momentum and finishing off.

3

Thinking about methods

Introduction

Many, perhaps most, introductory books on doing research pay a great deal of attention to the extensive variety of research methods which are available and in use. If you are already well into your research project, detailed guidance on the use of particular methods may, of course, be invaluable. If, on the other hand, you are just beginning research, or lack confidence, such detail and its associated jargon can be both discouraging and demotivating.

The approach we have taken in this chapter is to present your choice and use of research methods as an integral part of the whole process of doing research, and to relate this to the rest of your life. From this perspective, we would argue not just that you can do research, but that you already possess many useful research skills.

> If you have not already done so, you might usefully read the section in Chapter 1 on **Getting a flavour of possibilities** at this point.

The chapter is organized in the following sections:

- **Everyday research skills.** Applying life skills and experience to research.
- **Which method is best?** Thinking about research philosophy and design.
- **Families, approaches and techniques.** Alternative approaches to thinking about research methods.
- **Action research.** Using your research project to study and change something you care about.
- **Case studies.** Focusing your research project on a particular example or examples.
- **Experiments.** Testing your research hypotheses through controlled studies.
- **Surveys.** Collecting data from people, materials and artefacts.
- **Which methods suit?** Different ways to think about your choice.
- **Deciding about methods.** Issues to bear in mind when deciding upon your research design.

Everyday research skills

Many everyday skills – such as reading, listening and watching – are important research skills. Researchers use such skills for the collection, selection, analysis and presentation of data. Researchers, however, make use of these taken-for-granted skills in a conscious, considered and systematic fashion, and aim to be rigorous, critical and analytical. And they also keep records of their activities.

Research involves the professionalization of these everyday skills. And it also requires the researcher to pay particular attention to alternative values, views, meanings and explanations; while remaining alert to biases and distortions. Your experience and understanding of everyday skills provide a ready route into thinking about research design and methods. Consider, for example, the following skills.

Reading

We regularly read from a wide variety of sources: books, newspapers, magazines, instruction manuals and so on. We are not only literate, but familiar with the particular conventions involved in reading different sorts of materials. Thus we are likely to be critical in reading election literature or double glazing publicity material, but more relaxed when reading popular novels or magazines. You will have developed many skills through reading, not least how to understand and relate to what you are reading.

> Chapter 4 focuses on **Reading for research**. If you have not looked at it yet, you might usefully scan it now.

Listening

Unless we have a hearing impairment, we will spend much or all of our time, consciously or subconsciously, listening: to friends and members of our families, to our colleagues and associates, to the people we meet in the street or in the shops, to radio and television programmes, to records, tapes or CDs, to the 'background' sounds of our environment. Through this constant listening, you will have developed skills in identifying different people's voices, their attitudes and emotions, their openness and honesty. You will have learnt how to extract useful information from listening, and how to relate this information to that coming to you from other sources.

> The issues involved in listening for research are considered further in the section on **Interviews** in Chapter 7.

Watching

We watch our children, pets and those we care for at home; we watch the behaviour of our colleagues at work; we watch what we are doing ourselves as we cross the street or negotiate our way through a crowded room; we watch television for information, entertainment or relaxation; we watch sporting or cultural events in our leisure time. Through watching, you will have learnt to identify a wide range of visual signals, indicative of, for example, friendliness, unease or danger. Watching, like listening and reading, involves categorizing.

> The issues involved in watching for research are considered further in the section on **Observations** in Chapter 7.

Choosing

Every day of our life we make many deliberate choices. These range from the fairly trivial – which breakfast cereal to have, which route to take to work, when to go to bed – to the momentous – whether to move house or change our job, whether to get married, split up or have a child. In making choices, we are aware that there are a variety of options open to us, each with different implications. Through choosing, you will have developed skills of relevance to selecting topics for research, methods to be used in research, and the subjects or objects to be sampled during the research.

> **Sampling and selection** are considered in Chapter 6.

Questioning

In performing everyday skills, we are implicitly questioning the information we receive through our senses, placing this within acceptable frameworks, critically assessing its relevance, and challenging it when we find it wanting. You will have built up considerable skill in questioning, both directly, through asking questions of others, and indirectly, through reviewing the information you have gathered from various sources. These skills are particularly relevant when using documentary sources and questionnaire techniques.

> The use of **Documents** and **Questionnaires** for data collection is considered further in Chapter 7.

Summarizing

We do not treat all of the information which we constantly receive in everyday life as being of equal value, but reject most of it as being of little or no value, and critically question much of the rest. What we choose to retain in our memory for future application will typically be in summary form. Thus, if a colleague asks us what happened at a meeting yesterday, we will provide a summary response: we are highly unlikely to give, or be able to give, a verbatim report. Through such everyday actions, you will have learnt a great deal about summarizing information: what to leave out, what to stress, what is of key importance.

> The issues involved in summarizing data are considered in the section on **Managing your data** in Chapter 8.

Organizing

In addition to summarizing the information you receive in everyday life, you will have become quite adept at organizing it. Thus, in recounting to your colleague what happened at the meeting, you will organize your account in a particular way. You might do this by giving them the key points first, and then filling in the detail; or by focusing on the most momentous events; or by telling your story in its historical sequence.

> The techniques involved in organizing your research project are the subject of Chapter 5, **Managing your project**; while the organization of your writing is considered in the section on **How to argue** in Chapter 10.

Writing

Adults' experience of writing, as of reading, varies quite considerably. Some of you will have recent experience of extended pieces of writing, such as reports or essays, perhaps even books. Others will be more familiar with shorter and more immediate forms of writing, such as emails, letters or memos. Or you may have done very little writing at all since your school days, having a job and a lifestyle which do not require much written communication.

> Writing for research purposes is the subject of Chapter 10, **Writing up**.

Presenting

Presentation may be seen as related to writing. However, while you may have little current day-to-day experience of writing at any length, you are highly likely to have some experience of presenting your ideas in non-written forms: verbally and/or visually. You will probably have had to do this to your colleagues, to your fellow students, to your family and friends. Presenting forms part of the general process of discussion and argument. It is a key way in which you exert your influence on others and establish your place in the world.

> The presentation of your research is considered further in the section on **What do I do now?** in Chapter 11.

Reflecting

The final everyday skill to be considered here, reflection, is perhaps the most researcherly. It has to do with the ability to stand back from, and think carefully about, what you have done or are doing. You will almost certainly have done this many times, in reflecting on, for example, how the day at work went, or whether, had you said or done something differently, things might have worked out better. In research terms, it is particularly important to reflect upon your own role in the research process.

> The issues of reflection and reflexivity are considered further in the section on **Which methods suit?** later in this chapter.

In carrying out your research project, you will probably make use of all of the everyday skills we have identified in this section. You will use them in combination as well as individually, and you will devote a lot of conscious thought to your use and development of them.

Which method is best?

You can never empirically or logically determine the best approach. This can only be done reflectively by considering a situation to be studied and your own opinion of life. This also means that even if you believe that one approach is more interesting or rewarding than another, we . . . do not want to rank one approach above another. In fact, we cannot *on any general ground*. The only thing we can do is to try to make explicit the special characteristics on which the various approaches are based.
(Arbnor and Bjerke 1997: 5, emphasis in original)

There are many ways of thinking about, and categorizing, the wide variety of methods available for designing, carrying out and analysing the results of research. As we have already noted, there are numerous texts available that either attempt to provide a comprehensive overview of these methods, or focus on a smaller selection or just one method. Understandably, then, for those new to research a key question is, which method is best? It is easy to be confused.

You may ask, 'why can't we "just" collect data and make statements?' (Arbnor and Bjerke 1997: 3). However, the choice of the 'best' method is not simply the technical or practical question that it might at first appear. Different kinds of research approaches produce different kinds of knowledge about the phenomena under study. The question 'which method is best?' is not solely about whether, for example, to use interviews, questionnaires or observations. Underpinning these research tools are more general philosophical questions about how we understand social reality, and what are the most appropriate ways of studying it.

A key distinction may be made here between *method* and *methodology*. The term *method* can be understood to relate principally to the tools of data collection or analysis: techniques such as questionnaires and interviews. *Methodology* has a more philosophical meaning, and usually refers to the approach or paradigm that underpins the research. Thus, an interview that is conducted within, say, a qualitative approach or paradigm will have a different underlying purpose and produce broadly different data from an interview conducted within a quantitative paradigm.

See the section in this chapter on **Families, approaches and techniques** for a discussion of quantitative and qualitative research paradigms.

An awareness of the implications of methodological issues, their impact on the kinds of knowledge that research produces, and what kinds of knowledge it is possible to produce, is an important but often neglected issue in small-scale research. Our purposes here are to draw your attention to the broader philosophical issues associated with researching social reality. We aim to do this in two ways:

- By providing some guidance about how you can develop an understanding of the underlying philosophical issues that impact on your research
- By indicating the main issues that you should consider in the initial design of your research.

In Chapter 2 (see Box 2.3) we set out five questions as a way of helping you focus your research. We want to build on these questions here by encouraging you to explore more fully your own, and others', assumptions about social reality and how knowledge is produced about that reality. We all have theories – though we may not refer to them in this way – about how the world works, what the nature of humankind is, and what it is possible to know and not know. In social science, these issues are often categorized and referred to as paradigms. The usefulness of the term 'paradigm' is that it offers a way of categorizing a body of complex beliefs and worldviews.

The most common paradigms that new researchers are introduced to are those termed *quantitative* and *qualitative* (see also the following section). These terms are often presented as competing alternatives, and this should alert you to the political and contested nature of knowledge construction. As Oakley (1999) comments:

> [Paradigms] are ways of breaking down the complexity of the real world that tell their adherents what to do. Paradigms are essentially intellectual *cultures*, and as such they are fundamentally embedded in the socialization of their adherents: a way of life rather than simply a set of technical and procedural differences.
>
> (Oakley 1999: 155, emphasis in original)

Because of the degree of adherence such socialization can produce about the 'correct' way of researching the social world, discussion about the relative merits of quantitative or qualitative approaches has at times become very heated.

The quantitative and qualitative paradigms offer a basic framework for dividing up knowledge camps. Yet, within these two broad camps there are debates about how social research should proceed, and about what forms of knowledge are perceived to be valid and invalid. The difficulty for all of us is that these debates are complex and often invoke the use of very inaccessible language. It is no wonder, then, that students ask what is wrong with simply focusing on the collection of data, as this involves using a set of technical skills that can be fairly easily learnt. Moreover, these are the skills, as we have already pointed out, with which you are most familiar in terms of having prior experience.

Our advice to those who are new to these paradigm debates is twofold. First, you might begin by focusing on the following five paradigms: positivist and post-positivist, interpretive, critical and postmodern. The first three of these are the most common in social research. More recently, there has been a growth of interest in the potential and limitations of research that operates within postmodern assumptions. Box 3.1 provides definitions of these paradigms.

Box 3.1 Social research paradigms: some definitions

Positivism: This is the view that social science procedures should mirror, as near as possible, those of the natural sciences. The researcher should be objective and detached from the objects of research. It is possible to capture 'reality' through the use of research instruments such as experiments and questionnaires. The aims of positivist research are to offer explanations leading to control and predictability. Positivism has been a very predominant way of knowing the social world; what Guba and Lincoln (2005) refer to as the 'received view'. This can be seen by the ways in which many still perceive positivist approaches to be simply a commonsensical way of conducting research. While there are many varieties of positivism (see Crotty 1998), quantitative approaches that use statistics and experiments are seen as classic examples.

Post-positivism: This is a response to the criticisms that have been made about positivism. As its name suggests, post-positivism maintains the same set of basic beliefs as positivism. However, post-positivists argue that we can only know social reality imperfectly and probabilistically. While objectivity remains an ideal, there is an increased use of qualitative techniques in order to 'check' the validity of findings. 'Postpositivism holds that only partially objective accounts of the world can be produced, for all methods for examining such accounts are flawed' (Denzin and Lincoln 2005: 27).

Interpretivism: Interpretivist approaches to social research see interpretations of the social world as culturally derived and historically situated. Interpretivism is often linked to the work of Weber, who suggested that the social sciences are concerned with *verstehen* (understanding). This is compared to *erklaren* (explaining), which forms the basis of seeking causal explanations and is the hallmark of the natural sciences. The distinction between *verstehen* and *erklaren* underlies that (often exaggerated) between qualitative and quantitative research approaches. Interpretivism has many variants. These include hermeneutics, phenomenology and symbolic interactionism.

Critical: As you might expect, critical social paradigms critique both positivism and interpretivism as ways of understanding the social world. 'Critical inquiry . . . [is not] a research that seeks merely to understand . . . [it is] a research that challenges . . . that [takes up a view] of conflict and oppression . . . that seeks to bring about change' (Crotty 1998: 112). Included in this category would be feminism, neo-Marxism, anti-racist and participatory approaches.

Postmodern: While the other paradigms offer grand theories for understanding the social world, 'advocates of postmodernism have argued that the era of big narratives and theories is over: locally, temporally and situationally limited narratives are now required' (Flick 1998: 2). Postmodernist approaches seek to overcome the boundaries that are placed between art and social science. Postmodern approaches do not offer a view of rational progression to a better world. All we might expect is that social life will be in some ways different. As with the other paradigms, there are a variety of positions within the broad label of postmodernism. These would include post-structuralism.

Second, to aid your understanding of the relevancy of broader issues of methodology to your own research, particularly at the research design stage, Box 3.2 sets out some questions to illustrate the distinctions and similarities

Box 3.2 Thinking methodologically about research design

- What are the main purposes of your research? For example, are you trying to change injustices in the world, or are you trying to understand how social reality is perceived through the perspectives of the researched?
- What is your role in the research? For example, are you an 'expert' or a change agent?
- What is the nature of knowledge? For example, do you believe that there are facts or laws that can be known, or is knowledge informed historically through insights that occur from time to time and replace ignorance and misapprehensions?
- What are the criteria that you are bringing to judge the quality of your research? For example, should the research be objective and generalizable, or should it contribute to a fundamental change in social life?
- Do you think your values should affect your research?
- What is the place of ethics in your research? For example, do you consider it sufficient to abide by a code of professional ethics, or should the way the research is conducted closely match your own ethical frameworks?
- What 'voice' do you adopt (or are you encouraged to adopt) when writing a research report? For example, do you write as a disinterested scientist, a transformative intellectual or a passionate participant?

- What do you (and your teachers, managers and/or colleagues) think are the essential issues that you need research training in? For example, should you be trained primarily in technical knowledge about measurement, design and quantitative methods, in this and qualitative approaches, or do you need to be resocialized away from your existing assumptions about the nature of research?
- Can you accommodate several methodologies in your research?
- Who are the audience for your research? For example, are you hoping to persuade government administrators, funders and policy committees, feminists and Marxists or your colleagues and fellow researchers?

(*Source*: Adapted from Guba and Lincoln 2005)

between key research paradigms. These questions should cause you to reflect on some of the methodological issues associated with the design, conduct and knowledge generation implicit in your own research.

Families, approaches and techniques

In this section, we take a simpler and more straightforward way into the discussion of methods and methodologies by looking at three successive levels:

- Two research *families*, or general strategies for doing research (two alternative formulations are offered).
- Four *approaches* to designing your research project.
- Four *techniques* for collecting data.

These families, approaches and techniques are summarized in Box 3.3. The two alternative pairings of families are discussed in this section, while the four approaches are the subject of the following four sections. The four techniques are separately considered in Chapter 7, **Collecting data**.

Families

Research is a systematic investigation to find answers to a problem. Research in professional social science areas, like research in other subjects, has generally followed the traditional objective scientific method. Since the 1960s, however, a strong move towards a more qualitative, naturalistic and subjective approach has left social scientists divided between two competing methods: the scientific empirical tradition, and the naturalistic phenomenological mode. In the scientific method, quantitative research methods are employed in an attempt to establish general laws or principles.

Box 3.3 Research families, approaches and techniques

Research families

- Quantitative or Qualitative
- Deskwork or Fieldwork

Research approaches

- Action research
- Case studies
- Experiments
- Surveys

Research techniques

- Documents
- Interviews
- Observations
- Questionnaires

Such a scientific approach is often termed nomothetic and assumes social reality is objective and external to the individual. The naturalistic approach to research emphasizes the importance of the subjective experience of individuals, with a focus on qualitative analysis. Social reality is regarded as a creation of individual consciousness, with meaning and the evaluation of events seen as a personal and subjective construction. Such a focus on the individual case rather than general law-making is termed an ideographic approach.

(Burns 2000: 3)

As the above quotation indicates, researchers are adept at classifying themselves and their peers into two groups: us and them. In this subsection we will consider two alternative research dichotomies: qualitative/quantitative and deskwork/fieldwork. The first of these distinctions has been the subject of much debate. The second distinction is much more pragmatic, and hence less debated, and has to do with the individual researcher's preferences and opportunities for going out to do their research (fieldwork) or staying in their office, library or laboratory (deskwork).

Qualitative or quantitative?

Quantitative research is empirical research where the data are in the form of numbers. Qualitative research is empirical research where the data are not in the form of numbers.

(Punch 2005: 3)

Quantitative research tends to involve relatively large-scale and representative sets of data, and is often, falsely in our view, presented or perceived as being about the gathering of 'facts'. Qualitative research, on the other hand, is concerned with collecting and analysing information in as many forms, chiefly non-numeric, as possible. It tends to focus on exploring, in as much detail as possible, smaller numbers of instances or examples which are seen as being interesting or illuminating, and aims to achieve 'depth' rather than 'breadth'.

There has been widespread debate in recent years within many of the social sciences regarding the relative merits of quantitative and qualitative strategies for research. The positions taken by individual researchers vary considerably, from those who see the two strategies as entirely separate and based on alternative views of the world, to those who are happy to mix these strategies within their research projects. Because quantitative strategies have been seen as more scientific or 'objective', qualitative researchers have felt the need to argue their case strongly. Qualitative research has become increasingly popular. The continuing debate over its relative merits can be seen more broadly as being about the status and politics of different kinds of research.

How distinctive are qualitative and quantitative forms of research? On first consideration, the use of questionnaires as a research technique might be seen as a quantitative strategy, whereas interviews and observations might be thought of as qualitative techniques. In practice, however, it is often more complicated than that. Thus, interviews may be structured and analysed in a quantitative manner, as when numeric data is collected or when non-numeric answers are categorized and coded in numeric form. Similarly, surveys may allow for open-ended responses and lead to the in-depth study of individual cases.

Box 3.4 sets out the perceived differences between the qualitative and quantitative research families, while Box 3.5 sets out their similarities.

Fieldwork or deskwork?

The distinction between fieldwork and deskwork offers an alternative way of thinking about basic research strategies.

Fieldwork refers to the process of going out to collect research data. Such data may be described as original or empirical, and cannot be accessed without the researcher engaging in some kind of expedition. It might, for example, involve visiting an institution to interview members of staff, or standing on a

Box 3.4 The differences between qualitative and quantitative research

Qualitative paradigms	Quantitative paradigms
• Concerned with understanding behaviour from actors' own frames of reference	• Seeks the facts/causes of social phenomena
• Naturalistic and uncontrolled observation	• Obtrusive and controlled measurement
• Subjective	• Objective
• Close to the data: the 'insider' perspective	• Removed from the data: the 'outsider' perspective
• Grounded, discovery oriented, exploratory, expansionist, descriptive, inductive	• Ungrounded, verification oriented, reductionist, hypothetico-deductive
• Process oriented	• Outcome oriented
• Valid: real, rich, deep data	• Reliable: hard and replicable data
• Ungeneralizable: single case studies	• Generalizable: multiple case studies
• Holistic	• Particularistic
• Assumes a dynamic reality	• Assumes a stable reality

(*Source*: Adapted from Oakley 1999: 156)

Box 3.5 The similarities between qualitative and quantitative research

- While quantitative research may be used mostly for testing theory, it can also be used for exploring an area and generating hypotheses and theory.
- Similarly, qualitative research can be used for testing hypotheses and theories, even though it is used mostly for theory generation.
- Qualitative data often includes quantification (e.g. statements such as more than, less than, most, as well as specific numbers).
- Quantitative approaches (e.g. large-scale surveys) can collect qualitative (non-numeric) data through open-ended questions.
- The underlying philosophical positions are not necessarily as distinct as the stereotypes suggest.

street corner administering questionnaires to passers-by, or sitting in on a meeting to observe what takes place. In some disciplines, such as anthropology and sociology, fieldwork assumes particular importance.

Deskwork, on the other hand, consists of those research processes which do not necessitate going into the field. It consists, literally, of those things which can be done while sitting at a desk. These may include, for example, the administration, collection and analysis of postal surveys, the analysis of data collected by others, certain kinds of experimental or laboratory work, literature searches in the library, research using the internet, and, of course, writing.

As in the case of the qualitative–quantitative divide, the fieldwork–deskwork distinction is also something of a false dichotomy, since most, though not all, research projects will make use of both sets of approaches. No matter how much time a researcher spends in the field, it is difficult to avoid some deskwork, even if this consists only of writing up results. Similarly, although it is possible to carry out useful research without ever leaving an office environment, information is usually still being accessed somehow.

The distinction between fieldwork and deskwork is, obviously, also not clear cut. It is debatable, for example, into which category one would place telephone or email interviews, which can be conducted at the desk but effectively take the researcher, at least electronically, into the field. And how would you categorize using your laptop while out in the field collecting data? The development of information and communication technologies, in particular the growth of the internet, is undoubtedly blurring the fieldwork/deskwork distinction.

From the perspective of practice, however, this distinction may be more significant to researchers than that between qualitative and quantitative methods. An appreciation of it may help you in planning and implementing your research project. Your opportunities and preference for either fieldwork or deskwork – and you will most likely prefer one or the other – may help you in choosing, where this is possible, not just the topic of your research but also the kinds of methods you use.

Approaches

Box 3.3 identified four basic approaches to, or designs for, research in the social sciences: action research, case studies, experiments and surveys. These are discussed individually in more detail in the following four sections of this chapter.

It should be said at once that this classification is not meant to be either definitive or exclusive. It simply recognizes the most common approaches used by those carrying out small-scale research projects. Individual projects may, of course – as the examples given later in this chapter illustrate – involve more than one of these approaches: thus, a case study may be carried out through action research, while particular projects may involve both experiments and surveys.

Techniques

Box 3.3 also identified four basic social science research techniques: the study of documents, interviews, observations or questionnaires. These techniques are considered in more detail in Chapter 7, where the focus is on **Collecting data**.

Linking families, approaches and techniques

It should be stressed that the various families, approaches and techniques identified here do not map simply on to each other. Thus, it is possible to use action research, case study or survey approaches within either a qualitative or a quantitative research strategy; but experiments tend to be quantitative in nature. Similarly, case studies, experiments and survey approaches might be employed as part of desk-based or field-based research strategies; but action research tends to imply some fieldwork. Documents, interviews, observations and questionnaires may be used as part of all of the research strategies and approaches identified, though the way in which they are used and analysed will vary.

In other words, the families, approaches and techniques represent dimensions of the research process. The researcher may use alternatives from the different dimensions in combination as appropriate to study a particular set of research questions. You may focus on specific approaches or techniques, and concentrate on either deskwork or fieldwork, or a qualitative or quantitative strategy; or you might mix or vary your usage. It is up to you, given your preferences, the resources you have available, the constraints you are operating under, and the particular issues which you wish to research.

Action research

> AR [action research] is a complex, dynamic activity involving the best efforts of both members of communities or organizations and professional researchers. It simultaneously involves the co-generation of new information and analysis together with actions aimed at transforming the situation in democratic directions. AR is holistic and also context bound, producing practical solutions and new knowledge as part of an integrated set of activities . . . AR is a way of producing tangible and desired results for the people involved, and it is a knowledge-generation process that produces insights both for researchers and the participants. It is a complex action-knowledge generation process . . . the immense importance of insider knowledge and initiatives is evident, marking a clear distinction from orthodox research that systematically distrusts insider knowledge as co-opted.
>
> (Greenwood and Levin 1998: 50)

> Action research is referred to variously as a term, process, enquiry, approach, flexible spiral process and as cyclic. It has a practical, problem-solving emphasis. It is carried out by individuals, professionals and educators. It involves research, systematic, critical reflection and action. It aims to improve educational practice. Action is undertaken to understand, evaluate and change.
>
> (Costello 2003: 5)

Action research is an increasingly popular approach among small-scale researchers in the social sciences, particularly for those working in professional areas such as education, health and social care. It is well suited to the needs of people conducting research in their workplaces, and who have a focus on improving aspects of their own and their colleagues' practices. For example, the teacher who is concerned to improve performance in the classroom may find action research useful because it offers a systematic approach to the definition, solution and evaluation of problems and concerns.

Yet, action research is also an important approach for those with wider concerns for social justice. It lends itself to the direct involvement and collaboration of those whom it is designed to benefit. This is particularly the case for participatory action research, which is not designed and undertaken by research 'experts' alone, but in partnership with people who are involved in the issues that the research is addressing. In some fields of study, such as mental health or social work, user involvement may even be a requirement. Box 3.6 summarizes two contrasting examples of action research, one from further education, the other from a commercial company. Box 3.7 lists seven criteria distinguishing action research from other approaches.

Box 3.6 Two examples of action research projects

The type of action research proposed was that of practical-deliberative action research, where researchers and practitioners come together to identify potential problems, underlying causes and possible interventions. The aim is to move towards a form of action research which is concerned with development and change, participatory action research . . . A conventional action research approach was envisaged to:

- examine the nature of the problem situation;
- devise an appropriate product-based intervention;
- trial this (and the supporting mechanisms);
- evaluate the impact.

Focus groups, scenario planning and soft systems techniques (including use of rich pictures) were variously used to support shared discussion during the initial consideration of the problem and possible interventions. Similar techniques were used to reflect on lessons learned at the evaluation stages.

(Rowley et al. 2004: 239)

Mr B . . . manages a team of 19 staff. At regular meetings, Mr B requests contributions from the group that focus on work undertaken, progress made, issues and problems that arise, etc. Mr B is keen to explore the role his questioning plays in enhancing the group's learning and development . . . He would like to find out whether his own perceptions of his questioning are confirmed through research and so decides to initiate a project . . .

He decides to gather research data using two methods. The first involves a senior colleague observing his questioning during meetings in order to ascertain the number and nature of the questions asked. Mr B devises an observation chart using a category system that focuses on: open questions; closed questions; affective questions ('How do you feel about . . .?'); probing questions ('What aspects of your behaviour do you think might be relevant here?'); checking questions ('What you plan to do is . . . Is that right?'); and reflective questions ('In what way were your colleagues' questions confusing?'). He asks his colleague to indicate on the data sheet provided how many questions are asked in each category.

(Costello 2003: 51–3)

Box 3.7 Criteria distinguishing action research

We have selected seven criteria to distinguish different types of action research, and would argue that these seven, in dynamic interaction, distinguish action research from other methodologies . . . Action research:

1 is educative;
2 deals with individuals as members of social groups;
3 is problem-focused, context-specific and future-orientated;
4 involves a change intervention;
5 aims at improvement and involvement;
6 involves a cyclic process in which research, action and evaluation are interlinked;
7 is founded on a research relationship in which those involved are participants in the change process.

(Hart and Bond 1995: 37–8)

From these descriptions, you may have formed the impression that action research can be a very demanding, but also very rewarding, research approach. For this reason, it should not be lightly engaged in, and is probably inappropriate for most small-scale research projects. Box 3.8 identifies a number of inappropriate uses of action research.

Action research is clearly a very applied approach, one which could also be seen as experimental. It offers a research design which links the research process closely to its context, and is predicated upon the idea of research having a practical purpose in view and leading to change. As the diagram in Box 3.9 indicates, it also fits well with the idea of the research process as a spiral activity, going through repeated cycles and changing each time.

Box 3.8 Inappropriate uses of action research

Never use action research to:

1 Drive an unpopular policy or initiative through.
2 Experiment with different solutions without thinking through very carefully their soundness and the ethics involved.
3 Manipulate employees or practitioners into thinking they have contributed to a policy decision when it has already been made.
4 Try to bring a dysfunctional team or workgroup together (whether or not they actually are dysfunctional, any doubts you may have suggest you need to examine your 'systems' first, before engaging in a time-consuming and potentially disruptive project).
5 Bolster a flagging career. Action research will expose any weaknesses you may have extremely quickly!

(*Source*: Adapted from Morton-Cooper 2000: 24–5)

Box 3.9 The participatory action research spiral

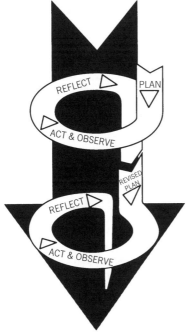

(*Source*: Atweh et al. 1998: 22)

See the section on **Getting a flavour of possibilities** in Chapter 1.

For these reasons, action research is likely to involve an extensive component of fieldwork, as opposed to deskwork. How might it be located, however, with reference to the distinction between quantitative and qualitative strategies? Try Exercise 3.1.

If you have concluded that action research is chiefly or necessarily qualitative, you might like to look again at the second example of action research given in Box 3.6. Would you say that this project adopted a qualitative strategy, either wholly or in part?

Case studies

Unlike the experimenter who manipulates variables to determine their causal significance or the surveyor who asks standardized questions of large, representative samples of individuals, the case study researcher typically observes the characteristics of an individual unit – a child, a clique, a class, a school or a community. The purpose of such observation is to probe deeply and to analyse intensively the multifarious phenomena that constitute the life cycle of the unit with a view to establishing generalizations about the wider population to which that unit belongs.

(Cohen et al. 2000: 185)

Case studies, as the name indicates, concentrate on special cases. Generalizations from case studies must be handled with care. To serve as a foundation for generalizations, case studies should be related to a theoretical framework, which in turn may be adjusted as case study results provide new evidence. The 'generalizability' of case studies can be increased by strategic selection of *critical cases*.

(Mikkelsen 2005: 92, emphasis in original)

The case study is, in many ways, ideally suited to the needs and resources of the small-scale researcher. It allows, indeed endorses, a focus on just one example, or perhaps two or three. This might be the researcher's place of work, or another institution or organization with which they have a connection: a company, a voluntary organization, a school, a ship or a prison. Or it might be just one element of such an organization: a class, a work team, a community group or a football team. Or the focus might be on one individual, or a small number of individuals, as in life history studies or analyses of how top managers have reached their positions.

Many of you may be familiar with case studies, and their analysis, through their use as examples on courses (especially in business studies, health care or law). In this sense, case studies are often used to illustrate problems or indicate good practices. The distinction between this usage of case studies and case study as a social research method lies in the explicit recognition, in the latter usage, of an underlying methodological philosophy about how we know the social world, and its linkage to a body of theory and practice in the literature.

Box 3.10 summarizes two contrasting examples of case study research. One involves the study of five national cases, the other just one family. While the latter is explicitly qualitative in approach, the former shows concerns with representativeness, and might also be described as a survey.

Restricting your research to a detailed study of one or a small number of cases does not, however, mean that the context for those cases can be ignored. It is a temptation, as it is with action research, for the researcher to immerse

---

Box 3.10 Two examples of case study research

Save the Children's Health Sustainability study looked at the way in which primary health care in developing countries was financed and organised through five case studies in countries with different character-istics. The study had a strong theoretical framework, and a standard set of information was gathered through substantial fieldwork in each country . . . In each case study country an analysis was undertaken of the histor-ical development of the health sector, an appraisal of the key factors (political, organisational and economic) which determine the context of health sector operation and development, and an analysis of the role of government, donors and communities.

(Laws et al. 2003: 345)

In essence this is a case study methodology in which I study one case – my family – within the context of being a family with one member that has a physical impairment.

(Davis and Salkin 2005: 210)

This latter research project examined the impact of physical impairment on family dynamics, and specifically on siblings. The first author's interest in this came from her own experience. She looked in the literature for evidence that others had shared her experiences, and found that little had been written on the sibling relationship. She was 'aware of the moral ethics of speaking for [her sister]' (Davis and Salkin 2005: 210), so, in writing, 'it was important to me that I not attempt to give my accounts of Kathy's experiences'. Instead, she made a 'conscious effort to give both of us voice' (p. 211). The article includes recollections, feedback and conversations, with the researcher's thoughts after the conversations written in parentheses.

themself wholly in the details of the case. This is a tendency which should be guarded against. Box 3.11 identifies this tendency, alongside other advantages and disadvantages of this research approach.

Box 3.11   Advantages and disadvantages of case studies

Advantages

1   Case study data is drawn from people's experiences and practices and so it is seen to be strong in reality.
2   Case studies allow for generalizations from a specific instance to a more general issue.
3   Case studies allow the researcher to show the complexity of social life. Good case studies build on this to explore alternative meanings and interpretations.
4   Case studies can provide a data source from which further analysis can be made. They can, therefore, be archived for further research work.
5   Because case studies build on actual practices and experiences, they can be linked to action and their insights contribute to changing practice. Indeed, case study may be a subset of a broader action research project.
6   Because the data contained in case studies are close to people's experiences, they can be more persuasive and more accessible.

(*Source*: Adapted from Cohen et al. 2000: 184)

Disadvantages

The disadvantages of case studies are linked to their advantages. In particular:

1   The very complexity of a case can make analysis difficult. This is particularly so because the holistic nature of case study means that the researcher is often very aware of the connections between various events, variables and outcomes. Accordingly, *everything* appears relevant. It is not, however; and to write up your case as if it is does not make for good research. You might think about this in terms of a Russian doll metaphor, where each piece of data rests inside another, separate but related. You need to show the connections but not lose sight of the whole.
2   While the contextualization of aspects of the case strengthens this form of research, it is difficult to know where 'context' begins and ends.

You might like at this point to look again at the section on **Focusing** in Chapter 2, and particularly at Box 2.6.

One other caution about adopting a case study approach to your research project has already been mentioned in this book. It also applies to action research, as well as to other research approaches. This concerns the tendency of small-scale researchers, particularly those in employment who are receiving support from their employers, to base their research projects within their places of employment. While you may in practice have little or no choice about this, if you do have some choice, you should consider alternatives.

See the section in Chapter 2 on **Researching in your workplace**.

Case studies may be progressed in a variety of ways. Yin (2003: 5) identifies six types of case study, defined along two dimensions:

- In terms of the number of cases: single or multiple.
- In terms of the purpose of the study: exploratory, descriptive or explanatory.

Thus, we can talk in terms of single descriptive case studies, and multiple exploratory case studies, and so forth. Exercise 3.2 explores these categorizations a little further.

Experiments

The experiment is a situation in which the *independent variable* (also known as the exposure, the intervention, the experimental or predictor variable) is carefully manipulated by the investigator under known, tightly defined and controlled conditions, or by natural occurrence. At its most basic, the experiment consists of an *experimental group* which is exposed to the intervention under investigation and a control group which is not exposed. The experimental and control groups should be equivalent, and investigated systematically under conditions that are identical (apart from the exposure of the experimental group), in order to minimise variation between them.

(Bowling 2002: 216, emphasis in original)

For many people undertaking small-scale research in the social sciences, the idea of conducting experiments may seem rather strange. The experimental method is particularly associated with the physical sciences, where materials and non-human life forms are more amenable to experimentation. Indeed, experiments are at the heart of what is known as the scientific method, with its practice of formulating and testing hypotheses through carefully designed and controlled tests. The associated terminology appears very precise and suggestive.

Experiments are, however, widely used as a research approach in a number of the social sciences, particularly psychology (though this is often classified as a science rather than a social science), but also economics, health care and education. Box 3.12 summarizes two contrasting examples of experimental research, one hypothetical in nature, in the social sciences.

Box 3.12 Two examples of experimental research

I am sitting in a pub near Paddington station, clutching a small brandy. It's only about half past eleven in the morning – a bit early for drinking, but the alcohol is part reward, part Dutch courage. Reward because I have just spent an exhausting morning accidentally-on-purpose bumping into people and counting the number who said 'Sorry'; Dutch courage because I am now about to return to the train station and spend a few hours committing a deadly sin: queue jumping.

(Fox 2004: 1)

The disciplinary practices used by mothers to control their children in four ethnic groups in Australia are compared from a developmental perspective. A vignette approach was used in which each mother was asked to say how she would deal with 12 situations involving her oldest child at 8 years of age and at 4 years of age. The responses were coded as power assertion, love withdrawal, induction and permissiveness. Twenty mothers from each of the ethnic groups, Greek, Lebanese, Vietnamese and Anglo, from the same socioeconomic level and geographic area, were randomly chosen from lists of families that met the criteria for inclusion in the study.

(Papps et al. 1995: 49)

There are good reasons, though, for more caution in the use of experiments as a research approach in the social sciences. As already indicated, the social sciences are concerned with human behaviour and perspectives. A strict application of an experimental approach to research in these areas would suggest exposing one group of individuals to the experiment – which might be beneficial or disadvantageous, and difficult to judge in advance – while denying it to others. There are, in other words, ethical issues around the use of experiments involving people. Yet, while they appear particularly evident in the case of experiments, these issues are just as strong for other research approaches. They apply to action research, to case studies and to surveys as well.

These issues are discussed further in the section on **Access and ethical issues** in Chapter 6.

Some of the considerations to be borne in mind when designing a useful social experiment are addressed in Exercise 3.3. The advantages and disadvantages of experiments are summarized in Box 3.13.

Box 3.13 Advantages and disadvantages of experiments

Advantages

1   Through the random assignment of people to intervention and control groups (i.e. randomization of extraneous variables) the risk of extraneous variables confounding the results is minimized.
2   Control over the introduction and variation of the 'predictor' variables clarifies the direction of cause and effect.
3   If both pre- and post-testing are conducted, this controls for time-related threats to validity.
4   The modern design of experiments permits greater flexibility, efficiency and powerful statistical manipulation.
5   The experiment is the only research design which can, in principle, yield causal relationships.

Disadvantages

1   It is difficult to design experiments so as to represent a specified population.
2   It is often difficult to choose the 'control' variables so as to exclude all confounding variables.
3   With a large number of uncontrolled, extraneous variables it is impossible to isolate the one variable that is hypothesized as the cause of the other; hence the possibility always exists of alternative explanations.
4   Contriving the desired 'natural setting' in experiments is often not possible.
5   The experiment is an unnatural social situation with a differentiation of roles. The participant's role involves obedience to the experimenter (an unusual role).
6   Experiments cannot capture the diversity of goals, objectives and service inputs which may contribute to outcomes in natural settings.

(*Source*: Adapted from Bowling 2002: 218–19)

Surveys

A social survey is a type of research strategy. By this we mean that it involves an overall decision – a strategic decision – about the way to set about gathering and analysing data. The strategy involved in a survey is that *we collect the same information about all the cases in a sample*. Usually, the cases are individual people, and among other things we ask all of them the same questions.

(Aldridge and Levine 2001: 5, emphasis in original)

Surveys involve *systematic* observation or *systematic* interviewing. They ask the questions which the *researcher* wants answered, and often they dictate the range of answers that may be given. Standardization lies at the heart of survey research, and the whole point is to get consistent answers to consistent questions. We ask everyone precisely those questions that we want answered. More than this, we try to ask the questions in precisely the same way in each interview – to *standardize* the questionnaire as a measuring instrument.

(Sapsford 1999: 4–5, emphasis in original)

As these quotations indicate, surveys are usually associated as a research approach with the idea of asking groups of people questions. There is, however, a related meaning of survey which is also relevant to the social sciences. This is when the subjects which are being questioned by the researcher are really objects: materials or artefacts rather than people. Thus, most small-scale research projects will involve some kind of literature survey; but in some cases, as when documentary analysis is extensively used, this may be the basis for the whole project.

The issues involved in conducting a literature survey are considered in the section on **Coping with the research literature** in Chapter 4. The analysis of documents is discussed in the section on **Analysing documents** in Chapter 9.

Box 3.14 summarizes two contrasting examples of survey research, one a large-scale questionnaire survey, the other a smaller-scale example of 'research by correspondence'. Note the common concern with sampling strategy. The advantages and disadvantages of surveys are considered in Box 3.15. Like experiments, surveys have their own peculiar terminology, or jargon, which includes such terms as census, population, sample, case and variable.

Exercise 3.4 asks you to consider the value of questionnaire surveys in the light of the previous discussion of alternative research strategies and approaches.

Box 3.14 Two examples of survey research

A postal questionnaire was sent to a random sample of people aged 18 and over in England and Wales who were on the electoral register in 2000. The sample of 2777 was selected using an equal probability sampling design. Addresses were stratified by region, and within region by local authority. The survey was carried out between October 2002 and February 2003. Respondents were sent three reminders in addition to the first mailing. The original sample was reduced to 2489, as 288 had died or moved away. 1187 (48%) completed the questionnaire, 75 (3%) refused and 1227 (49%) did not reply.

(Calnan et al. 2005)

[M]y experience of postgraduate research led me, by accident rather than design, to another method that I had not previously considered. In the absence of a readily available sampling frame, I advertised for respondents in a variety of publications including local and national newspapers, women's magazines and 'infertility' and 'involuntary childless' support group magazines. This brought forth individuals who either preferred to write rather than talk about their experience (sometimes anonymously) and/or individuals who lived a considerable distance away. With these respondents, I engaged in . . . 'research by correspondence': an exchange of letters. Early on in the process I sent respondents a letter detailing the issues that I was interested in. I presented these as a mixture of questions and topic areas. From the perspective of respondents, it is possible to see a letter as something between a questionnaire and an in-depth interview.

(Letherby 2004: 182)

Box 3.15 Advantages and disadvantages of surveys

Advantages

1 With an appropriate sample, surveys may aim at representation and provide generalized results.
2 Surveys can be relatively easy to administer, and need not require any fieldwork.
3 Surveys may be repeated in the future or in different settings to allow comparisons to be made.
4 With a good response rate, surveys can provide a lot of data relatively quickly.

Disadvantages

1 The data, in the form of tables, pie charts and statistics, become the main focus of the research report, with a loss of linkage to wider theories and issues.
2 The data provide snapshots of points in time rather than a focus on the underlying processes and changes.
3 The researcher is often not in a position to check first hand the understandings of the respondents to the questions asked. Issues of truthfulness and accuracy are thereby raised.
4 The survey relies on breadth rather than depth for its validity. This is a crucial issue for small-scale researchers.

Questionnaires and interviews, the techniques which are at the heart of one type of survey research, occupy a major place in small-scale social science research projects. This is the case to such an extent that, when students or employees are asked to carry out a research study, they almost automatically think of using these techniques, often both at once. Interviews and questionnaires can also, of course, play a part in action research, case studies and experimental approaches to social science research. Yet they are not the only techniques available, with the use of documents and observations also widespread.

Which methods suit?

The question 'quantitative or qualitative?' is commonly asked, especially by beginning researchers. Often, they are putting the 'methods cart' before the 'content horse'. The best advice in those cases is to step back from questions of method [and tools], and give further consideration to the purposes and research questions, bearing in mind that the way questions are asked influences what needs to be done to answer them.

(Punch 2005: 240)

As this quote reminds us, you need to consider some of the broader issues of research design and philosophy before focusing on the tools and techniques for data collection. Box 3.16 poses some further questions to help you revise, reflect upon and reformulate your plans. In addition, there are other issues which you may need or wish to consider to help you reach your decision. Eight are considered in this section.

What do you need or want to find out?

One of the key determinants of the approach you might use in your research is undeniably the nature of the research proposed. You may want, or need,

---

Box 3.16 Which method to choose?

---

1   *Research questions.* What exactly are you trying to find out? Focus on the 'exactly' as this can lead you into either the quantitative or the qualitative direction.
2   Are you interested in making standardized and systematic comparisons or do you really want to study this phenomenon or situation in detail?
3   *The literature.* How have other researchers dealt with this topic? To what extent do you wish to align your own research with standard approaches to the topic?
4   *Practical considerations.* Issues of time, money, availability of samples and data, familiarity with the subject under study, access to situations, gaining cooperation.
5   *Knowledge payoff.* Will you learn more about this topic using quantitative or qualitative forms of research? Which approach will produce more useful knowledge? Which will do more good?
6   *Style.* Some people prefer one approach to another. This may involve paradigm and philosophical issues or different images about what a good piece of research looks like.

(*Source*: Adapted from Punch 2005: 239–40)

---

to answer a particular question or set of questions. This may immediately suggest a method or technique to you. For example, if you want to find out what members of the general public think about a given issue, an obvious way forward is to ask some of them. Or, if you need to understand why a traffic management plan does not appear to have reduced traffic congestion, observing traffic behaviour in the relevant area may seem appropriate.

You might want to have another look at Box 2.3 at this point.

In the research literature, it is sometimes suggested that if your research questions are well enough focused or refined, they will effectively determine the methods you use to answer them. In practice, however, in almost every case there will be alternative techniques which could be used, either instead of or in conjunction with the one(s) you first think of. Thus, to follow up the two examples just given, you might observe the public's actual behaviour, where this impacts upon the issue under consideration, or you might attempt to model traffic behaviour using a computer program.

The words 'want' and 'need' in the title of this subsection also suggest an important distinction, one which has to do with focusing as well as method. Here, as when considering your research plans in general, you need to think about which methods are practicable given the time and other resources you have available.

What skills do you have?

As we suggested in the opening section of this chapter, on **Everyday research skills**, one of the key resources you have available for your research is yourself. You will have many skills as an adult which have been developed through everyday life. So you might find it useful to think about which are your best skills and which skills you like using.

Do you like talking to people? How comfortable are you with the give and take of conversation? Do you like watching people? Would you prefer to sit at a desk and read documents? Or work on data stored on a computer? Each of these preferences suggests that you might be most comfortable using a particular technique: some form of interviews, observation or documentary analysis. You might, therefore, find it easiest, where possible, to research an area which allows you to use the skills you have best developed, or which you are most comfortable with. Use Exercise 3.5 to help you decide.

Alternatively, you might, in carrying out an audit of your everyday and research skills (see Exercise 1.1), decide that you want to use your research project to deliberately develop skills which you feel you lack but which could be useful to you. This might be a good way of adding interest or personal benefit to a research project which could otherwise be rather boring or limiting. Be careful, however, not to overreach yourself if this might affect the likelihood of your successfully completing your project.

Will your methodological preferences answer your questions?

Bearing the two previous questions in mind, you now need to consider whether the everyday research skills which you wish to use are actually suited to the issues you are going to investigate.

To return to the two examples used above, if you like talking to people, and feel that you are reasonably good at it, you will probably be comfortable with the idea of researching public opinion by talking to people. Or, if you are experienced with computer modelling, you may be engaged by the prospect of researching traffic management options using these techniques. If the circumstances were reversed, however, you might have some qualms.

There may, as has already been suggested, be ways around such problems, short of changing your research topic. In the latter case, if computers turn you off and you'd much rather talk to people, you might research traffic management by questioning a number of drivers and pedestrians, perhaps referring to existing computer-based studies as necessary. Or, in the former case, you might approach the study of public opinion by re-examining some of the many sources of published information, rather than by questioning people directly.

In many cases, however, particularly where you do not have an entirely free choice over the subject of your research, you will find yourself needing to use methods you may not feel entirely happy with.

How will your methods affect the answers you get?

Just as it is sometimes argued that your research questions should determine your approach and techniques, so, in an analogous fashion, it is often suggested that the methods you use will significantly affect the answers you get. There is, of course, a good deal of sense in this argument.

If you carry out a questionnaire survey, the information you collect will be rather different from what you would get if you used in-depth interviews, though there might be a good deal of overlap. The questions, and thus the nature and scope of the answers, in a questionnaire are determined in advance by the researcher. Interviews, by contrast, even when highly structured, allow for more flexibility in asking and answering questions. While the responses to the former tend to be brief, those to the latter may be very lengthy, so fewer interviews may be carried out in the same time.

It is also the case, of course, that the choice of the subjects or objects of your research – people, classes, traffic, books, etc. – assuming that you are not able to study every possible subject or object of relevance to your questions, will influence your findings. This issue is discussed further in the section on **Sampling and selection** in Chapter 6.

How will you affect your research?

> Y soon realized that in fieldwork interactions, her nationality was often subordinate to her social position. The respondents perceived her as someone from 'abroad' first, and as an Indian later. She also realized that her native tongue (Hindi) did not allow her to pass as an 'insider'. In her experiences, many of the respondents attempted to create a 'good impression' by constructing their responses in broken English despite her repeated desire to conduct the interviews in their native dialects. The dilemma for Y then was whether to work with incomplete responses or to make a concerted effort to 'de-glamorize' her location. These problems also meant that Y chose not to reveal to her respondents that she was engaged to a white, European man because she feared that she would be understood by the respondents as an illegitimate 'outsider'.
>
> (Thapar-Bjorkert and Henry 2004: 367–8)

Researchers are themselves a powerful, and often under-recognized, influence on their research and their findings. This influence extends beyond the choice of the research topic itself, and the methods used to explore it, to the impact of you as a person and of your ideas. As a researcher, you will have certain opinions and views about a wide range of issues, and these are likely to find some expression in your research and your reporting of it. Thus, as well as having a set of research questions to ask, you may already have a view on the likely answers. Your views may have been shaped by what you have read. This will affect the way in which you ask questions, of people or of documents, and the significance you attach to their answers. It will also affect who or what you ask, using your contacts or networks, and the ways in which your questions are answered.

As an adult, you also have a range of individual demographic characteristics, including your sex, age, class, ethnic background and size. These will impact upon your research in more or less complex ways, and will raise issues related to the contexts of your research. For example, if you are a white, middle-class male, conducting fieldwork in a women's refuge, or in inner city areas with large black populations, will require you to consider the ways in which your sex, class and ethnicity contribute to your research findings. While such clear differences between the researcher and the researched throw these issues into relief, they are relevant in other cases as well.

If somebody else carried out your research, using the same approach, techniques and sample, the results would be, at the very least, subtly different. There is no easy way in which the effect of the researcher on the research can be minimized. You cannot be wholly objective, and, in many ways, it is foolish to try to be so. The play of emotions between researcher, researched and research is often something to be welcomed. Yet there is a need to be aware of your influence on your research, and to be as open as you can in recording and recognizing these affects. Box 3.17 lists ten questions to help develop your reflexivity.

Box 3.17 Developing reflexivity: some questions to ask yourself

Think about a situation you have been in, preferably in piloting your research.

1   What was your role in this situation?
2   Did you feel comfortable or uncomfortable? Why?
3   What actions did you take? How did you and others react?
4   Was it appropriate? How could you have improved the situation for yourself, and others?
5   What could you change in the future?
6   Do you feel as if you've learnt anything new about yourself or your research?
7   Has it changed your way of thinking in any way?
8   What knowledge, from theories, practices and other aspects of your own and others' research, can you apply to this situation?
9   What broader issues – for example ethical, political or social – arise from this situation?
10 Have you recorded your thoughts in your research diary?

Which methods are acceptable?

Another key issue in deciding about your approach to your research is the question of which methods may be acceptable. You may be working under direction or in collaboration with others, for example, and these people may have an influence on your choice of methods. Your research may be funded by an organization which has very definite views on the value of alternative techniques, or has produced a research brief which limits or directs your choice. Or you may be working within a subject or disciplinary tradition which expects you to take a given methodological perspective.

In all of these cases, however, it should be useful to you to be able to reach a considered opinion on the advantages and disadvantages of using particular approaches or techniques. You may also be able to go a little further and modify or add to the choice of methods.

Using more than one method

It is common for researchers to use more than one method. This is even more likely if you are carrying out your research project as part of a group, rather than on your own. Your main method may, for example, be a questionnaire survey, or a set of interviews, or a series of observations, but this is likely to be complemented at the very least by some documentary analysis to enable you to explore relevant literature or policy. Most research projects in the social sciences are, therefore, in a general sense, multi-method.

There are, however, good reasons for deliberately seeking to use more than one method in the main body of your research. You may follow up a survey with some interviews in order to get a more detailed perspective on some of the issues raised. The telling anecdote may be much more revealing and influential than almost any amount of figures. You might follow the reverse process, using interviews in order to identify the key issues which you would then ask questions about in your survey. You might complement interviews within an institution with the analysis of available documents in order to compare written and spoken versions.

Where two or more methods are used in this way, to try to verify the validity of the information being collected, the process is referred to as triangulation. This kind of approach should be carefully considered if your resources allow. Mixed methodological approaches are considered further in Chapter 7.

Allowing for changes of direction

Another reason for not restricting yourself in your planning to just one method or technique is to allow for possible changes of direction in the research project. You may find, for example, that your postal survey is not getting sufficient responses, or that it is not being answered satisfactorily. Or you may be unable to get access to many of the people you were planning to interview, or to the sites where you were going to carry out observations. Or, as you read the literature, you may find that your research questions have already been addressed thoroughly by others. In such cases, which are not uncommon, having planned to use more than one method should allow you to change your approach and direction more easily.

Deciding about methods

By now, you may have a fairly clear answer to the following questions:

- How are you going to do the research?
- What is your strategy and approach?
- What techniques or methods are you going to use?

Or you may still be pretty vague. If you are in the latter position, you might wish to read around your subject more, and return to this point later. If you do have some ideas, think about them for a few minutes, and then try to succinctly summarize your intended research design using Exercise 3.6.

In reflecting on your plans, think about the details of what you are going to do for your research project. You may have said, for example, that you are going to read so many books or articles, complete a certain number of interviews, administer so many questionnaires, or observe a group of people over a given period; or you may have mentioned more than one of these. Can you, however, say why you have chosen these particular methods? In other words, do you have a methodological perspective?

If you can answer the kinds of questions posed in Exercise 3.6, you already have, or are well on the way to having, a methodological perspective on your research. If you have some understanding of the range of possible research strategies, approaches and techniques available to you in undertaking research, you are going to be in a much better position to make an informed choice about which methods to use yourself, and how best to apply them.

Summary

Having read this chapter, you should:

- appreciate that you already have many everyday skills which will be of use to you in your research;

- have a good understanding of the different approaches, techniques and methods which are available to you as a small-scale researcher in the social sciences;
- have decided, or be closer to deciding, which methods you are going to use, and be able to justify that choice;
- have a clearer idea of your own methodological preferences.

Exercises

3.1 Is action research primarily or necessarily qualitative research? Give reasons for your answer. What research paradigm(s) do you think action research best fits within?

3.2 Using Yin's typology – single or multiple; exploratory, descriptive or explanatory – how would you characterize the examples of case studies included in Box 3.10?

3.3 The police are experimenting with a zero tolerance policy against drunk and disorderly behaviour in selected town centres. How would you judge whether their approach had been successful? How does this strategy differ from action research?

3.4 Are the results of survey research necessarily more accurate than those arrived at using other approaches? Do surveys lend themselves to qualitative as much as quantitative research strategies?

3.5 At the beginning of the chapter, ten everyday research skills were identified. For each of these skills, give yourself a rating on a scale from 1 (low) to 10 (high). Is your mix of skills appropriate for the research approaches or techniques you plan to adopt?

3.6 Note down the research methods you plan to use. What are their advantages and disadvantages? What other methods might you use as alternatives?

Further reading

In this section, we list a selection of books that are of particular relevance to the topics discussed in this chapter. The list is extensive because a large number of books have been written on the subject of alternative research methods, their uses, advantages and disadvantages. Some, as you will see, are subject- or discipline-specific, whereas others are more generic in their coverage.

Abbott, P. and Sapsford, R. (1998) *Research Methods for Nurses and the Caring Professions*, 2nd edition. Buckingham: Open University Press.

Aimed at readers who wish to evaluate and contribute to professional practice. Includes practical exercises and examples. Methods covered include interviews, observations, controlled trials, surveys and secondary sources. Also discusses reading and writing research.

Adams, J., Khan, H., Raeside, R. and White, D. (2007) *Research Methods for Graduate Business and Social Science Students*. London: Sage.

Aims to explain the basics of qualitative and quantitative research.

Ader, H. J. and Mellenbergh, G. J. (eds) (1999) *Research Methodology in the Life, Behavioural and Social Sciences*. London: Sage.

The focus is exclusively on quantitative methods. Topics covered include experimental design, clinical trials, cross-sectional research, longitudinal analysis, measurement models, graphical modelling, structural equation modelling and meta-analysis.

Aldridge, A. and Levine, K. (2001) *Surveying the Social World: Principles and practice in survey research*. Buckingham: Open University Press.

Oversight of the whole survey process, from planning, through sampling, data collection, design and analysis to presentation.

Anderson, G. and Arsenault, N. (1998) *Fundamentals of Educational Research*, 2nd edition. London: Falmer Press.

An introductory text to the methods and sources of educational research. Contents include literature surveys, research design, historical, descriptive, experimental, correlational, ethnographic, case study and policy research, and programme evaluation issues. Advice is given on surveys, questionnaire construction, interviewing and focus groups.

Atweh, B., Kemmis, S. and Weeks, P. (eds) (1998) *Action Research in Practice: Partnership for social justice in education*. London: Routledge.

A collection of stories from action research projects in schools and a university.

Balnaves, M. and Caputi, P. (2001) *Introduction to Quantitative Research Methods: An investigative approach*. London: Sage.

Takes a detective approach to showing how quantitative methods can be used to solve real-life problems.

Barbour, R. (2007) *Introducing Qualitative Research: A student's guide to the craft of doing qualitative research*. London: Sage.

Designed for those new to the 'craft' of qualitative research.

Bassey, M. (1999) *Case Study Research in Educational Settings*. Buckingham: Open University Press.

Suggests how case study research can be a prime strategy for developing educational theory which illuminates policy and enhances practice.

Bechhofer, F. and Paterson, L. (2000) *Principles of Research Design in the Social Science*. London: Routledge.

Designed for researchers who know what they want to study but have yet to decide how best to study it. Chapters discuss experiments, representativeness, choice of locale and group, interviews, questionnaires, fieldwork, time, policy analysis, journalism and literature.

Bennett, J. (2003) *Evaluation Methods in Research*. London: Continuum. Considers the variety of evaluation methods available and their use in practice.

Bernard, H. R. (2000) *Social Research Methods: Qualitative and quantitative approaches*. Thousand Oaks, CA: Sage. Discusses the fundamentals of social research, preparation, interviewing, scaling, observation, qualitative and quantitative analysis.

Black, T. R. (1999) *Doing Quantitative Research in the Social Sciences: An integrated approach to research design, measurement and statistics*. London: Sage. This book is organized in six parts covering research design; measurement design; the use of statistics; ex post facto, experimental and quasi-experimental designs; non-parametric tests; and non-causal relationships.

Blaikie, N. (2009) *Designing Social Research: the logic of anticipation*, 2nd edition. Oxford: Polity Press. Focuses on research questions, designs, proposals and strategies.

Bowling, A. (2002) *Research Methods in Health: Investigating health and health services*, 2nd edition. Buckingham: Open University Press. Five sections examine the scope of health research; the philosophy, theory and practice of research; quantitative research (two sections); and qualitative and combined research methods.

Breakwell, G., Hammond, S., Fife-Schaur, C. and Smith, J. (2006) *Research Methods in Psychology*, 3rd edition. London: Sage. Organized in three main sections considering the research question and design, the choice of data-gathering method, and the selection of data treatment.

Brewer, J. D. (2000) *Ethnography*. Buckingham: Open University Press. Offers guidelines for good practice, and advice on the collection, analysis, interpretation and presentation of ethnographic data.

Brewerton, P. and Millward, L. (2001) *Organizational Research Methods: A guide for students and researchers*. London: Sage. Successive chapters address starting off, obtaining access, project design, data collection, sampling, assessing performance, data analysis and reporting findings.

Bryman, A. (2004) *Social Research Methods*, 2nd edition. Oxford: Oxford University Press. Substantive text organized in four main parts exploring social research strategies and designs, quantitative research, qualitative research, and other issues such as ethics, the internet and breaking down the quantitative/qualitative divide.

Burns, R. B. (2000) *Introduction to Research Methods*, 4th edition. London: Sage. Organized in four parts which focus on general issues, quantitative methods, qualitative methods and survey methods. Includes many self-testing questions for the reader to check their understanding.

Burton, D. (ed.) (2000) *Research Training for Social Scientists: A handbook for postgraduate researchers*. London: Sage.
A substantial text covering philosophy, ethical and legal issues, getting started, qualitative methods and analysis, survey research, quantitative analysis and finishing off.
Clough, P. and Nutbrown, C. (2007) *A Student's Guide to Methodology*, 2nd edition. London: Sage.
The authors aim to show how every element of research is a function of methodology. They clearly distinguish between methodology and methods, and explain how their relationship is articulated in practice.
Coglan, D. and Brannick, T. (2004) *Doing Action Research in your own Organization*, 2nd edition. London: Sage.
Covers theory and methods, politics and ethics, the role of the researcher and writing up.
Cohen, L., Manion, L. and Morrison, K. (2007) *Research Methods in Education*, 6th edition. London: Routledge.
Covering the range of methodological approaches in social research, this text drawn on examples from predominantly school-based education. Chapters include discussion of triangulation, role playing, interviewing, personal constructs, action research, case study, developmental research, ex post facto research and experimental designs.
Costello, P. (2003) *Action Research*. London: Continuum.
Short text covering planning, data collection and analysis, and reportage of action research projects.
Cournoyer, D. and Klein, W. (2000) *Research Methods for Social Work*. Boston: Allyn & Bacon.
Topics discussed include scientific thinking, critical reasoning, ethics, research questions and design, measurement, sampling, numerical and non-numerical data collection and analysis.
Cresswell, J. W. (2008) *Research Design: Qualitative, quantitative and mixed methods approaches*, 3rd edition. Thousand Oaks, CA: Sage.
Which to choose: qualitative or quantitative approaches? How do you write a journal article? These are two of the issues addressed in this text.
Cresswell, J. W. and Plano, V. L. (2006) *Designing and Conducting Mixed Methods Research*. Thousand Oaks, CA: Sage.
Combines the latest thinking about mixed methods research designs with practical, step-by-step guidelines for the decisions that must be made in designing a mixed methods research study.
Davies, C. A. (1998) *Reflexive Ethnography*. London: Routledge.
A practical and comprehensive guide to ethnographic methods. Engages with significant issues associated with modernism/postmodernism, subjectivity/objectivity and self/other.
Easterby-Smith, M., Thorpe, R., Jackson, P. and Lowe, A. (2008) *Management Research*, 3rd edition. London: Sage.

Examines both the philosophy and politics of management research, and the application of qualitative and quantitative methods.

Evans, J. (2005) *How to do Research: A psychologist's perspective*. London: Routledge.
Covers research design, hypothesis testing, statistical inference, theory development, supervision and communication.

Fetterman, D. M. (1998) *Ethnography: Step by step*, 2nd edition. Thousand Oaks, CA: Sage.
How does one manage a mountain of data and make meaningful statements? These are the key questions addressed by this book. Chapters cover anthropological concepts, methods and techniques, ethnographic equipment, analysis, writing and ethics.

Field, D., Clark, D., Corner, J. and Davis, C. (eds) (2000) *Researching Palliative Care*. Buckingham: Open University Press.
Aimed at those involved in palliative care who wish to pursue research. This book identifies key methods, provides examples of issues and practices, and discusses related methodological and ethical issues.

Fink, A. (2005) *How to Conduct Surveys: A step-by-step guide*, 3rd edition. Thousand Oaks, CA: Sage.
Does pretty much what the title suggests.

Flick, U. (2009) *An Introduction to Qualitative Research*, 4th edition. London: Sage.
Deals with how to construct and interpret verbal, visual and observational data, with practical guidance on documentation, analysis, coding and categorization. Lots of examples, summaries and suggestions for further reading.

Flick, U., Kardoff, E. von and Steinke, I. (eds) (2004) *A Companion to Qualitative Research*. London: Sage.
Covers theory and practice, with contributions from researchers in Europe and North America.

Fowler, F. (2001) *Survey Research Methods*, 3rd edition. Thousand Oaks, CA: Sage.
Aims to improve question design, survey administration, response rates and analysis.

Gilbert, N. (ed.) (2008) *Researching Social Life*, 3rd edition. London: Sage.
Aims to cover the whole range of methods from quantitative to qualitative in a down-to-earth and unthreatening manner.

Gill, J. and Johnson, P. (2002) *Research Methods for Managers*, 3rd edition. London: Sage.
Chapters cover theory, experimental design, quasi-experiments and action research, survey research, ethnography and methodological choices.

Gillham, B. (2000) *Case Study Research Methods*. London: Continuum.
Chapters discuss principles and practice, including evidence, electronic material, observation, interviewing, quantitative data and physical artefacts.

Gillham, B. (2008) *Small-Scale Social Survey Methods*. London: Continuum.

A comprehensive guide to the successful design and implementation of surveys as a research method.

Goldblatt, D. (2000) *Knowledge and the Social Sciences*. London: Routledge.
Provides an introduction to key philosophical and epistemological issues in the social sciences. Addresses both positivist and interpretative methodologies through a comparison of contemporary debates about social change.

Gorard, S. (2001) *Quantitative Methods in Educational Research: The role of numbers made easy*. London: Continuum.
Emphasizes the selection of appropriate techniques, and understanding their strengths and weaknesses. Discusses secondary data, surveys and controlled trials, and their analysis.

Gorard, S. and Taylor, C. (2004) *Combining Methods in Educational and Social Research*. Maidenhead: Open University Press.
Practical guidance on how to combine quantitative and qualitative methods, including discussion of triangulation, life histories and design studies.

Gray, D. (2009) *Doing Research in the Real World*, 2nd edition. London: Sage.
Starts by setting out best approaches to the design of appropriate research tools, and then leads the reader into issues of data collection, analysis and writing up.

Greenwood, D. J. and Levin, M. (1998) *Introduction to Action Research: Social research for social change*. Thousand Oaks, CA: Sage.
The three parts of the book consider the nature of action research; science, epistemology and practice; and varieties of action research praxis.

Hakim, C. (2000) *Research Design: Successful designs for social economic research*. London: Routledge.
A practical overview of the issues involved in the design of social and economic research, covering both theoretical and policy-related research.

Hayes, N. (2000) *Doing Psychological Research: Gathering and analysing data*. Buckingham: Open University Press.
Organized in two parts. 'Gathering data' addresses techniques such as experiements, observational studies, questionnaires, interviews, case studies and documentary analysis. 'Making sense of data' examines different methods of qualitative and quantitative analysis.

Henn, M., Weinstein, M. and Foard, N. (2009) *A Critical Introduction to Social Research*, 2nd edition. London: Sage.
Seeks to introduce students and researchers to the key ideas and issues that inform research practice.

Johnson, P. and Duberley, J. (2000) *Understanding Management Research*. London: Sage.
Covers the principal epistemological debates in social research, including positivism, postmodernism, critical theory, pragmatism and more reflexive approaches.

Jupp, V., Davies, P. and Francis, P. (eds) (2000) *Doing Criminological Research*. London: Sage.

Thirteen chapters examine issues in planning, doing and experiencing research in criminology. Topics covered include interviews with female prisoners, realistic evaluation of criminal justice, the measurement of crime, and understanding the politics of criminological research.

Krueger, R. K. and Casey, M. A. (2000) *Focus Groups: A practical guide for applied research*, 3rd edition. Thousand Oaks, CA: Sage.

For those interested in marketing and gauging public opinion, this text takes the reader through the processes of conducting focus group interviews and analysing the results.

Kumar, R. (2005) *Research Methodology: A step-by-step guide for beginners*, 2nd edition. London: Sage.

Organized in terms of eight organizational steps: formulating a research problem, conceptualizing a research design, constructing an instrument for data collection, selecting a sample, writing a research proposal, collecting data, processing data and writing a research report.

Laws, S., Harper, C. and Marcus, R. (2003) *Research for Development: A practical guide*. London: Sage.

Aimed at those managing or doing research for development. Coverage includes writing a research brief, managing research staff or consultants, engaging stakeholders, models of supervision, evaluating research results and promoting research findings for impact. Many international examples.

Lee, R. M. (2000) *Unobtrusive Methods in Social Research*. Buckingham: Open University Press.

Focuses on research methods other than surveys and interviews, including found data, captured data (i.e. observation), running records, personal documents and the internet.

Linkogle, S. and Lee-Treweek, G. (2000) *Danger in the Field*. London: Routledge.

An analysis of the potential pitfalls in qualitative research in a variety of research settings.

Litosseliti, L. (2003) *Using Focus Groups in Research*. London: Continuum.

Short guide to the planning, conduct and analysis of focus groups.

Marshall, C. and Rossman, G. (2006) *Designing Qualitative Research*, 4th edition. Thousand Oaks, CA: Sage.

Introduces students to the processes of qualitative research. Includes sections on data collection, data management, analysis and resource allocation decisions.

Mason, J. (2002) *Qualitative Researching*, 2nd edition. London: Sage.

Focuses on the practice and process of qualitative research. Chapters consider research design, the generation of data through interviewing, observation and documents, sampling and selection, and the organization and analysis of data.

Maxim, P. S. (1999) *Quantitative Research Methods in the Social Sciences*. New York: Oxford University Press.

Reviews general statistical theory and methods, and explores the problems that quantitative social scientists face in conducting research. Topics discussed include scientific method, theory formalization, causality, statistical inference, sampling, experimental design, measurement theory and errors, and hypothesis testing.

Maxwell, J. (2005) *Qualitative Research Design: An interactive approach*, 2nd edition. Thousand Oaks, CA: Sage.
Attempts to move away from the conventional, linear approach to design by offering a flexible and user-friendly approach.

May, T. (2001) *Social Research: Issues, methods and process*, 3rd edition. Buckingham: Open University Press.
The text explores issues of perspective, social theory, values and ethics. Data collection methods such as official statistics, questionnaires, interviewing, participant observation, documentary sources and comparative research are included. Questions at the end of each chapter are designed to deepen understanding and reflection.

May, T. and Williams, M. (eds) (1998) *Knowing the Social World*. Buckingham: Open University Press.
Ten contributions examine the relations between philosophy, social theory and empirical research, how we can claim to 'know' the social world, and what the properties of the social world and their implications might be.

McIntyre, L. (2005) *Need to Know: Social science research methods*. Boston, MA: McGraw-Hill.
Broad coverage of research design, experiments, survey research, unobtrusive methods and qualitative research. Text includes exercises, ancedotes, glossary and appendices.

McNeill, P. and Chapman, S. (2005) *Research Methods*, 3rd edition. London: Routledge.
Written by two sociologists, this text examines surveys, experiments, comparative methods, ethnography, secondary data and values.

McNiff, J. and Whitehead, J. (2006) *All You Need to Know About Action Research*. London: Sage.
Organized around the what, why and how questions.

McNiff, J. and Whitehead, J. (2009) *Doing and Writing Action Research*. London: Sage.
Offers guidance on presenting findings, producing reports that can inform policy, and demonstrating the quality of one's research.

McNiff, J., Whitehead, J. and Lomax, P. (1999) *You and Your Action Research Project*, 3rd edition. London: Routledge.
Offers practical guidance on doing an action research project as part of an award-bearing course.

McQueen, R. and Knussen, C. (2002) *Research Methods for Social Science: A practical introduction*. Harlow: Prentice Hall.
Does pretty much what the title suggests.

Mikkelsen, B. (2005) *Methods for Development Work and Research: A new guide for practitioners*, 2nd edition. New Delhi: Sage.

Emphasizes participatory methods, development studies, monitoring and evaluation.

Morton-Cooper, A. (2000) *Action Research in Health Care.* Oxford: Blackwell Science.
Considers the ethos and principles of action research, strategies and advice for practitioners and researchers, giving support to those engaged in action research, and critiques of action research.

Moule, P. and Goodman, M. (2009) *Nursing Research: An introduction.* London: Sage.
Aims to lead the novice nurse researcher and student nurse through the main techniques and skills required of a practising nurse researcher.

Neuman, W. L. (2000) *Social Research Methods: Qualitative and quantitative approaches,* 4th edition. Boston, MA: Allyn & Bacon.
Comprehensive introduction organized in five parts: foundations; planning and preparation; quantitative data collection and analysis; qualitative data collection and analysis; and social research and communication with others.

Partington, D. (ed.) (2002) *Essential Skills for Management Research.* London: Sage.
Organized in three parts covering philosophy and research, research processes, and approaches and techniques.

Payne, G. and Payne, J. (2004) *Key Concepts in Social Research.* London: Sage.
Sections on concepts – such as qualitative and quantitative approaches, internet polling and visual methods – include definitions, key points, examples and further reading.

Pierce, R. (2008) *Research Methods in Politics.* London: Sage.
Provides an overview of the philosophy and principles of research, with a critical review of selected methods.

Plummer, K. (2001) *Documents of Life 2: An Invitation to Critical Humanism,* 2nd edition. London: Sage.
This revised edition considers recent developments in the use of life stories and other personal documents in social research. Issues examined include the emergence of an auto/biographical society, writing and narrative, memory and truth, and humanism.

Punch, K. (2003) *Survey Research: The basics.* London: Sage.
A practical guide focusing on small-scale quantitative research.

Punch, K. (2005) *Introduction to Social Research: Quantitative and qualitative approaches,* 2nd edition. London: Sage.
Comprehensive introduction, which covers developing models for empirical research, the logic of quantitative and qualitative research (design, data collection and analysis), mixing methods, evaluation and writing.

Punch, K. (2009) *Introduction to Research Methods in Education.* London: Sage.
This book focuses on helping the reader to develop a clear conceptual understanding of the nature of empirical research in education, and of how those ideas lead to, and underlie, the principal research techniques.

Reason, P. and Bradbury, H. (eds) (2006) *Handbook of Action Research*. London: Sage.
Thirty-two chapters organized in terms of the groundings, practices, exemplars and skills of action research.

Ritchie, J. and Lewis, J. (eds) (2003) *Qualitative Research Practice: A guide for social science students and researchers*. London: Sage.
Covers theoretical, methodological and practical issues.

Robson, C. (2000) *Small-Scale Evaluation: Principles and practice*. London: Sage.
Designed for those undertaking small-scale evaluations for the first time. Chapters deal with the nature and purpose of evaluation, collaboration, ethical and political issues, design, analysis, practicalities and communicating findings.

Rossi, P. H., Lipsey, M. and Freeman, H. E. (2004) *Evaluation: A systematic approach*, 7th edition. Newbury Park, CA: Sage.
For those concerned with the utility and effectiveness of social intervention programmes, this text is designed to outline appropriate methods of data collection, analysis and interpretation. The text contains discussion of diagnosis, measurement and monitoring, with numerous examples from evaluation research.

Ruane, J. (2004) *Essentials of Research Methods: A guide to social research*. Malden, MA: Blackwell.
Includes discussion of ethics, validity, measurement, causal analysis, design strategies, sampling, questionnaires, interviews, field research and statistics.

Rugg, G. and Petre, M. (2006) *A Gentle Guide to Research Methods*. Maidenhead: Open University Press.
This book explains what research is, and guides you through choosing and using the method best suited to your needs, with examples chosen from a range of disciplines.

Ruspini, E. (2002) *Introduction to Longitudinal Research*. London: Routledge.
Considers characteristics, data collection techniques, problems and major analytical techniques.

Sapsford, R. (1999) *Survey Research*. London: Sage.
Considers the nature of survey research, sampling, methods of data collection, tabular analysis, correlation, regression and factor analysis, analysis of variance, using existing data sources and reporting results.

Schostak, J. F. (2000) *Understanding, Designing and Conducting Qualitative Research in Education*. Buckingham: Open University Press.
Offers a strategy focusing on the project as the organizing framework that ensures that the methods chosen are appropriate to the subject of study.

Seale, C. (ed.) (2004) *Social Research Methods: A reader*. London: Routledge.
A substantive collection of 79 selected extracts, covering issues including methodological awareness, critiques of quantification, the limits of science, ethnography, reflexivity, postmodernism and paradigm disputes.

Seale, C., Gobo, G., Gubrium, J. and Silverman, D. (eds) (2004) *Qualitative Research Practice*. London: Sage.

A substantive collection in which researchers reflect on their own experiences.

Silverman, D. (ed.) (2004) *Qualitative Research: Theory, method and practice*, 2nd edition. London: Sage.
Selected researchers discuss theory and practice using their own work and analyses.
Silverman, D. (2009) *Doing Qualitative Research*, 3rd edition. London: Sage.
A practical guide to the design, administration and delivery of qualitative research. Includes case studies, examples and checklists.
Simons, H. (2009) *Case Study Research in Practice*. London: Sage.
The four sections of the book cover rationale, concept and design, methods, ethics and reflexivity, interpreting, analysing and reporting, and generalizing and theorizing in case study research.
Somekh, B. and Lewin, C. (eds) (2004) *Research Methods in the Social Sciences*. London: Sage.
Specialists address all of the key quantitative and qualitative techniques in separate chapters.
Stake, R. (2005) *Multiple Case Study Analysis*. New York: Guilford Press.
Practical guide to studying groups of cases within one research project.
Strauss, A. L. and Corbin, J. (1998) *Basics of Qualitative Research*, 2nd edition. London: Sage.
Written for students, and located within the 'grounded theory' school, this text includes coding, theoretical sampling, using the literature and writing a thesis.
Tashakkori, A. and Teddlie, C. (1998) *Mixed Methodology: Combining qualitative and quantitative approaches*. Thousand Oaks, CA: Sage.
The three sections of this book focus on the paradigms and politics of research (positivism versus constructivism, research design), methods and strategies, and applications, examples and future directions.
Tashakkori, A. and Teddlie, C. (eds) (2002) *Handbook of Mixed Methods in Social and Behavioral Research*. Thousand Oaks, CA: Sage.
A collection of articles by leading scholars.
Teddlie, C. and Tashakkori, A. (2008) *Foundations of Mixed Methods Research: Integrating quantitative and qualitative approaches in the social and behavioural sciences*. Thousand Oaks, CA: Sage.
This text begins with an introduction to and overview of the development of mixed methodology, and then takes students through all aspects of working with mixed methods from research design and data collection through to analysis and conclusions.
Travers, M. (2001) *Qualitative Research Through Case Studies*. London: Sage.
Case studies are used to illustrate approaches such as grounded theory, dramaturgical analysis, ethnomethodology, critical discourse analysis and postmodern ethnography.
Vaus, D. de (2001) *Research Design in Social Research*. London: Sage.
Organized in five main parts, looking first at research design in general, and

then focusing on experimental, longitudinal, cross-sectional and case-study designs.

Vaus, D. de (2002) *Surveys in Social Research*, 5th edition. Sydney: Allen & Unwin.
With the novice researcher mainly in mind, this text discusses how to plan, conduct and analyse social surveys. Combines questionnaire construction and administration, sampling and formulating research questions with techniques for coding and developing indicators and statistical methods.

Verma, G. and Mallick, K. (1998) *Researching Education: Perspectives and techniques*. London: Routledge.
Aims to help the reader understand the concepts and terminology used in educational research, and to provide guidance on initiating and implementing research studies.

Wellington, J. and Szczerbinski, M. (2007) *Research Methods for the Social Sciences*. London: Continuum.
Aims to provide an introductory but not simplistic guide to research in the social and behavioural sciences.

Williams, M. (2003) *Making Sense of Social Research*. London: Sage.
Covers quantitative methods in more detail than qualitative, with chapters addressing, among other topics, selecting and sampling, survey research, questionnaire design and the analysis of survey data.

Yin, R. K. (2003) *Applications of Case Study Research*, 2nd edition. Thousand Oaks, CA: Sage.
Aiming to provide guidance for those who wish to carry out a case study, the text uses examples from actual research. The text is organized into four parts: theory, descriptive case studies, explanatory case studies, cross-case analyses. The contexts used for illustration include education, management information systems, youth programmes and community-based prevention programmes.

Yin, R. K. (ed.) (2004) *The Case Study Anthology*. Thousand Oaks, CA: Sage.
Includes 19 full cases, complete with discussion and guidelines. Sections consider theoretical perspectives, multiple cases, quantitative evidence and embedded units of analysis.

Yin, R. K. (2008) *Case Study Research: Design and methods*, 4th edition. Thousand Oaks, CA: Sage.
Seen as a classic text, Yin considers design, data collection, analysis and reporting case studies. The text includes exercises at the end of each chapter.

4

Reading for research

Introduction • Why read? • Coping with the research literature •
Basic reading strategies • Using libraries • Using the internet • Good
enough reading • Reading about method as well as subject • Recording
your reading • The literature review • Issues in reading • Summary •
Exercises • Further reading

Introduction

Carrying out a research project in the social sciences will almost invariably
involve the researcher in a significant amount of reading, particularly if they
are not already well read in their subject area. The work and skills associated
with reading for research – how to read, what to read, how to make sense of
your reading – can be a major worry and barrier for the relatively inexperienced researcher. The purpose of this chapter, therefore, is to support you in
developing and using your research reading skills.

The chapter is organized into the following sections:

- **Why read?** The importance of reading for research.
- **Coping with the research literature**. Dealing with the volume and variety
  of reading available.
- **Basic reading strategies**. Guidance on what and where to read.
- **Using libraries**. How to get the best out of them.
- **Using the internet**. Navigating the universe of information.
- **Good enough reading**. How to read.
- **Reading about method as well as subject**. The importance of understand-
  ing and exploring research approaches and techniques.
- **Recording your reading**. Being meticulous.

- **The literature review**. How to put it together.
- **Issues in reading**. Problems with too much or too little literature.

Why read?

> Read not to contradict and confute, nor to believe and take for granted, nor to find talk and discourse, but to weigh and consider. Some books are to be tasted, others to be swallowed, and some few to be chewed and digested; that is, some books are to be read only in parts; others to be read but not curiously; and some few to be read wholly, and with diligence and attention.
>
> (Francis Bacon, quoted in Peacock 1903: 21–2)

It is possible to carry out research without engaging in much direct reading, though it would be unusual to do so without any new reading. This may happen, for example, where the constraints on the time available do not allow for much reading, or where the method and context are familiar, or where the researchers involved are being employed simply to administer questionnaires or carry out interviews for someone else.

We would argue strongly, however, especially where the research has an academic connection, that it is highly desirable, if not essential, to engage in related reading while carrying out a research project. Your research project needs to be informed and stimulated by your developing knowledge as you carry it out. Box 4.1 gives ten reasons for reading for research.

As you look through Box 4.1 you may recognize many of the reasons given. You may be able to add others as well. You should also see, however, that a

---

Box 4.1 Ten reasons for reading for research

1 Because it will give you ideas.
2 Because you need to understand what other researchers have done in your area.
3 To broaden your perspectives and set your work in context.
4 Because direct personal experience can never be enough.
5 To legitimate your arguments.
6 Because it may cause you to change your mind.
7 Because writers (and you will be one) need readers.
8 So that you can criticize effectively what others have done.
9 To learn more about research methods and their application in practice.
10 In order to spot areas which have not been researched.

mixture of positive and negative reasons is given. You may read both for the delight of discovery and to cover your back. You may read in order to contextualize what you are doing or to impress your own readers with your knowledge of the literature.

Box 4.1 also suggests two other important points about reading for research. Thus, it is not just essential to read, but to read at different stages of the research project and to read for a variety of purposes (see Box 4.2). For the committed researcher, reading becomes a continuing and wide-ranging activity.

Box 4.2 Reading at different stages and for different purposes

Stages

- At the beginning of your research, in order to check what other research has been done, to focus your ideas, shape your hypotheses and explore the context for your project.
- During your research, to keep you interested and up to date with developments, to help you better understand the methods you are using and the field you are researching, and as a source of data.
- After your research, to see what impact your own work has had and to help you develop ideas for further research projects.

Purposes

- Accounts of research on similar topics to your own.
- Accounts of research methods being applied in ways which are similar to your own plans.
- Accounts of the context relating to your project.
- To protect against duplication and enrich your arguments.

Coping with the research literature

To the novice researcher, it can seem as if there is so much that needs reading, and that it is so difficult to get on top of or make sense of it. More experienced researchers – you may or may not be relieved to know – can have much the same concerns. But the new researcher may feel overwhelmed by the magnitude of these demands for quite a long time.

You may be concerned about any or all of the following:

- *The volume of literature.* The amount of material written on most subjects is already huge, and expanding at an ever increasing rate. How does the researcher get to grips with this?

- *The variety of literature*. There are so many kinds of literature (e.g. textbooks, journals, magazines, newspapers, policy documents, academic papers, conference papers, internet materials, internal reports, novels, etc.) which may be relevant. How does the researcher use this range of sources?
- *Lack of boundaries*. Unless a project is very tightly defined, it may be impossible to judge which areas of the literature are relevant. How does the researcher avoid reading too widely or aimlessly?
- *Conflicting arguments*. As soon as you start reading, you are likely to be confronted by different opinions, arguments and interpretations. It may seem that no two writers agree about even the most basic issues. How does the researcher assess these arguments, and place themselves within them?

> **Hint**: If you find very conflicting arguments in your reading around, you may well have identified an issue or debate which would be worth exploring in your research project.

If you recognize these problems, are not sure where to start in reading the research literature, or what to do with it when you have read it, try Exercise 4.1 at the end of this chapter.

If you found this exercise relatively easy to do, you may not need to read this chapter in detail. If you found it difficult, don't despair, there are lots of helpful suggestions in the remainder of the chapter. Whatever you do, don't worry too much now: you don't have to do it all at once! If you can, allow yourself some time, especially at the beginning of your project, to be baffled and enthralled by the scope and variety of the literature available.

Basic reading strategies

This section offers some basic guidance on four related questions:

- Where to read
- What to read
- Whom to read
- How to find what you need to read

Where to read

The obvious place to read – at least, up until the last decade or so – may seem to be the library, particularly if you are doing a research project in an academic setting. Libraries come in different guises. They may be wide-ranging or specialized resources, general or academic in function, for reference only or available for borrowing. This last distinction highlights a critical point: that of access. While public libraries are available to everyone, and university libraries normally allow access to all bona fide researchers, some may impose restrictions on borrowing or charge fees, and others may prohibit access altogether.

> **Using libraries** is the subject of the next section in this chapter.

The other obvious place to read, nowadays, is on your computer, making use of some of the vast range of materials available through the internet. Compared to libraries, the material available on the internet is much more variable in quality. You do, of course, need to have, or have access to, a computer and internet connection. Given this, access is easy, though at times it may be frustrating and can be expensive.

> **Using the internet** is the subject of the next but one section in this chapter.

Beyond these sources, however, there are many other places in which you might read. Bookshops are an underused resource from this point of view. They have the advantage of being up to date, but may be restricted to certain kinds of material (e.g. just books) and will usually have little that is out of print. You don't have to buy the books on display, though you will be restricted in what you can do if you don't buy them, but bookshops (and online bookshops) can be a very useful place to get an idea of what and who is current in a particular subject area.

Your employer, colleagues, supervisors, friends, fellow students and research subjects may have access to relevant materials which they may be willing to share with you. A key strategy here for the researcher, particularly those working in fields where written resources are restricted, is to exploit as many possible sources and venues for reading as are feasible. Books which are unavailable in your main library may turn up unexpectedly elsewhere, while your colleagues or the subjects of your research may have access to materials of which you are completely unaware. So, where possible, use a variety of sources for your reading.

What to read

The short answer to the question of what to read has to be to read as much, and as many different kinds or sources of texts, as possible. This will enable you to encounter a range of views and forms of presentation within the different kinds of writing appropriate to your topic.

The kinds of things you might read could include:

- *Books*: of all kinds.
- *Journals*: local, national and international, home and overseas, practitioner oriented or research based, popular and academic, and abstracting journals.
- *Reports*: produced by institutions or organizations of different kinds, including employers, representative associations, political parties, trade unions, voluntary bodies, community groups, central and local government, and international bodies.
- *Popular media*: the daily and weekly press, magazines, radio and television broadcasts.
- *Online materials*: including both textbook and journal materials as well as discussion groups and websites.
- *Memos, minutes, internal reports*: produced by organizations you are studying, or which are relevant to your research topic.
- *Letters, diaries*: and other personal documents produced by individuals of interest.

In using these different kinds of written sources, it will be useful to bear in mind a number of other distinctions between types of material for reading:

- *Published and unpublished literature.* Much that is of relevance to your research, perhaps because it is a relatively new field, may not be published. Unpublished material (e.g. committee minutes), though more difficult to access as an outsider, may be of critical importance to your research.
- *Contemporary and classic works.* While it is important to be as up to date as possible, this does not mean that you should ignore older materials. There may be key classic texts in your discipline which you should refer to. Or you may find that much the same issues which you are addressing have been tackled by others quite some time ago.
- *Introductory and overview texts.* All disciplines have produced one or more basic texts which summarize their development and current state of thinking. Typically designed for sixth-form or undergraduate audiences, these texts can be very useful means for reading quickly into a new or unfamiliar subject area, or for refreshing your understanding.
- *Edited collections and literature reviews.* These may also be of particular use to you when starting your research, particularly if they have been recently published. Edited collections can be an excellent introduction to a given topic. Literature reviews may be invaluable as well, but do not place too much reliance on their opinions or selection. Wherever possible, refer to the original materials as well so that you can form your own views.
- *Methodological and confessional accounts.* In addition to reading books and papers which relate directly to the issues you are researching, you should also consider reading material on the approaches, techniques and methods you are using in your research project. These may focus on the methods

themselves or on other people's experience of applying them. More guidance on this is given in the section on **Reading about method as well as subject** later in this chapter.

Finally, in your reading you should be aware of the extent to which texts present and make use of original data. A common distinction made is that between primary, secondary and tertiary sources. Primary sources mainly consist of original data, while secondary sources comment on and interpret data, and tertiary sources (e.g. textbooks) offer summaries of knowledge in a particular area. You would be unwise to restrict your reading mainly to tertiary sources, though these can be valuable as an initial guide.

Whom to read

Faced with a bookshelf containing twenty or thirty books on the same topic, or decades of dozens of journals, or a list of hundreds of hits provided by a search engine, it can be very difficult to decide where to start. You might choose one item at random, or take a more considered view, perhaps selecting the most recent book written and published in your country.

In doing so, it is important to be aware of whom you are reading, where they are coming from, how authoritative a voice they have, and what their motivations in writing might be. In part, your aim should be to read a range of views, exploring both the founding thinkers or the great names of your field and the diversity of current opinions. Remember, however, that everybody is capable of being mistaken in their opinions or interpretations. That is, after all, the purpose of research writing: to stimulate further thinking.

You should be able to get plenty of guidance on whom to read, at least to start with, from your supervisor, manager, colleagues or fellow researchers. Some of the kinds of sources mentioned above, particularly literature reviews, are also excellent places to go for suggestions on whom to read. As you read more and more literature, you will begin to build up a view of the most quoted or cited authors and the classic texts, but you should also follow your own hunches and seek out less read materials.

> **Hint**: Take some time just to browse – serendipity can be a wonderful thing.

How to find what you need to read

If you are a researcher tackling an unfamiliar field of study for the first time, you need to be able to get to grips with the relevant literature as quickly as possible. Your aim should be to become familiar with the key texts on your subject area, and to supplement this understanding with a broader and more selective reading around the topic.

You might find it useful at this point to look at the section on **Focusing** in Chapter 2.

Box 4.3 presents an eight-stage approach to finding what you need to read. For advice on how to read it, see the later section on **Good enough reading**.

Box 4.3 Eight stages for finding what you need to read

1 Take advice from available sources: your supervisor, manager, fellow researchers or students.
2 Locate books, journals or other materials that appear relevant by asking advice, browsing around, or using a library catalogue or internet search engine (see the following two sections on **Using libraries** and **Using the internet** for further advice). You will find that keyword searches can be particularly useful.
3 Once you have identified relevant shelf or internet locations, look at other materials there which are relevant to your topic.
4 Once you have identified relevant journals – in print or online – look through recent issues to find the most up-to-date writing on your topic.
5 Read outwards from your original sources by following up interesting-looking references.
6 Identify key texts by noting those that are referred to again and again. Make sure that you read the most popular or relevant of these. Seek out the latest editions.
7 As you develop a feeling for the literature relevant to your field, try to ensure that you have some understanding of, and have done some reading within, its different areas.
8 Use the time and resources you have available to do as much pertinent reading as possible.

Using libraries

Almost any library, and particularly academic libraries, will have a wide range of facilities and resources available to support you in your research. Libraries are not just about books! If you doubt this, or haven't been in a good library for a while, try Exercise 4.2.

You may have identified a wide variety of potential sources of information or advice, depending on your experience of using libraries. Box 4.4 details

Box 4.4 Sources of information in the library

- **Librarians**. These are an endangered species, yet are usually keen and interested to help. Researchers owe a duty to librarians to make good use of them, and there is much that a librarian may be able to advise you on or help you with, if approached in the right way.
- **Catalogues**. These are now almost invariably online. You need to understand how a library is catalogued if you are going to make best use of it. Once you know how your subject interests are coded, you should be able to search for other materials sharing these codes. You should also familiarize yourself with searching using key words, subject titles or authors' names.
- **Databases**. Larger libraries normally provide access online to a wide range of materials that they do not physically house themselves. Databases (e.g. Academic Search Premier, ERIC) allow the reader to search for relevant materials using key words, and to scroll through summary or detailed information on these texts. Practice may be needed to make full use of the range of facilities available.
- **Abstracts and reviews**. Abstracts are mostly now published only in online form, and contain up-to-date summary material on recent publications in their fields. Reviews are contained in a wide variety of popular or specialist periodicals (available in print form and/or online), and can be an invaluable guide to what has been recently published that might be worth reading or is influential.
- **Dictionaries and encyclopedias**. Larger general and any specialist dictionaries and encyclopedias can also be a useful starting point, though they typically will not go far enough into any particular topic to be of continuing use.
- **Open shelves**. Finally, and perhaps most obviously, most libraries have a considerable area of open shelving, containing both books and journals (bound and current issues). Browsing these can guide you to which areas of the library are likely to be of most use, and indicate the scope of the library's holdings in particular areas. Many key texts are unlikely to be on the shelves at any one time, of course, as they will be on loan or in use, and older materials are likely to be in store, so this method should only be used in conjunction with other, more comprehensive forms of searching. Recall books on loan immediately if you think they may be of interest.

six main sources with which you will probably need to be familiar if you are going to do a reasonable amount of reading and you wish to be up to date.

Note that we have started the list in Box 4.4 with librarians, and only ended it with what is perhaps the most obvious source, the shelves of books and journals themselves.

> **Hint**: Remember that all of the books on one topic, and with the same class mark, may not be gathered together on the same shelf or shelves. Oversize books and pamphlets are often separately shelved, some older books may be kept in store, while very popular books may be in a reserve section. You need to be able to identify and use all of these locations.

There are a number of other points which you should bear in mind when using your library, particularly if you are conducting your research at least partly for academic credit.

Reading journals as well as books

Don't neglect to read the journals relevant to your topic. These are the only reasonably up-to-date guide to thinking in your subject area, and will include much material that has not yet made, and may never make, it into books. If you are studying at a university, you should find that many of these are available to you online – note that some journals only publish online, and printed journals now commonly publish accepted articles online first before they are printed – as well as, or instead of, in the form of printed copies.

Accessing materials not in the library

You will probably run up against the problem of identifying materials which look of interest and then finding that they are not available in the library you are in. Three obvious strategies for responding to this problem are: the use of alternative libraries or sources, accessing materials through the inter-library loan system, or accessing them online. Each of these has associated costs. In practical terms, there are limits on what can be expected of any individual library and on how much reading a researcher can be expected to do.

> The question of how much to read is considered in the section on **Issues in reading** later in this chapter.

Before you do try to access materials which are not in, or freely available through, your library, make sure you have checked what is in them using available databases, abstracts or digests.

Photocopying

Where you cannot borrow materials, or do not have the time to bring them back, you may wish to photocopy selected items. Cost will likely be a limiting factor here, as will the legal restrictions on copyright. Nevertheless, many researchers make considerable use of photocopying facilities, spending limited time in the library and then reading what they have copied as and when convenient. Always make sure, however, that you have the full reference for any articles, chapters or extracts you photocopy.

> **Hint**: When using a photocopier, you may find that it saves you money and time, so long as your eyesight is good enough, to use the 'reduce' button, printing two pages at half-size on one.

Using the internet

The opportunities for searching for information via the internet are enormous, and the accessibility of this information makes it a very attractive source for research. However, having the world's knowledge at your fingertips can also be bewildering, as one link leads you on to the next. This is why an internet search needs to be systematic and carefully managed, and requires you to keep an eye on the quality of the information you are accessing.

> See the section later in this chapter on **The literature review** for further advice on systematic searching.

Box 4.5 indicates some of the internet resources that will be useful for social science and humanities researchers. For many researchers, a first step on the internet is to use a search engine, such as Google or Yahoo!. Google Scholar specializes in academic publications and resources. These should help you to locate the various sites that would be relevant to your topic. The search engine identifies these sites by using the key word or words that you enter. These key words are matched against millions of documents catalogued on the web to produce an index of sites of likely relevance.

Remember, though, that the web is a huge resource, and the information it contains is placed on it by a huge variety of institutions and individuals. It is, therefore, absolutely essential to be able to distinguish between useful, less useful and useless information, and to assess the varied quality of the information found. Search engines use a scattergun approach, selecting *any* site that fits your key words regardless of the source or quality.

> **Health warning**: Searches need careful refining if you are not to be inundated with lots of useless information.

Box 4.5 Key sites for social science researchers

Examples of internet gateways

http://www.intute.ac.uk/socialsciences/
This site provides access to, and reviews of, key sites. Coverage includes sociology, economics, government policy, anthropology, statistics and data, travel and tourism, law, women's studies. There is a virtual training suite to help gain skills in research tools.

http://www.ncrm.ac.uk
This is the ESRC National Centre for Research Methods. It is an important source for up-to-date research and training into social science methodologies.

http://bbc.co.uk
Provides access to information on business, history, science and society, and many other topics.

Examples of specific sites for reports of research, bibliographic databases, research databases, and choosing and using software

http://www.esrc.ac.uk
This is the site for the Economic and Social Research Council (ESRC), the key funding body for social science research and postgraduate studentships in the UK. Offers a fully searchable database of research it has funded.

http://www.data-archive.ac.uk/
Also funded by the ESRC, this archive is based at the University of Essex and houses the largest collection of accessible computer-readable data in the social sciences and humanities in the UK. The archive can provide data to help in masters and PhD research, especially for those working in the fields of economics, statistics, politics, sociology, accountancy, business studies, public health, welfare and history. It offers links to a range of other relevant information resources.

http://www.essex.ac.uk/qualidata/
Also funded by the ESRC and housed at the University of Essex, this is an archive of qualitative research data, mainly arising from ESRC funded projects. One of the aims of the site is to encourage the secondary use of archived qualitative data. It offers links to a range of other relevant information sources.

http://caqdas.soc.surrey.ac.uk/
This is the Computer Assisted Qualitative Data Analysis Software site, again set up by the ESRC. Its aims are to disseminate information needed to choose and use a range of software programs that have been designed to assist with qualitative data analysis.

http://onlineqda.hud.ac.uk
Another ESRC-funded site, aimed at researchers and postgraduates, offering support in qualitative data analysis.

http://www.statistics.gov.uk/
The home of official UK statistics on retail sales, the public sector, inflation, population, employment and many other themes.

http://www.bl.uk/
This is the British Library site; it includes information on millions of books, periodicals, newspapers, manuscripts, maps, music scores and photographs.

Examples of search engines

http://www.ask.co.uk
http://www.google.com
http://www.googlescholar.com
http://search.yahoo.com

Examples of metasearch engines

http://www.allonesearch.com/
All-in-One houses hundreds of the internet's search engines, databases, indexes and directories in a single site.

http://www.metacrawler.com
You will find twitter tools on this site.

Examples of directories

http://www.ipl.org/ref/
The Internet Public Library offers directories and research facilities for academics.

Web training

http://www.vts.rdn.ac.uk/
The Intute Virtual Training Suite aims to improve internet information literacy and IT skills. It offers a set of free 'teach yourself' tutorials in a growing number of social science subject areas for students, lecturers and researchers who want to find out what the internet can offer.

http://tramss.data-archive.ac.uk/
This is the website of the Teaching Resources and Materials for Social Scientists (TRAMSS). Its target audience is MA and research students in quantitative social science research.

Because of concerns about quality and the sheer amount of information, attempts have been made to classify material on the web into useful categories. This is done through what are called *internet gateways*. These are sites that edit sources of information, so they can direct you more immediately to what is relevant and appropriate. A key gateway for social scientists is Intute (see Box 4.5). This accepts only worthwhile databases and sources and classifies them into subject areas. You can search the whole system by key word, or just browse to see what is there. Intute also offers free online training to students, researchers and lecturers through the RDN Virtual Training Suite. These training sessions are designed to help you learn what the internet can offer in your subject area.

The adequacy of an internet search – as when you are searching a library catalogue online – relates to the key words that you have entered. You need to take care that you refine your search appropriately. Most search engines use Boolean operators and syntax. This means that you can group words together, or exclude words, to ensure that your search is as precise as possible. For example, a search using the single word 'Education' or 'Business' will produce thousands of items of information. By refining the search to a specific area of education or business, using additional key words and one or more Boolean operators (e.g. AND, OR, AND NOT), you are more likely to find the sites that you are particularly interested in.

If, for example, you key in 'Adult AND Education', this should list all those items or titles that contain both words. Or, if you key in 'Business AND NOT Small', the search should exclude all items referring to small business. Box 4.6 reproduces the Economic and Social Research Council's advice on how to restrict and extend your search on its database. This uses Boolean operators, but it also illustrates the usefulness of checking the 'help' tips on any system you are using to facilitate your search.

Good enough reading

How to 'read' a book in five minutes

If you are engaged in a research project, you will normally have to understand a great deal of published material of various kinds. If you attempt literally to read all of this it will take you ages. Most likely, you simply will not have the time to do so on top of all of your other plans and responsibilities. So, you will have to be much more selective in your reading of most of it.

Can you read books, reports and articles quickly and effectively for research purposes? Can you get to the gist of the argument and pull out the material or details you want within minutes? If you are not sure, try Exercise 4.3.

If you were able to complete Exercise 4.3 to your satisfaction, you probably

---

Box 4.6 Too much or too little information?

Finding too many records?
Try narrowing your search by:

- Using AND to combine terms, e.g. social AND exclusion.
- Use phrase searching, connect terms using underscore, e.g. social_ exclusion.
- Use the advanced search option and restrict your search to a section of the record, e.g. title.
- Exclude words or phrases by using NOT.

NB: AND will automatically be used to connect terms unless you type in a connector: e.g., if you type social exclusion the search will be social AND exclusion, but if you type social NOT exclusion, then AND will be overridden by NOT.

Not finding enough records?
Try broadening your search by:

- Using OR to combine terms, e.g. forest OR woodland.
- Using truncation – type the stem of a word followed by an asterisk to find any other endings: e.g. econ* will retrieve economy, economics, economist, etc. Be careful, however, as truncation can retrieve unwanted results: e.g. car* will find cars but will also retrieve carnation and carnage.

NB: If you switch on truncation by adding an asterisk in the search all the terms in that search will also be truncated. For example, econ* AND forest will retrieve economics, economist etc., but will also retrieve forestry, forester and so forth.

---

need read no further in this section. If you didn't find the exercise so straight-forward, have a look at Box 4.7 for some hints and advice.

You should, with some practice, be able to get the gist of a book, report or article in five minutes. In many cases, this will be quite enough, and you can move on to read or do something else. In other cases, however, your initial reading will allow you to identify which parts of the book or article need to be read more carefully. But you should rarely need to read more than 25 per cent of any book to get the best out of it for your own purposes.

Even this more detailed reading can be done selectively. You may find it particularly useful to scan relevant sections looking for passages which

---

Box 4.7 Getting the gist: some hints and tips

- Note down the author(s), title, publisher and date of the book, report or article. Keep this record, and any notes on the content, safely.
- Look for an introduction, concluding chapter, abstract or executive summary. If there is one, read it quickly, scanning the pages. If the book or report has a cover, the publisher's blurb may also be useful.
- If it is a book or report, look for the contents page. Identify any chapters which you think may be of particular relevance and focus on them, again starting from the introduction and/or conclusion. You can find your way through a chapter or section by using the subheadings.
- If it is a book or report, look for an index. If there are specific points you are interested in (people, institutions, events, etc.), you should be able to locate from the index where they are discussed in the text.
- In the text itself, key points will often be highlighted, or placed in the first or last paragraphs. Similarly, the first and last sentences of paragraphs are often used to indicate and summarize their contents.

---

succinctly summarize or advance the argument. These sections are often worth noting down as potential quotations.

Hint: If you can afford it, print off or take photocopies of key chapters or articles. You will then be able to mark these with highlighter pen, and make notes in the margins. Do this with books that you have purchased as well, or use Post-it notes.

Finally, in case you are worried that the approach suggested here is in some way inadequate, let us assure you of the contrary. All researchers use these techniques, or something similar. We couldn't pursue our work, let alone have time to do things other than research, if we didn't. Many suggested reading techniques (see Box 4.8) are based on this kind of approach, and encourage you to interact with the text rather than repeat it uncritically or verbatim.

We must stress, however, that a superficial knowledge of the research literature relevant to your topic is not adequate. You will need to know enough about what has been written to intelligently criticize and summarize it. This means being able to give both a broad picture of the appropriate literature and a more focused account of those parts of that literature which are of particular significance.

Box 4.8 SQ3R and SQ4R: strategies for reading

SQ3R

The SQ3R reading method is a structured approach to reading that can be very helpful for learning or revision.

- *Survey.* Scan the material you want to learn to get a picture of the overall argument or the area covered by the book or article you are reading.
- *Question.* Ask questions of the text. Turn any headings or subheadings into questions, and then try to answer them in your own words.
- *Read.* Go through the text in the light of the questions you have asked, and take notes at your own pace and in your own words.
- *Recall.* Close the book and try to remember what you have read. Try to write down what you remember in your own words. Only by testing your recall will you know how successful your learning has been.
- *Review.* Later, go back over all your notes to make sure you don't forget and to see how what you have learned relates to the course as a whole, your other reading and what you still need to do.

(Hay et al. 2002: 29)

SQ4R

1 Survey and Question
2 Read to Answer Questions
3 Recite and Write Answers and Summaries
4 Review

Advantages and disadvantages:
SQ4R is designed to help you focus on learning what is important to you . . . You learn to organise and structure your studying. You state your goals as questions, seek answers, achieve your goals and move on. You focus on grasping the key concepts . . . It is difficult to change old study habits . . . It takes more energy to ask questions and develop summaries than it does to let your eyes passively read printed pages.

(Walter and Siebert 1993: 89, 96)

How to critically assess what you are reading

Reading academic material is not just about becoming an elegant reader who can grasp the overall sense of a piece, translate jargon in order to extract facts from a text, while taking notes efficiently. Ideally, readers should learn to engage with a text in a way which enables them to assess its worth . . . [B]eing critical is learning to assess the logic and rationale of arguments and the quality of the substantiating data . . . [I]t is being able to ask how important the flaws are, and so to weigh the worth of evidence. This means being able to ask questions of the text beyond what it means, what it is saying.

(Peelo 1994: 59)

Critical reasoning is centrally concerned with giving reasons for one's beliefs and actions, analysing and evaluating one's own and other people's reasoning, devising and constructing better reasoning. Common to these activities are certain distinct skills, for example, recognizing reasons and conclusions, recognizing unstated assumptions, drawing conclusions, appraising evidence and evaluating statements, judging whether conclusions are warranted; and underlying all of these skills is the ability to use language with clarity and discrimination.

(Thomson 1996: 2)

In everyday language, if someone is 'critical' we may be referring to a dressing down or personal disparagement. In research terms, however, critical reading, critical thinking and critical assessment refer to a considered, though not necessarily balanced, and justified examination of what others have written or said regarding the subject in question. An important skill at the heart of these processes is the ability to recognize, analyse and evaluate the reasoning and forms of argumentation in the texts and articles that you will read. This skill is called critical reasoning. Developing a systematic approach to the analysis of the arguments of others is an essential research skill. Box 4.9 provides a summary of the key points involved in analysing and evaluating arguments, while Box 4.10 summarizes what is meant by a critical assessment of your reading.

Reading and writing critically can be difficult skills to learn. Exercise 4.4 encourages you to practise critical reasoning by applying the points in Box 4.9 to an article or short passage of your choosing.

Hint: Being critical does not mean rubbishing or rejecting someone else's work. As a researcher and thinker you should be able to entertain two or more contradictory ideas at one time.

The topic of writing critically is considered further in the section on **How to criticize** in Chapter 10.

Box 4.9 Assessing an argument

Analysing

1   Identify conclusion and reasons: look for 'conclusion indicators' [key words to look for are 'therefore', 'so', 'hence', 'thus', 'should']; look for 'reason indicators' [key words to look for are 'because'; 'for', 'since']; *and/or*

- Ask 'What is the passage trying to get me to accept or believe?'
- Ask 'What reasons, evidence is it using in order to get me to believe this?'

2   Identify unstated assumptions:

- assumptions supporting basic reasons
- assumptions functioning as additional reasons
- assumptions functioning as intermediate conclusions
- assumptions concerning the meaning of words
- assumptions about analogous or comparable situations
- assumptions concerning the appropriateness of a given explanation

Evaluating

3   Evaluate truth of reasons/assumptions: how would you seek further information to help you do this?
4   Assess the reliability of any authorities on whom the reasoning depends.
5   Is there any additional evidence which strengthens or weakens the conclusion? Anything which may be true? Anything you know to be true?
6   Assess the plausibility of any explanation you have identified.
7   Assess the appropriateness of any comparisons you have identified.
8   Can you draw any conclusions from the passage? If so, do they suggest that the reasoning in the passage is faulty?
9   Is any of the reasoning in the passage parallel with reasoning which you know to be faulty?
10   Do any of the reasons or assumptions embody a general principle? If so, evaluate it.
11   Is the conclusion well supported by the reasoning? If not, can you state the way in which the move from the reasons to the conclusion is flawed? Use your answers to questions 5 to 10 to help you do this.

(*Source*: Thomson 1996: 99–100)

Box 4.10 What is a critical reading?

- One that goes beyond mere description by offering opinions, and making a response, to what has been written.
- One that relates different writings to each other, indicating their differences and contradictions, and highlighting what they are lacking.
- One that does not take what is written at face value.
- One that strives to be explicit about the values and theories which inform and colour reading and writing.
- One that views research writing as a contested terrain, within which alternative views and positions may be taken up.
- One that shows an awareness of the power relations involved in research, and of where writers are coming from.
- One that uses a particular language (authors assert, argue, state, conclude or contend), may be carefully qualified, and may use an impersonal voice.

Reading about method as well as subject

Why read about method?

We have already stressed a number of times the importance of understanding your research approaches and techniques as well as the subject of your research. As the lists of further reading in this book indicate, there is a considerable published literature on research methods. As a researcher, you could gain a great deal from studying some of this literature. If you doubt this, consider Box 4.11, which identifies nine linked reasons for reading about method as well as subject.

Where to read about method

There are a variety of sources in which you can read more about methods:

- *Methodological texts*. These may review a range of methods or focus in more detail on just one or two. The extensive bibliographies included in this book include many examples of such texts.
- *Methods journals*. These specialize in articles on the use and development of particular methods. Some examples are given in Box 4.12. Subject journals sometimes also have special issues which focus on methodological questions.
- *Confessional accounts*. These are articles or books which tell the story of what it actually felt like doing research, what problems were encountered and how they were dealt with. They help to undermine the idea of research as a

---

Box 4.11 Nine reasons for reading about method

1   You are going to be using one or more research techniques or methods in your project work, so it is as well that you understand as much as possible about them and their use.
2   You may need to evaluate a number of alternative approaches and techniques before deciding which ones you are going to use.
3   If you are likely to engage in a series of research projects, you will need to develop your understanding of the broad range of research methods used in your disciplinary or subject area.
4   In doing so, you will be developing your knowledge of research practices, and will be better able to reflect upon your own practice.
5   It will help you to justify what you are doing, or proposing to do, and why.
6   It will allow you to see research for what it is, a social process with its own varying conventions and changing practices, rather than as an artificial and objective set of procedures.
7   Your methods may be of more interest to you than the subject of the research.
8   You may need, or be expected, to write a methodological section or chapter in your research report or dissertation.
9   Simply to expand your knowledge.

---

clear, fault-free process, and you may find them very supportive when you encounter difficulties of your own. You will come across quotations and references to these throughout this book.

- *Reports on methodology in published research*. Any research paper will probably give some indication of the methods used to conduct the research described. This may be minimal or fulsome, and may include reflections on problems that occurred and suggestions for changed practice in the future.

The last of these sources, we suggest, is possibly the most problematic, as Exercise 4.5 may well reveal. Many published reports of social research contain relatively little discussion of the methods and techniques employed. Where methods are described, the tendency is to present them in a relatively unproblematic light, so that the research strategy is difficult to evaluate or question. In subject areas where methodology has not been a major preoccupation, as in policy analysis, a growing emphasis can be detected, however, towards making underlying concepts and processes more visible.

It would certainly be difficult to replicate most pieces of research using just the information contained in a journal paper. This is partly a function of the restricted length of most research articles and of the pressures to focus on reporting and interpreting results in the available space. Yet it scarcely represents what might be called good practice.

Box 4.12 Some examples of methods journals

- *Behaviour Research Newsletter*
- *Cognitive Psychology*
- *Development Psychology*
- *Education and Psychological Measurement*
- *Evaluation and Methodology*
- *Evaluation and the Health Professions*
- *Evaluation Review*
- *Historical Methods*
- *International Journal of Qualitative Studies in Education*
- *International Journal of Social Research Methodology*
- *Journal of Applied Behavioural Science*
- *Journal of Contemporary Ethnography*
- *Journal of Philosophy, Psychology and Scientific Methods*
- *Qualitative Health Research*
- *Qualitative Inquiry*
- *Sociological Methodology*
- *Sociological Methods and Research*
- *Studies in Qualitative Methodology*

(*Note*: This list is illustrative rather than comprehensive. It includes journals which specialize in discussing and analysing methods, those which have a methods section, those which regularly contain articles which focus on methods, and those which report research using particular methods. An increasing number of methods journals are available online.)

It is usually necessary to study lengthier, and often unpublished, research reports, where these are available, in order to get a full understanding of the process of research. Even these may be inadequate, however, in which case a direct approach to the researcher(s) concerned is the only option.

Recording your reading

Meticulousness, along with creativity, flexibility, persuasiveness and the ability to get funding, has to be one of the most prized qualities in the researcher. Being meticulous, from the beginning of your research project right through to its end and beyond, will save you time and trouble in the long run.

This is particularly important when it comes to recording your reading. You should resolve, right from the start, to note down full details of everything you read. These details should include:

- the author or authors;
- the title of the paper, report or book;
- the date of publication;
- if it is a book or report, the publisher and place of publication (and the edition, if there has been more than one);
- if it is a chapter in an edited book, the title and editor of the book, and the page numbers of the chapter;
- if it is a paper in a journal, the title of the journal, volume and issue number, and pages;
- if it is a website, the address and the date you accessed the information.

All of the references listed in this book contain this information. In addition, you should note the location and page number(s) of any material which you may quote.

There are a number of ways in which you might collect and store this information. Index cards used to be the conventional way, since they can be kept in alphabetical or some other kind of order, as best suits your needs. Box 4.13 contains some examples of what your records might look like. Whatever recording method you use, the information you store will be similar.

The contemporary practice is to input all of your referencing details, together with a note of the contents and of possible quotations, directly into your computer. Computer systems usually have facilities for sorting your records, and for placing selected quotations directly into your text without the need for retyping. Specially designed software, such as Endnote, Procite or RefWorks (which can also do a lot more), can be very useful for these purposes.

> See also the section in Chapter 5 on **Using computers**.

It may seem tedious, but if you aren't meticulous in this way, you will give yourself much trouble and irritation later, when you are trying to locate and check details, particularly when you come to the writing-up phase.

The literature review

A research literature review is a systematic, explicit, and reproducible method for identifying, evaluating and synthesizing the existing body of completed and recorded work produced by researchers, scholars and practitioners.

(Fink 2005: 3)

Box 4.13 What to put in your records

Partington, D. (ed.)
Essential Skills for Management Research
London, Sage, 2002.
Organized in three parts: philosophy and research (philosophical underpinnings, ethical considerations); research processes (theory development, successful writing, acknowledging the individual); approaches and techniques (research design, ethnographic approaches, grounded theory, case studies, cognitive mapping, repertory grids, laddering, action research).

Stake, R.
Qualitative Case Studies
pp. 443–66 in N. Denzin and Y. Lincoln (eds), *The Sage Handbook of Qualitative Research*.
Thousand Oaks, CA, Sage, 3rd edition, 2005.
This chapter reviews, with examples, theory and practice of case study research.

Mullins, G. and Kiley, M.
'It's a PhD, not a Nobel Prize': how experienced examiners assess research theses.
Studies in Higher Education, 2002, 27(4): 369–86.
Using a sample of 30 experienced Australian examiners, reports on the processes they go through in assessing PhDs.

Winter, G.
A comparative discussion of the notion of 'Validity' in qualitative and quantitative research.
The Qualitative Report, 4(3/4), March 2000
(Available: http://www.nova.edu/sss/QR/QR3–4/winter.html)
This article explores issues surrounding the use of validity in social research. It begins by exploring 'validity' in quantitative and qualitative approaches, and proceeds to examine the various claims to 'validity' made by researchers. The article concludes by suggesting that an understanding of the nature of 'truth' is central to the ways in which 'validity' is theorized.

[R]esearch is greatly strengthened by placing your new information in the context of what is already known about the issue. Researchers call this process 'doing a literature search', 'survey', or 'doing a literature review' or 'study'. 'The literature' refers to all the available research on a subject. 'Literature search' refers to the process of finding the material, and a 'literature survey' simply describes the literature which exists. The terms 'review' or 'study' point to the importance of critically assessing the information you collect, and making sense of it in relation to your own research question. A good literature review is a key feature by which the quality of a piece of research is judged.

(Laws et al. 2003: 213)

The ability to carry out a competent literature review is an important skill for the researcher. It helps to place your work in the context of what has already been done, allowing comparisons to be made and providing a framework for further research. While this is particularly important, indeed will be expected, if you are carrying out your research in an academic context, it is probably a helpful exercise in any circumstances. Spending some time reading the literature relevant to your research topic may prevent you from repeating previous errors or redoing work that has already been done, as well as giving you insights into aspects of your topic which might be worthy of detailed exploration. Box 4.14 provides an example of some of the questions a literature review can answer.

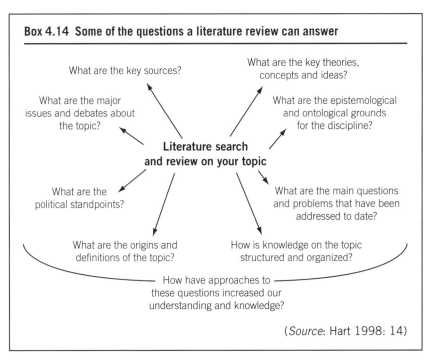

Box 4.14 Some of the questions a literature review can answer

What are the key sources?

What are the key theories, concepts and ideas?

What are the major issues and debates about the topic?

What are the epistemological and ontological grounds for the discipline?

Literature search and review on your topic

What are the political standpoints?

What are the main questions and problems that have been addressed to date?

What are the origins and definitions of the topic?

How is knowledge on the topic structured and organized?

How have approaches to these questions increased our understanding and knowledge?

(*Source*: Hart 1998: 14)

Nevertheless, it is possible to approach your literature review in a variety of ways, and with a range of different purposes in mind. Box 4.15 contrasts the range of different perspectives adopted by beginning research students with the more comprehensive strategy taken in carrying out systematic reviews.

Box 4.15 Literature and systematic reviews

A typology of literature reviews

- *As a list.* The primary focus is on the listing rather than on the knowledge contained within the literature represented.
- *As a search.* Source materials act as an intermediary directing the researcher towards or providing an awareness of existing literature.
- *As a survey.* The student's focus is on the literature, with his/her interest centred on the knowledge base of the discipline.
- *As a vehicle for learning.* The student's focus is beyond the literature and on his or her personal development.
- *As a research facilitator.* The impact of the literature moves beyond influencing the researcher to have an impact on the research project.
- *As a report.* The report is not only a synthesis of literature relevant to the research, it is a final representation of interaction with the literature.

(*Source*: Adapted from Bruce 1994: 224–5)

Aims of a systematic review

- To address a specific (well focused, relevant) question.
- To search for, locate and collate the results of the research in a systematic way.
- To reduce bias at all stages of the review (publication, selection and other forms of bias).
- To appraise the quality of the research in the light of the research question.
- To synthesize the results of the review in an explicit way.
- To make the knowledge base more accessible.
- To identify gaps; to place new proposals in the context of existing knowledge.
- To propose a future research agenda; to make recommendations.
- To present all stages of the review in the final report to enable critical appraisal and replication.

(*Source*: Adapted from Torgerson 2003: 7–8)

A key point to note is that good literature reviews go beyond the stage of simply listing sources to offer an analytical study of the area, through which you can develop your own position, analysis and argument. A literature review is a critical summary and assessment of the range of existing materials dealing with knowledge and understanding in a given field. It may be restricted to books and papers in one discipline or sub-discipline, or may be wider-ranging in approach. Generally, its purpose is to locate the research project, to form its context or background and to provide insights into previous work. A literature review may form part of an empirical study or it may be a study in itself.

In undertaking a literature review, you should find the general advice given in the rest of this chapter of some use. For more specific guidance, have a look at Boxes 4.16 and 4.17, which offer a number of suggestions designed to make your review more focused, relevant and enjoyable. Box 4.16 focuses on the processes involved in planning the literature, including getting advice on its size and scope, while Box 4.17 offers guidance on what the review might contain.

Box 4.16 Planning a literature review

- Ask your supervisor, manager, colleagues or fellow students for advice on what is expected. If you are researching in an academic context, there may be quite precise expectations.
- Look at previous examples of literature reviews in your area of research. They may have been completed by former students or researchers in your institution, or published in books or journals. Many articles include at least a brief literature review. While you may take account of such previous reviews, try not to slavishly follow their structuring or argument. Wherever possible, read for yourself the sources referred to, rather than relying on others' interpretations.
- The two previous points should help you to get an idea of the scale of the exercise, i.e. how long a literature review should be, and how many items might be referred to.
- Make sure you include what are thought of as the key texts in your field, and that you locate this work within the broader traditions of your discipline, sub-discipline or subject area.
- If your work is going to be examined, and you are aware of the examiners' identities and/or their preferences, it is sensible to address these in your review. Examiners are human beings too. Refer to some of your examiners' work, demonstrate that you have read it, and do not be unduly critical.
- Structure your review in sections to reflect different approaches, interpretations, schools of thought or areas of the subject you are tackling.

Recently, there have been a small number of publications produced that have been specifically written to help students with literature reviews. Examples are listed at the end of the chapter.

You will find guidance on writing up your literature review in Chapter 10, **Writing up**.

Box 4.17 Writing a literature review

A separate chapter or integrated throughout?

- The former is the safer, more conventional strategy.
- A literature review might be spread over two or more chapters if, for example, there is a substantive policy as well as a research literature of relevance.
- In some cases, your whole work may, in effect, be a literature review; if, for example, you have undertaken a library-based project or focused on theory development.

Don't just use, but critique, the literature

- Don't produce lots of lists, tables, figures, bullet points and summaries.
- Don't overuse quotations with little in the way of your discussion, comment and critique linking them.
- Make sure your opinion on the literature you discuss is clear (though not overly dogmatic).

Make sure that you link the literature review – assuming that you adopt the conventional, separate chapter, strategy – to the rest of your writing

- Relate the literature review to your research questions.
- Return, selectively, to the literature in your analysis, discussion and conclusions.
- Don't suddenly introduce new bodies of literature in the final sections of your writing.

In the introductory section of your literature review, explain how it has been organized and why

- Impose your own categorization on the literature: don't use somebody else's, if one exists, unless you have a good reason to do so.
- Make sure that you also explain what has been left out (you can't discuss everything of possible relevance), and why.
- Explain the method(ology), including the sampling strategy, that underlies your literature review.

Make sure that you cover the following points

- Important, particularly contemporary, debates of relevance.
- Key authors, both contemporary and classic: ones whose names keep recurring in your reading.

- Alternative schools of thought and disciplinary approaches.
- How theory, method(ology) and data interact in the literature.

Key purposes of a literature review

- To establish the present condition of the field.
- To provide a rationale for your work (e.g. gaps, limited perspectives, methodological weaknesses).
- To enable you to make a claim for originality.
- To clarify relevant concepts and theories.
- To set up comparisons (with your own data and analysis).

Key processes involved in carrying out a literature review

- Categorization
- Summary
- Selective quotation
- Synthesis
- Evaluation
- Critique

Final points

- Make sure it's up to date.
- Don't forget the methodological literature.

Issues in reading

As a novice researcher, you are quite likely to encounter some difficulties in reading for your research topic. The most common problems raised are:

- Nothing has been written on my research topic.
- There's too much.
- It's all been done.
- How many references do I need?

These issues are complementary. Indeed, they may all be uttered by the same researchers at different points in the research process.

Nothing has been written on my research topic

This is unlikely to be literally true, if only because it is difficult to be quite as original as this suggests.

It may be that you are defining your area of interest too narrowly. It is, after all, unlikely that anything will have been written on your particular issue or combination of issues, using your chosen methods, and focusing on the particular cases or sample you have selected (if it has, consider changing your topic or approach slightly). But there is likely to be material on some or all of the issues of concern to you, perhaps in different contexts. And there will be books and papers on the method or methods you are using. And there may well be discussions of your cases or sample for other purposes. All of this material should be of some interest.

It may be that you cannot find relevant material and that you need further advice on how to get started.

Have another look at the section on **Basic reading strategies** earlier in this chapter.

If you are in this position, you might start again by focusing on the disciplinary debates which relate to your research topic, or by looking for relevant sections in basic textbooks by key authors.

If, however, it is really the case that you have stumbled upon a topic about which very little has been written which is accessible to you, you should probably consider changing your topic. Ploughing a little-known furrow as a novice researcher is going to be very difficult, and you may find it difficult to get much support or help.

There's too much

See also the section on **Coping with the research literature** earlier in this chapter.

It is normal to be overwhelmed by the volume and complexity of the available research literature, and much of this chapter is about how you respond and get to grips with this. The only answer is to start somewhere, eventually (soon, hopefully) begin to see patterns and linkages, and to get as much support and guidance as you can. Set yourself reasonable and limited targets, and remember that you cannot be expected to do everything.

If, after a period of time, you still feel that there is too much, you should consider refocusing and limiting your research topic, so that you have to concentrate on just one aspect of the broader literature you have discovered.

> **Hint**: If you carry out a search of the literature using a computer database, and this results in hundreds of references, do not download them all. Narrow your search further, perhaps by limiting it to works published after a certain date, or by adding to or changing your key words.

It's all been done

The worry that you will one day come across a piece of published research which effectively replicates what you are doing is a common research nightmare. It very rarely happens. It is highly unlikely that someone else will have made exactly the same research choices as you. There will be differences, however slight, in location, sample, size, instruments, context and issues considered. It is common, on the other hand, to come across material which closely relates to what you are doing, and which may suggest some changes in direction or focus. This is usually helpful.

> See also the section on **Panics** in Chapter 10.

How many references do I need?

Even if you are carrying out a wholly library-based project, reading is only part of your research project. You need time to think about what you are reading, and to write. If you are doing fieldwork, you will also need lots of time to plan, carry out, evaluate and analyse this work, in addition to engaging in relevant reading.

Somehow, then, you need to be able to put boundaries on your reading. How and where? If you feel that you do not have much of an idea of the answer to these questions, try Exercise 4.6. This should give you a rough guide as to what you might aim for in terms of references – but only a rough guide. Some authors over-reference, seeming to show off by cramming in as many references in a page as possible. Others under-reference, appearing to assume that all of their readers have a good grounding in the field and are aware of the texts on which they are drawing, but perhaps giving the impression that they've read nothing. Some give bibliographies, but make little actual direct use of the works referred to in their text. Some never quote directly, while others produce texts which are little more than a series of linked quotations. There are also considerable differences in referencing styles between journals and publishers.

You should be aiming for a balanced approach between these extremes, but one which you are personally comfortable with, and which takes account of any regulations or expectations applying to your research. Box 4.18 makes some suggestions as to how you should, and should not, make use of references.

Box 4.18 Use and abuse of references

You should use references to:

- justify and support your arguments
- allow you to make comparisons with other research
- express matters better than you could have done so
- demonstrate your familiarity with your field of research

You should not use references to:

- impress your readers with the scope of your reading
- litter your writing with names and quotations
- replace the need for you to express your own thoughts
- misrepresent their authors

You cannot possibly read everything that might be of relevance to your research topic. So, as with other aspects of your research project, you have to reach a compromise between what you would ideally like to do and what is feasible, and do the best that you can within these constraints.

It is common to spend too much time on reading, proportionate to other aspects of the research project. You should try to get a good understanding of the literature as early as you can in your research, aiming to appreciate both the breadth of the literature and to understand in more depth the specific parts of it of most relevance to you. You should then move on to the actual research itself, but keep up with and return to reading to refresh, check and update yourself when you can.

Summary

Having read this chapter, you should:

- understand the vital importance of reading as part of the research process;
- feel more confident about how to find relevant materials to read;
- realize that reading for research is a very selective process;
- appreciate the importance of meticulously recording what you have read;
- have a better idea of what is involved in producing a literature review.

Exercises

4.1 Find half a dozen books, papers, articles, reports or other materials which seem relevant to your proposed area of research. Taking no more than 30 minutes, produce a brief annotated bibliography of these materials, writing no more than a short paragraph on each item. Think about what you had to do in order to complete this exercise.

4.2 Pay a visit to a library (physical or virtual) you envisage using for your research project. Look around the library and identify the main sources of information or advice that you think you will find useful.

4.3 Pick up a book of relevance to your research, one you have not read before. Taking no more than five minutes, summarize the key message(s) of the book that relate to your research.

4.4 Take a short article or part of an article. Make a list of its conclusions, and of the reasons for these conclusions. How adequate do you think the reasoning in the article is?

4.5 Choose a research report, article or book. Can you identify the methods used in carrying out the research reported? Are any problems in the use of the methods discussed? How well justified do you find the choice of methods?

4.6 Get hold of one or more of the dissertations, theses or reports produced by researchers in your department or organization. Work out how long each dissertation, thesis or report is, and note how many references there are.

Further reading

In this section, we list a limited selection of books that are of particular relevance to the topics discussed in this chapter.

Black, T. (2001) *Understanding Social Science Research*. London: Sage.
Focuses on the critical understanding of published research, particularly that using statistical analysis.

Brown, A. and Dowling, P. (2009) *Doing Research/Reading Research: A mode of interrogation for education*, 2nd edition. London: Routledge.
Designed to help the beginning researcher organize and evaluate the research that they read, and implement small-scale research projects of their own.

Fairbairn, G. J. and Fairbairn, S. A. (2001) *Reading at University: A guide for students*. Buckingham: Open University Press.
Deals with topics such as developing your skills as a reader, active reading, note taking, and where and when to read.

Fairbairn, G. J. and Winch, C. (1996) *Reading, Writing and Reasoning: A guide for students*, 2nd edition. Buckingham: Open University Press.
This text is in three parts: reading, writing and talking; writing as a student; developing coherent trains of thought. Advice is given on drafting, developing argument and understanding the text.

Fink, A. (2005) *Conducting Research Literature Reviews: From paper to the internet*, 2nd edition. Thousand Oaks, CA: Sage.
A thorough guide using checklists, examples and exercises. Topics covered include refining questions to guide the review, identification of subheadings and key words, use of databases and the internet, quality and reliability, and how to report the results.

Girden, E. R. (2001) *Evaluating Research Articles From Start to Finish*, 2nd edition. Thousand Oaks, CA: Sage.
Using examples of good as well as flawed articles, this book indicates how to critically read qualitative and quantitative research articles. Numerous questions are included to guide the reader.

Hart, C. (1998) *Doing a Literature Review: Releasing the social science research imagination*. London: Sage.
Considers the role of the literature review, the processes of reviewing, classifying and reading, argumentation and organization, mapping and analysis, and writing the review. Lots of practical examples.

Hewson, C., Yule, P., Laurent, D. and Vogel, C. (2002) *Internet Research Methods: A practical guide for the social and behavioural sciences*. London: Sage.
Covers both using the internet to access online material and its use for primary research.

Jones, S. (ed.) (1999) *Doing Internet Research: Critical issues and methods for examining the net*. Thousand Oaks, CA: Sage.
Includes chapters on methodological considerations for online research, studying online social networks, survey research, measuring internet audiences, naturalist discourse research and cybertalk.

Locke, L., Spirduso, W. and Silverman, S. (2004) *Reading and Understanding Research*, 2nd edition. Thousand Oaks, CA: Sage.
Covers how to locate, select, read and evaluate research.

Mann, C. and Stewart, F. (2000) *Internet Communication and Qualitative Research: A handbook for researching online*. London: Sage.
This book reviews online research practice and basic internet technology, details the skills required by the online researcher, examines ethical, theoretical and legal issues, and considers power, gender and identity issues in a virtual world.

Ridley, D. (2008) *The Literature Review: A step-by-step guide for students*. London: Sage.
Describes how to carry out a literature review in a systematic, methodical way, providing useful strategies for efficient reading, conducting searches, organizing information and writing the review itself, with examples of best and worst practice drawn from real literature reviews.

Rumsey, S. (2004) *How to Find Information: A guide for researchers*. Maidenhead: Open University Press.
Discusses how to formulate your search strategy, the use of conventional and online sources, referencing, copyright and plagiarism.
Torgerson, C. (2003) *Systematic Reviews*. London: Continuum.
Takes the reader through the stages involved in carrying out a systematic literature review, including the development of a protocol, quality appraisal, publication bias and data synthesis.

5

Managing your project

Introduction • Managing time • Mapping your project • Piloting •
Dealing with key figures and institutions • Sharing responsibility • Using
computers • Managing not to get demoralized when things do not go as
planned • Summary • Exercises • Further reading

Introduction

You've decided what topic to focus on in your research project. You've worked
out your research approach, and settled on the techniques and methods you
will use. You've located and begun to read some of the literature relevant
to your topic. How do you actually manage and progress your plans so
that you carry out and complete your project in the time and with the
resources you have available? That is the subject of this chapter.

The chapter focuses on the various skills which you will need to bring into
play, or to develop, in order to manage your research project effectively and to
cope with the problems that will arise as you proceed with your work.

The following issues are covered:

- **Managing time**. How to use your time for research.
- **Mapping your project**. Scheduling your research into the time you have
  available.
- **Piloting**. Testing your research plans before committing yourself.
- **Dealing with key figures and institutions**. The roles of supervisors,
  managers, employers and universities.
- **Sharing responsibility**. Using formal and informal relationships to support
  your research.
- **Using computers**. Getting the available technology to work for you.

- **Managing not to get demoralized when things do not go as planned.**
  The ups and downs of the research process.

Managing time

Even if you register only part-time, you should ideally put in some work on your research every day (to an equivalent of two days' solid work a week), if possible in a place where you can leave the work spread out in between times. It really *cannot* be fitted in to odd half days at the weekend. This doesn't mean cutting off your social, domestic life and active life entirely. On the contrary, you need these for balance: to ensure you stay healthy and supported.

(Leonard 2001: 77)

People think about, describe and manage their time in a wide variety of different ways. Box 5.1 outlines a number of different attitudes to time. Do you recognize yourself in any of these statements?

Box 5.1 Attitudes to time

- I'm a night owl.
- I'm an early bird.
- I juggle lots of tasks.
- I schedule everything in my diary.
- I over-schedule!
- I compartmentalize (e.g. I keep Sundays for the family).
- I slot things in when I can.
- There are too few hours in the day.
- I sleep fast.
- I don't have time even to go to the loo.
- I cook the children's dinner and write my essays on the corner of the table.
- I have to know I will be uninterrupted.
- The less time I've got, the more I get done.
- Time for me is really more about energy and motivation.

You should find it of help to you in carrying out your research project to have an appreciation of your own attitudes towards, and usage of, time. You need to understand your own ways of managing your time in relation to your energy levels and coping strategies, and to the demands made upon you. You also need to think about the rhythms of your day, week, month and year. For example, some people cannot work in the school holidays because of the demands of child care, while others see holiday time as a space which is sacrosanct and separate from work (and research). Some people like to keep Sunday free for family activities, while others see it as an ideal time to study.

Think about the demands on your time and your own preferences in relation to how others think about it. In our rushaway world, time is perhaps the most precious commodity. No one ever has enough of it. However, as people living in an industrialized society, we do have a particular view of time. Whereas agricultural societies viewed time as essentially cyclical, bounded by the pattern of seasons and days, industrial societies view it as linear and finite. Yet, we may still have glimpses of eternity.

It is relatively easy to identify a series of pragmatic time management principles. These should be of use to you in managing your research, almost regardless of your attitude towards time and the amount of it you have available. Box 5.2 contains a series of such hints and tips.

You may well, however, have other significant demands upon your time in addition to research. Particularly if you are a part-time student, but increasingly also if you are studying full time, you may have full-time or part-time employment. You may also have family responsibilities, caring for children or looking after elderly or infirm relatives. In such circumstances, carving out the time necessary for research, and doing so consistently week after week, can seem almost impossible.

But don't despair. Clearly, if the other demands on your time are pretty much all-consuming, you would be well advised to defer or suspend your research activities for the time being. There's no point in adding to your stress levels. Universities and employers are usually fairly flexible and understanding in such circumstances, particularly if your position is likely to improve in the foreseeable future.

If the pressures are not that bad, then you need to find ways of managing your time to cope with them as best you can. In your home life, this will probably mean that, for some of the time, your research activities will have to take priority over your family and social activities. Talk it over with those involved and try to get them on-side. Help them to understand how important this is for you, that they will still have priority for much of the time, and that your research will not last for ever.

In your work life, the key issue is whether you are undertaking this research for and/or with the support of your employer. If your employer is involved, they should be more willing to show some flexibility, though you may need to negotiate this repeatedly (and you may find that the support offered is more in principle than in practice). You may even be in the fortunate position of being able to do at least some of your research in work time: indeed, your research may be focused on your workplace. If your employer is not behind your research – and you may not wish them even to know about it – then your best option might be to make strategic use of your holiday entitlement for research

Box 5.2 Using time for research

Delegation

Can you delegate certain aspects of your research? For example, making appointments, carrying out interviews, tape transcription, inputting data to the computer, statistical analysis, typing of drafts.

Reading effectively

Train yourself to get through the literature, and to get at the nub of the arguments within it, more quickly.

> You will find that Chapter 4, **Reading for research**, contains much useful advice

Chunking

You may be able to divide some of your research tasks up into small chunks which can be tackled whenever you have a little spare time. For example, if you take photocopies of materials you need to read, you could bring these out (e.g. during a train journey) as and when you have time.

Relaxing with a purpose

Make sure all your downtime activities have a clear purpose. You might, for example, be idly looking through a book to gain a sense of what it is about. Or you might use time spent walking the dog or having a bath to give you time to think. Don't think of such time as wasted: one of the keys to doing worthwhile, effective research is to allow yourself plenty of space in which to mull over what you are doing.

You might commit such thoughts to your research diary. See the section on **Keeping your research diary** in Chapter 2.

purposes, or even, assuming you can afford it, reduce the number of hours you work.

From the start, however, you will need to be realistic. You cannot undertake a research project and not expect it to impact upon other aspects of your life. At the very least, you can expect to enjoy rather less in the way of sleep and loafing about. You will probably also have less time for dinner parties, sport and holidays. But always remember that research has its own consolations!

Mapping your project

Once you are clearer about your own preferences and possibilities regarding the usage of time, you should be able to draw up a draft schedule for your research. This will relate the time you have available in which to carry out the research – a given number of hours, days, weeks or perhaps years – to your other responsibilities and commitments. You can then slot in the various research activities you will need to engage in at times when you expect to be both free and in the mood to work on your research.

Just because you have drawn up a schedule, however, doesn't mean that you have to keep strictly to it. It is difficult, even with experience, to precisely estimate the time which different research activities will take. Some will take longer than expected, whereas others may need less time. Some will be abandoned, whereas other unanticipated activities will demand attention. So it is a good idea to allow for some spare time or flexibility in your scheduling. You should also revisit your schedule from time to time, and make revisions, to allow for such changes and to keep yourself on track.

There are a number of ways of scheduling your research time: one diagrammatic approach is illustrated in Box 5.3. Such charts have the disadvantage of suggesting a simplified, rational view of research. They are useful, however, in conveying the overlap or concurrence between the tasks to be carried out, and as a guide to progress. In practice, of course, there will be numerous minor changes to your plans as set out, and perhaps some major ones as well. When you have examined Box 5.3, see if you can draw up your own research schedule, if you have not already done so. Try Exercise 5.1, at the end of this chapter.

Piloting

Piloting, or reassessment without tears, is the process whereby you try out the research techniques and methods which you have in mind, see how well they work in practice, and, if necessary, modify your plans accordingly.

> The idea of 'informal piloting' was discussed in the section on **Focusing** in Chapter 2.

You may think that you know well enough what you are doing, but the value of pilot research cannot be overestimated. Things never work quite the way you envisage, even if you have done them many times before, and they have a nasty habit of turning out very differently from how you expected on

Box 5.3 Scheduling research using a grid

	Jan	Feb	Mar	Apr	May	June	July	Aug	Sept	Oct	Nov	Dec	Jan
Planning, discussion with partners	→→→▶												
Search for existing information	→→→▶												
Draft research tools (questionnaires etc)		→→▶											
Select and contact respondents			→→→▶										
Pilot tools and revise			→→▶										
Fieldwork 1. Focus groups				→→▶									
Fieldwork 2. Interviews						→→→▶							
Transcribing					→→▶		→→▶						
Analysis						→▶		→→→▶					
Writing									→→▶				
Editing and publication										→→▶			
Dissemination												→→▶	

(*Source*: Laws et al. 2003: 151)

occasion. So try a pilot exercise. If you don't, you will probably find that your initial period of data collection turns into a pilot in any case. In a sense, of course, all social research is a pilot exercise.

If you would like to pilot your research, and are not sure of the processes involved, try Exercise 5.2.

Dealing with key figures and institutions

There are a variety of key figures and institutions with which most researchers have to deal at some time or another. In this section, we consider the issues involved in dealing with the most common of these:

- At the individual level: your supervisor, tutor, mentor or manager.
- At the institutional level: your university, employer or sponsor.

Just how significant these individuals and organizations are will vary depending on your research project and circumstances. Here we will focus on those that are likely to be of most relevance to you in agreeing, progressing, reviewing and assessing your research.

> The issues involved in dealing with informants and case study institutions are covered in the section on **Access and ethical issues** in Chapter 6.

Key figures

The two individual figures we have identified as being likely to be of most importance to you as a researcher are your supervisor and your manager. A rough definition of these two roles would be:

- A supervisor has an academic responsibility for guiding and advising you on your research project.
- A manager has a responsibility for directing and overseeing your work in a more general sense.

You may have either, neither or both of these key figures involved in your research project. The two roles may even be combined in the same person, though in most circumstances this is probably not advisable.

If you are doing research for academic credit, you will almost certainly have a supervisor (or supervisors), though their importance to you may vary, depending on your topic, level of study, institutional practices and individual predilections. If you are doing research within your employing or work organization – and you may be doing this for academic credit as well – your manager may be of significance. Their importance will, similarly, vary depending upon a range of factors, including whether you are sponsored by your employer, and whether your employer or manager has determined your research topic.

> The question of what you might expect from your supervisor is considered in the section on **Finding and choosing your supervisor** in Chapter 2.

You may, in practice, have a splendid relationship with your supervisor and/ or manager, and receive good advice and sufficient support throughout your research work. If so, consider yourself fortunate, and be thankful. Other researchers have to make do with less engaged or with overworked supervisors, mentors or managers. One point to remember is that your supervisor or manager is probably a member of an organization which will have its own expectations regarding both this role and their other duties. You may want to discuss these with them.

Where your relationship gets off to a good start, it may change to your disadvantage during the course of your research (or vice versa). Or your supervisor or manager may themselves move on, and you will be passed on to somebody else. Box 5.4 details some general lessons about dealing with your supervisor and/or manager.

Box 5.4 Handling your supervisor or manager

- Investing too much authority or responsibility in key figures in your research life is likely to lead to disappointment. It is important to develop your own sense of authority and responsibility.
- In supervisor/researcher and manager/researcher relationships, responsibility is two-way. Just as you may rightly have expectations of your supervisor and/or manager, in terms of support and advice, so may they rightly have expectations of you. These may cover aspects such as scheduling, regularity of work and reporting back.
- Where you are carrying out a research project as part of a group, the situation is inevitably rather more complicated. A whole web of relationships and attendant responsibilities will exist between you, the other members of your group, and your joint supervisor(s) or manager(s). Because of this complexity, it is important to be as clear as possible about the nature of the relationships involved.
- You should ideally aim to be in a position of sharing responsibility for, and authority over, your research. After all, you are the person doing, and to a large extent managing, the research.
- If you ask for assistance or advice from your manager or supervisor, be prepared to have it refused, and still be able to move forward with your research.

How, then, can you, as a relatively inexperienced researcher, go about developing more authority in these relationships and greater responsibility for your own learning needs? If possible, and if you have not already done so, draw up and agree a contract with your supervisor and/or manager. This should set out the tasks involved in managing and progressing your research project, and detail the specific roles and responsibilities of the individuals concerned.

Although such contracts are by no means foolproof, they should give you rather more leverage to influence matters if something goes wrong, and they help to clarify roles and expectations for all involved. Having some kind of contractual agreement, with your research colleagues as well as your supervisor and/or manager, is doubly important if you are carrying out a group

---

Box 5.5 What a contract for a research student might include

Responsibilities at university level

- maintaining the regulations for postgraduate students
- admitting students and ensuring that admission standards are maintained
- checking that departments are monitoring students and dealing with complaints and problems
- approving recommendations for upgrading students from MPhil to PhD
- appointing examiners . . .

Responsibilities of supervisors

- to explore fully the student's background at the outset, and identify areas where further training is needed
- to give guidance on the nature of research and the standard expected, the planning of the research programme, attendance at appropriate courses, literature and sources . . .
- check on the student's progress at regular intervals
- allocate a reasonable period of time for supervisory sessions
- deal with urgent problems as soon as possible . . .

Responsibilities of research students

- to tackle the research with a positive commitment, taking full advantage of the resources and facilities offered by the academic environment and in particular contact with the supervisor, other staff and research students
- to discuss with the supervisor the type of guidance and comment believed to be most helpful, the training which might be required, and agree a schedule of meetings
- to attend supervision sessions, meetings, seminars, lectures and laboratory sessions as required by the supervisor or head of department . . .

(*Source*: Lancaster University 2005a)

---

research project. Box 5.5 gives some examples of the things a contract for a research student might include.

You might like to try to draft a contract for your own research work, on your own, with your research colleagues, or directly with your manager or supervisor. Try Exercise 5.3.

Research contracts can, of course, have disadvantages as well as advantages. These are summarized in Box 5.6: you may be able to think of others. If your supervisor or manager, or your research colleagues, are unwilling to agree a

---

Box 5.6 Advantages and disadvantages of research contracts

Advantages

1   They can help to specify your respective roles and responsibilities.
2   They can indicate the expectations held by both sides of the relationship, in terms, for example, of meetings or outputs.
3   They can help you to establish an initial working relationship, or to change an existing relationship.

Disadvantages

1   They may become rigid if not reviewed or revisited at intervals.
2   They may commit you to certain things you would rather avoid or keep fluid.

---

research contract with you, you should at least be able to talk with them about your aims, needs and constraints, and how you will work together.

The key message here is to ask yourself what you want from your relationship with your supervisor and/or manager, and do what you can to get it. Open discussions about these issues during your initial meetings. Renegotiate or revisit these discussions, and your contract, as necessary, throughout the life of your research project. Keep a record of these discussions, and of your contract, in the file you have opened on the regulations and expectations governing your project.

Health warning: In seeking to negotiate a contract with your supervisor, manager or mentor, be aware of the power relationships and institutional constraints involved.

Key institutions

The institutions we have identified as being likely to be of key importance to you in your research are your university or college, if you are carrying out your research project for academic credit, and your employer or sponsor. It may be the case, of course, that only one, or perhaps neither, of these institutions is of significance for you.

If you are researching, at least in part, for academic credit, you will, as we have stressed already, need to know as much as possible about the rules, facilities and practices of the university or college involved. You will need this information at an early stage, preferably even before you register and start your

Box 5.7 What you need to know from your institution

From your university or college

1   In terms of facilities, you should know:

- what resources are available (e.g. libraries, computers, software, language laboratories, rooms, training), and when they are available;
- what research services are offered (e.g. questionnaire design, data input, tape transcription, statistical advice, writing workshops, language teaching);
- what library services are offered (e.g. databases, internet, inter-library loans, photocopying), and on what basis;
- how these facilities are organized at university or departmental level.

2   You will also need to be aware of both your university's and department's written regulations and their unwritten, informal practices. These might include, for example:

- expectations of supervisors and/or tutors;
- rules about the roles of external supervisors and examiners;
- regulations about the time allowed to complete research, and regarding possible suspension or extension of registration;
- rules about the use of others' materials (e.g. plagiarism);
- training requirements;
- internal and ethical approval procedures;
- pre-publication rules associated with the submission of your thesis.

From your employer or sponsor

1   If you are being given some time out or work release, find out if you are getting cover or will be expected to do five days' work in four.
2   Will your manager accept that every Thursday you are not at work, or will you have to forgo your study day when a contract has to be completed or a colleague is off sick?
3   Will your employer or sponsor help to buy your books or give you an allowance?
4   Will you get access to computing facilities at work for research purposes?
5   In what format will your employer or sponsor require you to report back (e.g. verbal and/or written presentation)?
6   Will you be required to pay back fees and funding if you fail, the research is deemed unsatisfactory, or you leave within a certain period?

research project, if you are to manage your research effectively. Similar advice applies in the case of your employer and/or sponsor (who may also have a supervisory role). You should inform yourself as fully as possible about any expectations or conditions which they may set. Box 5.7 contains details of the kinds of issues you will need information on.

You should adjust your schedule to take account of all of the points covered in Box 5.7, and try to build them into your research contract. Don't forget to add all of this information to the file you have opened on the regulations and expectations governing your project.

Sharing responsibility

In the previous section we encouraged you to take responsibility for your research project by recognizing the roles of key figures and organizations, and establishing your independence from them. It is also important, however, to develop interdependence with fellow researchers and colleagues. These relationships can greatly strengthen your support network and the value of your research. They may be formal, required or implicit to your project, as in the case of group research or where you are under the direction of somebody else. Or they may be informal, and developed in part by you, as in the case of personal links with other researchers or colleagues.

Group research

The advantages and disadvantages of group, as opposed to individual, research have already been discussed in Chapter 2.

> You may like to have a look at the section on **Individual and group research** in Chapter 2.

In practice, of course, you may have little choice about engaging in group research: it may be a requirement of your work or your degree. You may, in such cases, be given guidance by your supervisor or manager on how to manage the group's dynamics. Nevertheless, there is no doubt that you will need, both individually and as a group, to work out early on your respective roles and tasks.

Researchers on group dynamics have identified a series of group roles which need to be filled if a group is to work effectively. One such formulation is given in Box 5.8.

Box 5.8 Team roles

[H]aving observed some hundreds of teams at work, I'd like to offer my own list of the team roles – i.e. team-building and maintenance roles, rather than task or individual roles – which are prerequisites for well-functioning teams:

- *Organizer*: Keeps meetings focused and in order, does his or her best to get through the agenda.
- *Encourager*: Brings good-humoured appreciation to proceedings, able to defuse tensions and revive flagging morale.
- *Facilitator*: Ensures that the quieter members of the group are heard and everyone's contribution acknowledged.
- *Recorder*: Keeps a note of decisions (especially decisions as to who will do what before the next meeting), ensures that everyone is aware of them.
- *Time-keeper and progress-chaser*: Keeps an eye on the calendar and ensures that everyone is aware of the 'state of play'.
- *Coordinator*: Sees the 'big picture' (the strategic overview), with an eye for gaps and overlaps, and presents this to the team.
- *Lookout*: Visualizes future scenarios, is alert to issues that may be looming over the horizon, keeps everyone informed.

(Levin 2005: 72–3)

To help you think about the working of your group, you may like to try Exercise 5.4.

Informal relationships

Even if you are not doing research as part of a group, or are not required to do so, you may like to set up a variety of informal relationships with others to help you in developing and progressing your work. Indeed, your employer or university may encourage you to do so, and may have a system of buddies, mentors or peer tutors in place already. Or it may be the case that some of your colleagues, or other researchers, are interested in the work you are doing and get in touch with you.

How can you establish and make the best use of such informal research relationships? Box 5.9 contains some pertinent suggestions.

The most general advice we would give about developing and using research relationships, of whatever kind, is much the same as that given for managing relations with key individuals or institutions. That is, view the relationship as a bargain which requires the active participation of the parties concerned, a shared understanding of what is going on, and a good deal of give and take.

Box 5.9 Managing informal relationships

- Find out what seminars, meetings and conferences you can attend, at your own institution and elsewhere. Attend a range of these, making contributions where possible. These will help you network, keep up to date, share anxieties and successes.
- Your university or employer may run a mentoring or buddy system, which will pair you, or put you in touch, with a student or colleague who has more experience and can show you the ropes.
- Get in touch with relevant research or professional organizations in the area in which you are working. These will have their own sets of meetings, will likely be interested in the research you are undertaking, and could provide useful contacts as well as a sounding board for your ideas.
- Check out relevant online discussion groups, particularly those run or housed by research or professional organizations.
- Talk about your research with interested relatives, neighbours, colleagues and others in your 'communities'. You may be surprised at how useful some of them can be, particularly as research is partly about communicating your ideas and findings.

Using computers

Information technologies are now an essential tool for the management of information. There are three aspects of particular importance:

- You should be able to type reasonably competently. You may be going to get your research report or dissertation typed out by somebody else, but you may have to type letters, drafts, notes and corrections yourself. It is probably also a good discipline to type up your own research: you are, after all, the person who knows most about it, and you can make changes and amendments as you go along.
- You should know of, and be able to access and use, the internet and the various computer databases of relevance to your field of research. You will almost certainly need to make use of email.
- You should be aware in general terms of the kinds of packages and programs available for analysing and presenting research data in your subject area. This awareness should extend to knowing how they work, what their requirements are, and what their advantages and disadvantages may be.

You may already be well versed in all of these areas: if so, well done, and please share your knowledge with somebody else! If not, however, you could see your research as giving you an opportunity to develop new skills in these areas, skills which are likely to have a wide future application. Alternatively, you may want to do the minimum in this respect, and avoid areas which heighten your insecurities. Whatever your perspective, however, you should find it useful to do a skills and resources check (see Exercise 5.5). The purpose of this is to get you to think about where you want to get to with your research, and how you might use computers as tools to help you get there.

Commonly available facilities

The kinds of technological facilities you are likely to have available, or be able to get access to, can be divided into three groups:

- *Word processing*. Beyond basic typing, you may find a wide range of facilities available on your computer, many of which are likely to be of some use to you in carrying out, and particularly in writing up, your research (see Box 5.10).

Box 5.10 Useful facilities available on word-processing software

- *Layout*. You should be able to use a variety of page layouts, typefaces and type sizes to emphasize or get over complex information in an engaging fashion.
- *Spellcheck*. Most word-processing packages will check your spelling for you and suggest possible corrections. Note, however, that many are based on American spellings.
- *Word count*. They will also count the number of words you have written, useful if you are working to a limit.
- *Thesaurus*. This will suggest alternative or synonymous terms, to stop you using the same words all of the time.
- *Grammar check*. This will check that your sentences obey the basic rules of grammar.
- *Searching*. Word-processing software can search through your text to find particular words or passages. It can do this with other texts as well once they have been input.
- *Tabulation*. Word-processing software often has special facilities for laying out tables and charts. Most have the ability to box or shade areas of text.
- *Graphs and maps*. Your software may have programs to produce graphs or maps from your input data. If not, there are special packages available.
- *Contents*. Your software should be able to draft and lay out a contents page for you.
- *Indexing*. If you enter certain labels as, or after, you type, your software will index your work for you.

- *Databases and communications.* An increasing variety of information databases and communications networks are available in libraries, educational and other institutions, and over the web.

> See the section in Chapter 4 on **Using the internet** for examples of databases and search engines.

- *Analytical packages and programs.* Many package programs are available which can be invaluable to the social science researcher in storing, recording and analysing their data.

> See the sections in Chapter 7 on **Interviews** and **Questionnaires** for discussion of the use of the internet and email in the collection of data.

> See the section in Chapter 8 on **Managing your data** for examples of packages and programmes.

> **Health warning**: You don't want your information technology skills to control the practice or outcomes of your research in unforeseen ways because you can't get the technology to work for you. Think ahead!

Managing not to get demoralized when things do not go as planned

Even in the most carefully managed research project, things do not always go quite as planned. Most changes are likely to be fairly trivial in nature, and are not recognized as such. Yet, when they are recognized, the things that went wrong can seem to mount up and assume an unwarranted importance. They can be very disheartening and demotivating. It would be difficult to find an honest researcher who had not made significant mistakes. You are going to make mistakes. Box 5.11 offers, for your amusement and enlightenment, a list of twenty things that can go wrong.

How can you overcome such difficulties and get beyond them? Perhaps the golden rule is to remember that research is a process of learning. Just as we learn by our mistakes, at least in part, so changes in plans are an essential part of research. It might even be said that research without such mistakes or changes

---

Box 5.11 Twenty things that can go wrong

---

1   You run out of time.
2   Access is refused by a key institution or individual.
3   A key contact in an organization you are studying leaves.
4   You discover that someone has already done your research.
5   You lose your job.
6   Your response rate is very low.
7   Your manager or supervisor interferes with your plans.
8   You fall ill.
9   You change your job, making access to the site of your research difficult.
10   You split up with your partner.
11   You lose the citation for a key reference.
12   You find that you have too much data to analyse, or too little.
13   Your tape recorder doesn't work, or runs out of batteries.
14   You run out of money.
15   You cannot find key references in your library.
16   You are absolutely fed up with your project.
17   The dog eats your draft, and then dies.
18   You have written too much, or too little.
19   Your computer crashes.
20   The margins on your text are not the right size for binding.

---

is not real research, and is unlikely to tell us much that we do not already know. Research is really about getting misdirected, recognizing this as such, understanding why it happened, then revising our strategy and moving on.

In Box 5.12 you will find some possible, more positive responses to the kinds of dilemmas you may face in managing your research project. Box 5.13 then gives some real-life examples of how social science researchers coped with problems or changes in their plans.

Box 5.12 Reponses to adversity

• Remind yourself that the purpose of carrying out a research project, particularly as a novice researcher, may be as much about developing your understanding of the research process and/or the use of particular research methods, as about exploring substantive issues.
• Remember that it may be just as valid, and possibly a lot more helpful to other researchers, to write up your research in terms of, for example, the problems of gaining access to a particular group, or of getting an adequate response from that group once access has been gained.

- Make it part of your business in writing up to reflect upon your research strategy, explore what went wrong and why, and include recommendations for doing it better 'next time'.
- View research as being about the skills you have learnt and developed on the way. As we have said already, few research projects are truly ground-breaking, or shocking in their conclusions. Part of doing research is about appreciating what is involved, and where it may be leading you.
- If you have time and resources you may, of course, choose to redirect your research strategy when you are stymied in one direction. This is very common, not an admission of failure.
- Welcome to the club! All is not lost.

Box 5.13 Researchers coping with problems and changes

Tofi, a MA student trying to complete a case study of industrial training during the early summer, found that access was agreed just as the factory's holiday fortnight began. He had to re-design his strategy to lay less emphasis on original data, while focusing more on the methodological issues. Having done so, he then received an invitation to talk to a shop stewards' meeting, just three days before his thesis was due for submission. He decided to go to the meeting to learn more about his subject, but not to write up his thesis on the assumption that he could use data from that meeting.

Whilst I had expected my interviews with the women to be upsetting (for them and for me), I had been much more complacent about my interviews with health professionals, and this was not always justified. During an interview with a practice nurse about domestic violence, I was taken by surprise when she became distressed. Rather than recounting her professional dealings with domestic violence as I had expected, my interview prompted her to recall her personal experiences of attempting to deal with domestic violence within her own family network. I learned a powerful lesson from this interview: you cannot always predict who will get distressed and who will not. Researchers need to be prepared for a whole range of emotional responses from a whole range of research participants.

(Hallowell et al. 2005: 17)

Jim finished writing his report on a laptop computer that he was able to borrow to take on holiday with him. He finished it in time to experiment with the layout and make each page look professional. He returned with two days left to print and bind the report, only to find that his printer was not set up to print from the package he had used. He did not want to panic, so decided to spend some money. He contacted an office business which had experience of solving such problems. And they did!

Part of the eventual emphasis on teachers was also due to the corresponding lack of data in other areas. I soon found, for example, that it would not be possible to write very much on curriculum development within public schools because, although I had interviewed several textbook writers and others heavily involved, each case was idiosyncratic and thus would have been impossible to write about without identifying individuals involved and thus the research schools. My major problem, however, was that I had great difficulty in gaining useful information from pupils.

(Walford 2001: 76)

Summary

Having read this chapter, you should:

- be better equipped to manage your time to carry out the activities necessary for your research project;
- understand how you might go about ordering your relationships with the key figures and institutions for your research;
- be more aware of how you might use computers more effectively for your research;
- be more confident that you can make changes to, or mistakes in, your research plans, without being a bad researcher.

Exercises

5.1   Make a list of all the key things you have to do (or milestones you have to reach) in order to successfully complete your research project. Note where these have to be done in a particular order, or depend upon each other. Assign realistic deadlines for each milestone you need to reach. Set all of this information out as a grid, table or some other kind of schedule.

5.2   Complete two or three practice interviews, observations or questionnaires, or whatever technique or combination of techniques you were planning to use. Analyse the results. Note how long the data collection and its analysis took, and how well your techniques worked. Do you need to revise your plans or techniques?

5.3 Draft a contract for your research project, specifying the duties and responsibilities of all of those involved. Relate the items you have identified to your schedule. Discuss the contract and its scheduling with your supervisor and/or manager.

5.4 List all of the members of your research group. Through discussion, identify each member's skills, motivations and preferences. Negotiate how you are going to collectively undertake the project. Note aspects or areas in which you seem to be relatively weak, and think about how you will cope with this.

5.5 Note down all of the computing facilities and software you have access to. How useful might these be to you in your research, and which do you plan to make use of? If you don't know how, or are insufficiently skilled, to use some of these facilities, how might you develop your abilities?

Further reading

In this section, we list a selection of books that are of particular relevance to the topics discussed in this chapter.

Delamont, S., Atkinson, P. and Parry, O. (2004) *Supervising the PhD: A guide to success*, 2nd edition. Maidenhead: Open University Press.
A practical guide for novice and experienced supervisors.
Delamont, S., Atkinson, P. and Parry, O. (2000) *The Doctoral Experience: Success and failure in graduate school*. London: Falmer Press.
An empirical study of the experiences of research students and their supervisors in a range of disciplines. Discusses how students cope with uncertainty and frustration, how research groups can act as socializing environments, and how supervisors handle the tensions between student autonomy and their academic responsibilities.
Levin, P. (2005) *Successful Teamwork! For undergraduates and taught postgraduates working on group projects*. Maidenhead: Open University Press.
Highly practical guide to making the best out of team projects.
Orna, E. with Stevens, G. (1995) *Managing Information for Research*. Buckingham: Open University Press.
Written for first time researchers, this text looks at issues such as managing time and information, producing the written text and dealing with the emotions associated with research.
Phelps, R., Fisher, K. and Ellis, A. (2007) *Organizing and Managing your Research: A practical guide for postgraduates*. London: Sage.
Focuses on the strategies, skills, and systems that increase the efficiency and effectiveness of research practice.

Phillips, E. and Pugh, D. (2005) *How to get a PhD: A handbook for students and their supervisors*, 4th edition. Maidenhead: Open University Press.
Best-selling guide to the whole process of doing a PhD, from motivation and application through to supervision and examination.
Stablein, R. and Frost, P. (eds) (2004) *Renewing Research Practice*. Stanford, CA: Stanford University Press.
In this collection, prominent North American scholars in the fields of management and organizational studies provide accounts of overcoming difficulties in their research projects and careers.

6

Preparing to collect data

Introduction

By now you will have done your initial preparation and be ready to start collecting data. However, although we recognize that many students are eager to get started on this, there remain a number of issues that need to be thought through before you can start collecting data. These include issues of access: how are you going to gain entry to the site of your research, to your interviewees, to the documents you need or to the mailing list for your online questionnaire? They also include ethical issues associated with respecting and, if necessary, protecting research participants. Further concerns, prior to but closely related to data collection, are concerned with the adequacy and robustness of any research conducted. For example, how can you ensure that your research is systematic and thoughtfully planned in such a way that it strengthens your findings? Here, issues of sampling and selection of research participants and research sites become important.

Much social research is also highly reflexive about the research process itself. One way of monitoring this is through keeping a research diary (see Chapter 2). This helps you to keep a record of the decisions you make about data collection, and serves as a tool for analysis and reflection. Other forms of paper and computer-based record keeping are important for a systematic and well planned research project, and protection of your research respondents includes ensuring that the information stored on your computer is safe. Finally, you might want to prepare for some of the emotional aspects of data collection. As we have indicated in this book, research can be a very consuming passion, but you may encounter some difficulties during your project.

The purpose of this chapter is, therefore, to acquaint you with, and guide you through, the steps you need to take immediately prior to data collection. The chapter is organized around the following themes and issues:

- **Access and ethical issues.** Gaining the cooperation and consent of your research subjects or institutions, and dealing with the illegal, unethical and unprofessional.
- **Sampling and selection.** Choosing the subjects or objects of your research.
- **Recording your progress.** Keeping a close check on your data collection.
- **The ups and downs of data collection.** Enjoyment, loneliness and obsession.

Access and ethical issues

Two key issues are likely to confront you as a researcher as soon as you begin to consider collecting data for your project: access and ethics. These issues are also likely to be, and perhaps should be, a continuing concern throughout the process of data collection, and possibly also afterwards. They have to do with what data you are able to collect, how you get it and how you use it.

Access

For researchers conducting research in schools one difficulty is their reliance on adult gatekeepers allowing access to the children. A good research relationship with the teacher may ensure access. Simultaneously, taking a social actor perspective I also wanted to afford children autonomy in the research process; more autonomy than the children themselves or the teachers are accustomed to them having in the school setting. Therefore, the researcher must perform or negotiate two identities which balance out the researcher's own theoretical perspective, the interests of the teachers and of the children.

(Davies 2008: para. 4.15)

Initially access issues focused upon the generic research need to locate and identify suitable participants who would be willing to partake in social research. A second more personal though not entirely unique access issue emerged whilst undertaking the fieldwork, in that as a wheelchair user I was constantly plagued by an often hostile, inaccessible physical environment.

(Andrews 2005: 204–5)

You should already have given some consideration to the issues raised by access in choosing and focusing your research topic.

See the section on **Choosing a topic** in Chapter 2.

Your research topic may necessitate your gaining, and maintaining, access to any or all of the following:

- Documents, held in libraries or by institutions.
- People, in their homes, places of work, in the wider community, or over the internet.
- Institutions, such as private companies, schools or government departments.

The kinds of questions you should consider before seeking such access are the subject of Exercise 6.1.

As part of the process of planning and managing your project, you may already have approached the key individuals or gatekeepers involved in enabling you to access the documents, people and institutions you need for your research. The progress of your project, in the way you envisage it, and your ability to collect the kind of data which you want, may be critically dependent on their cooperation. If they say yes, you are in and under way (but read on, for it is not usually as simple as that!); but if they say no, you may have to look elsewhere or revise your plans.

How, then, can you increase your chances of getting access? Box 6.1 contains some suggestions.

Box 6.1 How to increase your chances of gaining access

- Begin by asking for advice on how it would be most appropriate to negotiate access.
- Be modest in your requests: limit their scope to what you can handle, and don't start by asking for everything.
- Make effective use of your existing contacts, and those of your supervisor, manager and colleagues.
- Base your research (and perhaps register yourself as a student) within the institutions to which you need access: for example, if they have specialist library facilities, staff with particular expertise, or if they are institutions you wish to study.

- Offer something back to your research subjects: perhaps a report or a workshop. Ask their advice on what might be useful to them. If your research is of potential interest and use to them, they will be more likely to allow you access.
- Ask at the right time. Some institutions need to plan ahead, while others like to act immediately. Busy periods and holidays are not good times.
- Be as clear as possible about what you are asking for: which documents and people, and how long it will all take.
- Explain the reasons for doing your research, why it will be of value, and what the outcomes might be (don't claim too much!).

If you adopt a reasoned, planned and modest strategy, you are more likely to get the access you need. If, however, despite all of your skills of negotiation, you are rebuffed, you may need to consider other strategies. Some of these are outlined in Box 6.2.

Box 6.2 Strategies to consider if access is refused

- Approach other individuals. For example, if one person refuses to be interviewed or to answer your questionnaire, you might approach another person in a similar position or with similar characteristics.
- Approach other institutions. If the institution you had chosen for a case study, or as part of your sample, or because of its library facilities, is uncooperative, you may be able to get access to another institution of a similar kind.
- Approach another individual within the same institution. This is a more risky strategy, because of their possible communication, but there is usually more than one person who can grant you access, even if this is more limited.
- Try again later, when it may be less busy, attitudes may have changed, people may have moved on, and you may have more to show to demonstrate the value of your research. This is also a risky strategy, since it involves your going further down a chosen path which may still turn out to be blocked.
- Change your research strategy. This is something you should probably be prepared to do, and plan for, throughout the research process. It may involve using other, perhaps less sensitive, methods for collecting data, or focusing on a slightly different set of issues, or studying alternative groups or organizations.
- Focus your analysis and writing up on the process of undertaking research, why you were unable to gain the access you wanted, and the possible implications of this for your topic.

Relatively few researchers end up studying precisely what they set out to study originally. In many cases, of course, this is because their ideas and interpretations change during the research, but the unpredictability of access negotiations is also a major influence. For example, one of our PhD students had hoped to research accountancy firms. She spent a considerable time contacting relevant managers and finally thought she had found an opening. However, it transpired that further up the organizational hierarchy concerns were raised that her research would be inappropriate at a time of financial volatility. As these attempts to gain access had taken up a fair amount of time, it became urgent that she revised her research strategy if she was to complete her research in an appropriate time frame. Beginning with a friend, she therefore used a snowball sample to contact directly research respondents working in the financial services industries. The end result was a quite different research design from the one she had started with, and a consequent change of focus. Nonetheless, the research was no less innovative and original for these modifications.

You may be fortunate in gaining initial access and, if so, you will have to consider how you are going to extend that access, say to other people in a particular institution or to other documents that you discover are highly relevant to your research. This means that access is not simply a one-off exercise which you conduct immediately before beginning your data collection. Rather, it is continuous and can potentially be a very demanding process, as Munro et al. describe:

As the fieldwork progressed, further dynamics of power emerged, particularly in relation to the negotiation and renegotiation of access. Gatekeepers at various levels within the organizations influenced whom we contacted, the distribution of our survey and the nature of interview settings. This affected how we pursued the research process and the nature of the data we gathered, yet also provided insights into the structures in large organizations, degrees of departmental autonomy and lines of communication which became a part of our findings . . . gatekeepers at different levels of the organization had access to different sources of power and influence.

(Munro et al. 2004: 290)

Gatekeepers can be very influential in terms of whom you get to talk to and interview. This can be the case even when you are researching an organization of which you are an employee, or a group, such as step-parents or students, of which you are a member. The dilemma that researchers face is that every time you meet another individual, or meet the same people again, you will need to engage, whether explicitly or implicitly, in a renegotiation of access. For example, if your study has a longitudinal element and you want to follow the changes in people's lives over a period of time, then you need to be confident that your respondents will remain willing, say over a twelve-month period, to be interviewed, or keep diaries, or complete questionnaires. Or, alternatively, if you are researching an organization then you may well need to explain the purposes of your research to a large number of people at different points during the data collection phase.

See also the section on **Researching in your workplace** in Chapter 2 for a discussion of the pros and cons of 'insider' research.

As you will appreciate, simply because one person has said yes does not mean that their colleagues cannot say no. Indeed, in some circumstances, of which you may initially be blissfully unaware, it may increase the chances of their doing so. You may be unable to call upon your initial contact for help in these conditions: doing so may even exacerbate the problem. Similarly, while an individual may have happily undergone one interview, filled in one questionnaire, or responded helpfully and promptly to your requests for documentation, this does not mean that they will react as favourably to subsequent or repeated requests. Ultimately, therefore, research comes down to focusing on what is practically accessible. Research is the art of the feasible.

Ethics

With regards to my experience, it felt at times like I was suggesting doing an expose of the NHS, not a small scale study on pregnant women and their partners' involvement in screening. There was no sense of 'trust' between them as health professionals and myself as an academic researcher. Health professionals seem happy to place trust in the 'abstract systems' of these ethics and governance procedures, however, they don't seem able to place trust in academic researchers themselves. Caution towards research is understandable in the aftermath of the scandal at Liverpool's Alder Hey children's hospital where children's organs were harvested without parents' consent. However, the level of paranoia among NHS staff towards research makes it seem quite untenable. In the context of my study, I felt that every time I got close to gaining approval a new hurdle was placed in my way, a new piece of paperwork needed to be completed in order for approval to be granted. Again, it was not the amount of bureaucracy needed to gain approval that was the problem, but the politics behind the process which as an NHS outsider placed me at a disadvantage.

(Reed 2007: para. 2.6)

While electronic communication is in transit . . . the researcher has no control over it. The networks it will pass through are owned by other people who may employ unscrupulous system administrators to maintain them. These administrators have the power to access anything they want. When service provider Prodigy faced protests for raising its charges, it intercepted, read and destroyed messages from dissenting clients and dismissed some members. The latter had no legal recourse and no way to picket the provider. If online discussion relates to criminal activity, law organizations may 'tap' the line and researchers might lay themselves open to being subpoenaed to disclose participants' identities . . . Apart from 'listening in', other users can copy and distribute messages to unintended recipients without the knowledge of the writers. The content of messages can also be changed with great ease . . . although researchers can promise confidentiality in the way that they use the data, they cannot promise that electronic communication will not be accessed and used by others.

(Mann and Stewart 2000: 42–3)

Ensuring that your research is ethically appropriate is a significant aspect of the conduct of sound research, and one which institutions are paying increasing attention to. Indeed, it may be that you cannot begin your research at all until you have had your research proposal approved, perhaps by your university or department's research ethics committee or by the institution you wish to research in. These bodies will want to be assured that you understand the ethical implications of your research and have taken them into account in your planning.

The conduct of ethically informed research should be a goal of all social researchers. Most commonly, ethical issues are thought to arise predominantly with research designs that use qualitative methods of data collection. This is because of the closer relationships between the researcher and researched. Nevertheless, all social research (whether using surveys, documents, interviews or computer-mediated communication) gives rise to a range of ethical issues around privacy, informed consent, anonymity, secrecy, being truthful, and the desirability of the research. It is important, therefore, that you are aware of these issues and how you might respond to them. You owe a duty to yourself as a researcher, as well as to other researchers and to the subjects of and audiences for your research, to exercise responsibility in the processes of data collection, analysis and dissemination.

Box 6.3 outlines a range of ethical problems encountered in social research, which you might like to consider how you would respond to. You might think that some of these problems are rather extreme and of a sort which is unlikely to be encountered in most research projects, but these are all real dilemmas which were faced and dealt with by real researchers. These researchers include the authors of this book and some of the students we have supervised, as well as some examples of dilemmas reported in the research literature.

Ethical issues can be very wide-ranging, as Box 6.4 shows by comparing the formulations adopted by other writers. Box 6.5 summarizes some of the more common ethical issues you may have to face in your research project under the headings of confidentiality, anonymity, legality, professionalism and participation.

Box 6.3 Dealing with ethical problems

Consider how you would deal with the following situations:

1   You are researching the parenting behaviours of the parents of hospitalized children. You believe that when they are left alone some parents harm their children. You have a video camera. Do you set it up and use it?

2   You have been granted access to an archive of rare documents of crucial importance to your research. It would save you a lot of time if you could take some of the documents home, and security is very lax. Do you 'borrow' some of the documents?

3   You are part of a team researching issues of sexuality and you are using email to conduct interviews. You realize that the male members of your team have greater access to men and that the female members have greater access to women. To help with validity your team decides that female researchers should interview male respondents and vice versa. You log on, but your new respondents decline to discuss issues with a member of the opposite sex. You are worried that this will endanger the research project. Do you try again, but this time change your name and pretend that you are the same sex as the respondents?

4   Your research has highlighted unethical practices in your organization concerning the abuse of expenses claims. Do you publish it?

5   You find a newsgroup on the internet that is discussing issues central to your research. Do you 'lurk' (listen in without participating) and make use of the data?

6   You have been offered £1,000,000 to conduct research into genetically modified (GM) foods. The funder is a multinational chemical company with interests in GM crops. Do you accept the funding?

7   You have been offered £100 to conduct research into GM foods. The funder is a local direct action group opposed to the development of GM crops. Do you accept the funding?

8   You find a document on the internet that has done much of the background work for your topic. The deadline for the completion of your project has passed. Do you include the relevant detail in your dissertation but omit the reference?

9   Your research involves interviewing children under 5 years old. How do you ensure that they are able to give 'informed consent'?

10 You want to include a photograph (of your participants) in your report that has been published in a local newspaper. What issues do you need to consider?

Box 6.4 Alternative formulations of ethical principles and frameworks

---

1   Bryman 2004: 509
    harm to participants – lack of informed consent – invasion of privacy –
    deception
2   Burns 2000: 18–22
    voluntary and involuntary participation – informed consent – deception –
    role playing – debriefing – privacy and confidentiality – the right to
    discontinue – experimenter obligations – publication of findings –
    stress – intervention studies
3   Kent 2000: 63–5
    autonomy – beneficence – non-maleficence – justice – veracity – privacy –
    confidentiality – fidelity
4   Cohen et al. 2007: 51
    informed consent – gaining access to and acceptance in the research
    setting – the nature of ethics in social research generally – sources of
    tension in the ethical debate, including non-maleficence, beneficence and
    human dignity, absolutist and relativist ethics – problems and dilemmas
    confronting the researcher, including matters of privacy, anonymity, con-
    fidentiality, betrayal and deception – ethical problems endemic in particu-
    lar research methods – ethics and evaluative research – regulatory ethical
    frameworks, guidelines and codes of practice for research – personal
    codes of practice – sponsored research – responsibilities to the research
    community

Box 6.5 Common ethical issues

Confidentiality. It can be extremely tempting, in cases where confidentiality
has been agreed or demanded, to use material collected in this way. You may
think it is unimportant, or will never be detected, but its use could threaten
your sources and undermine your whole research project.

Anonymity. This is often linked to the issue of confidentiality. Where you
have assured individuals or organizations that they will not be identifiable in
your report or thesis, careful consideration may need to be given to how you
disguise them. For example, to refer to a university in a 'northern town of
150,000' rather gives the identity away. If you are quoting from interviews
with people in a named organization, disguising people's identities as 'woman,
30s, manager' may also be inadequate.

Legality. If you are a police officer, it is your duty to report any illegal activities
of which you become aware in the course of your research. The same applies,
though to a lesser extent, to certain other categories of employees, such as

social workers or fire officers. More generally, it could also be seen as an obligation shared by all citizens. In some circumstances, where the infringement is minor or occurred long ago, you may be happy to overlook it, but this may not always be the case.

Professionalism. If you are a member of a professional group, as many researchers are, this imposes or assumes certain standards of conduct in your professional life. These may overlap into your research work, particularly if you are conducting research among fellow professionals. You may need to think, therefore, about what you do if you discover what you believe to be unprofessional conduct during the course of your research.

Participation. Are the people you are doing the research *about* the same people you are doing the research *for* and *with*? The issue of involvement of different stakeholders will be of particular importance for some kinds of research, such as research in mental health or disability.

Informed consent, confidentiality and protection of individuals are central to guidelines on research ethics, and you need to consider how you can be clear about the nature of the agreement you have entered into with your research subjects or contacts. For example, do people who are taking part in your research understand what you are doing and why, and do they agree, voluntarily, to take part? Are you going to ensure that they are given pseudonyms as part of anonymizing who they are? Are there other details that need to be changed to ensure your participants are not identifiable? Are you going to show them everything you have written in order that they can delete anything with which they are uncomfortable? You may be concerned about the complications of gaining consent for research with vulnerable groups, such as children, mental health service users or frail older people. How can you be sure they are competent to understand the information provided? Can you provide a straightforward description of your research aims and objectives? How can you ensure that your research might benefit those you are researching? Even when using statistical data, there may be other details in your research that can contribute to identifying particular (perhaps unusual) individuals.

Thinking through these issues and drawing up research contracts can help you here. Ethical research involves getting the informed consent of those you are going to interview, question, observe or take materials from. It involves reaching agreements about the uses of this data, and how its analysis will be reported and disseminated. And it is about keeping to such agreements when they have been reached.

The use of research contracts is discussed in the section on **Dealing with key figures and institutions** in Chapter 5.

All of the problems and examples which we have quoted concern conflicts of interest. These may be between the demands of confidentiality or anonymity, and those of legality or professionalism. Or, more generally, they may be between your desire, as a researcher, to collect as much good data as you can, and the wishes or demands of your subjects to restrict your collection or use of data. The research process is in part about negotiating a viable route between these interests. The 'pursuit of truth' and the 'public's right to know' are not held as absolute values by everyone.

This point is evident in the ethical concerns that are arising from the increased use of the internet and associated communication technologies. For example, there can be no certainty about the confidentiality of materials sent by email, as they can be easily forwarded and copied. It is not unusual to hear about cases of hackers who gain access to the customer databases of public or private organizations. What is kept on computers is also of increasing legal and government concern as, for example, police and immigration agencies monitor particular internet sites and their usage.

Specific kinds of ethical issues also arise when computer-mediated communication is used as a data collection instrument. The lack of non-verbal and social cues makes it more difficult for the researcher to monitor how interviewees are responding to questions about sensitive issues. When computer-mediated communication is used for group activities and research, ethical questions are raised about how, when and if those who remain silent (often referred to as lurkers) should be 'made' to take part, and what effects lurking has on those who are more open and actively involved.

Many professional associations and employers working in the social sciences have drawn up their own ethical guidelines or codes of conduct for researchers. You should try to get hold of a copy of those that are relevant to your subject area. Box 6.6 gives details of where you can find many of these.

Box 6.6 Further ethical guidance and resources from professional associations

---

Economic and Social Research Council (ESRC): Research Ethics Framework

http://www.esrcsocietytoday.ac.uk/ESRCInfoCentre/Images/
ESRC_Re_Ethics_Frame_tcm6-11291.pdf
This document is divided into two parts. The first part provides an overview, the second provides more detailed policy guidelines, gives some background context and explains how it works in practice. It also includes some illustrative case studies.

Social Research Association (SRA): Ethical Guidelines

http://www.the-sra.org.uk/ethical.htm
Set out in three levels. Level A provides a simple basic statement of the

principles of the SRA code. Level B provides more discursive material that pinpoints specific dilemmas and principles and expands on why each of the principles are important. Level C contains very useful annotated bibliographies for follow-up and further examples of debate in this area.

British Sociological Association (BSA): Statement of Ethical Practice

http://www.britsoc.co.uk/equality/Statement+Ethical+Practice.htm
Includes discussion of professional integrity; relations with and responsibilities towards research participants; covert research; anonymity, privacy and confidentiality; relations with and responsibilities and obligations towards sponsors; clarifying obligations, roles and rights, pre-empting outcomes and negotiations about research. An appendix provides the web addresses for further ethical guidelines of different professional associations.

British Educational Research Association (BERA): Revised Ethical Guidelines for Educational Research

http://www.bera.ac.uk/files/2008/09/ethica1.pdf
BERA has kept the term 'revised' in the title of this document to signal that ethical issues are not cast in stone. The guidance sets out the values underpinning the guidelines in terms of an ethic of respect for the person, knowledge, democratic values, the quality of educational research and academic freedom. The guidance includes responsibilities towards children, vulnerable young people and vulnerable adults.

National Health Service (NHS): National Research Ethics Committee

http://www.nres.npsa.nhs.uk/
This site provides guidance on how to apply to your local NHS Research Ethics Committee.

Social Policy Association (SPA): Guidelines on Research Ethics

http://www.social-policy.com/documents/SPA_code_ethics_jan09.pdf
The guidelines discuss user involvement and the setting up of an advisory panel should your research involve complex ethical issues.

Socio-Legal Studies Association: Statement of Principles of Ethical Research Practice

http://www.kent.ac.uk/nslsa/content/view/60/259/
This sets out a number of principles and obligations to, for example, the academic and the wider community, research respondents and colleagues. It draws attention to the legal obligations of members of the Association, in that

they may be in receipt of information they are required by law to divulge and to bear in mind the implications of Freedom of Information Acts, Data Protection Acts, Human Rights, copyright and libel laws.

British Psychological Society (BPS): Member Conduct Rules, Code of Conduct and Ethical Guidelines

http://www.bps.org.uk/the-society/code-of-conduct/
The site provides a number of guidelines, including working with animals and for psychologists working in the NHS. The ethical code is based on four principles: respect, competence, responsibility and integrity.

Applied Ethics Resources

http://www.ethicsweb.ca/resources/
A host of resources here, including business ethics, professional ethics, international ethics and ethical decision making.

Don't forget that, while you may not have to go through lengthy procedures to gain ethical approval in many areas of social research, you are still very likely, if you are enrolled as a student, to be required to submit a proposal to either a departmental or a university ethics committee. The function of this committee is to consider whether your proposed research conforms to ethical guidelines set out by the relevant professional body, institution or employer, and to check that it does not infringe applicable laws. Check with your research supervisor for what is required.

Ethical issues do not relate solely to protecting the rights and privacy of individuals and avoiding harm. They can also relate to the methodological principles underpinning the research design. For example, those with social justice concerns will include the very topic of the research as part of their ethical framework, by asking whether it raises socially responsible questions or has the potential to create a more just world. Box 6.7 gives two examples of such research, and indicates how there is no easy resolution of the dilemmas that are raised. It also shows that ethical issues arise at all points in the research process, including analysis and interpretation. As such, the researcher's values, position and notions of truth are integral to ethical concerns. Researchers need to recognize the complexity and the many facets of ethical issues.

Finally, ethical concerns are not solely about protection of research respondents. Importantly, they should also include a concern for the safety and well-being of the researcher. It is not unusual, certainly in some forms of longitudinal, ethnographic research, or even in interview-based studies, to find that one may be in locales or with individuals with whom the researcher feels unsafe. The same 'rules of safety' apply to researchers as to other citizens.

Box 6.7 Ethical dilemmas for social justice research

Ethics have methodological implications in research on/for/with human beings, especially where that research is explicitly intended to improve social justice. An example is the use of control groups. These are, methodologically, extremely useful if repetition is not possible. Thus, they are widely used in botanical experiments, in order to test the influence of a single factor on a population (of flowers, say, or beans). Agency and interpretation can be taken into account by the use of 'double blind' tests, where neither the experimenter nor the subject know which is the control group or treatment. For instance, much medical research depends on the double blind use of placebo treatments. The ethical problem for education (as for medicine, but not for botany) is that the method depends on putting some subjects into a 'control' group and deliberately giving treatment thought to be inferior so that better treatments can be tested . . . For anyone wanting to do educational research for social justice, resolutions to these ethical issues of deception depend on judgements about 'on/for/with'.

(Griffiths 1998: 39–40)

[O]f all these [methodological] difficulties, the ethical issues associated with researching in prison have been the most problematic and ever-present . . . [A]t the most basic level . . . none of the young offender institutions has been identified, so as to protect the young men who volunteered to take part in this study . . . All the young men were guaranteed anonymity and so this has also meant that some aspects of the situations that they describe have also had to be changed and are often described in general, rather than specifically. Similarly, while it would have been helpful to reveal how each of these YO institutions was described by, for example, HM Chief Inspector of Prisons and the Howard League for Penal Reform, which formed the basis for how the fieldwork was triangulated, this has again not been possible, for to do so would reveal the identities of the young offender institutions and thus potentially also the young men themselves.

(Wilson 2004: 318)

These are that you discuss any concerns about your own security with your supervisor, in case you need to rethink your research plan; you always ensure that a friend or relative knows where you are and with whom you are meeting if you are conducting interviews, observations and so forth; and you consider the venue of meetings, particularly if you have never met the individual before.

The discussion in this subsection suggests three general conclusions about research ethics:

- That a consideration of possible or actual ethical issues is an essential part of any research project.
- That such a consideration is likely to need to take place throughout the research project, from initial planning through data collection to writing up and dissemination.
- That in many cases there will be no easy answers to the ethical questions which you may have to face.

Sampling and selection

[R]ather than people being systematically recruited to my study, they were drawn in, through their being a part of the friendship circle to which I was attached. In using a 'networking' approach, many people were a part of the study. If the sample is contained to those who formed the main focus, roughly 50 people were a part. Loosely these belonged to six different friendship groups. From the larger sample, six people were engaged in an in-depth research relationship, based on their central role in drug selling activity.

(Ward 2008: para. 2.5)

While most people would associate the words 'sampling' and 'selection' with survey approaches, there will be elements of these involved whatever approach you are taking to your research project. If your research involves observation, you will not be able to observe everybody of interest all of the time. If you are carrying out a case study, you will need to select the case or cases which you are going to focus on. Even with desk- or library-based research, sampling is an element of the procedure as you will not be able to access, or even read, every book or document that has been written on your subject. Whatever your approach, you should, therefore, give some consideration to the related issues of sampling and selection.

This may seem unnecessary if your research topic and strategy has been largely determined for you, or if you have a particular case study or action research project in mind. In such circumstances, however, you may still need to justify your choice and relate it to other examples. If you have not yet determined the subjects or objects of your research project, however, you should certainly think about how you are going to choose them and whether they will want to take part.

There are a wide variety of sampling strategies available for use. The main options are summarized in Box 6.8, and illustrated diagrammatically in Box 6.9. They are divided into two main groups: *probability* and *non-probability sampling*.

The most widely understood probability sampling approach is probably random sampling, where every individual or object in the group or 'population'

Box 6.8 Sampling strategies

Probability sampling

- Simple random sampling – selection at random
- Systematic sampling – selecting every nth case
- Stratified sampling – sampling within groups of the population
- Cluster sampling – surveying whole clusters of the population sampled at random
- Stage sampling – sampling clusters sampled at random

Non-probability sampling

- Convenience sampling – sampling those most convenient
- Voluntary sampling – the sample is self-selected
- Quota sampling – convenience sampling within groups of the population
- Purposive sampling – hand-picking supposedly typical or interesting cases
- Dimensional sampling – multi-dimensional quota sampling
- Snowball sampling – building up a sample through informants

Other kinds of sampling

- Event sampling – using routine or special events as the basis for sampling
- Time sampling – recognizing that different parts of the day, week or year may be significant

---

of interest (e.g. MPs, dog owners, course members, pages, archival texts) has an equal chance of being chosen for study. For some readers, this may accord with their understanding of what sampling is. But both more complex approaches, such as systematic and stratified sampling, and more focused approaches, such as cluster and stage sampling, are possible within a probabilistic framework.

Which approach is used will depend in part on your knowledge of the population in question, and the resources at your disposal. Thus, a small-scale researcher wishing to survey public attitudes may not be in a position to sample from the whole country, but will instead restrict their sampling to a local cluster. Or, if you do not know enough about the characteristics of a population to conduct stratified sampling, you might choose to sample from a list of subjects by taking every twentieth person.

Non-probability sampling approaches are used when the researcher lacks a sampling frame for the population in question, or where a probabilistic approach is judged not to be necessary. For example, if you are carrying out a series of in-depth interviews with adults about their working experiences, you

Box 6.9 Sampling strategies illustrated

RANDOM

STRATIFIED

SYSTEMATIC

CLUSTER

CONVENIENCE

SNOWBALL

PURPOSIVE

may be content to restrict yourself to suitable friends or colleagues. Or you may be studying an issue which is relatively sensitive, such as sexual orientation in the armed forces, and have to build up a sample confidentially and through known and trusted contacts. Market researchers commonly use a quota sampling approach, with targets for the numbers they have to interview with different socio-demographic characteristics.

Box 6.10 summarizes some real examples of the sampling strategies that were adopted for actual research projects. Exercise 6.2 asks you to consider which sampling approach you plan to adopt, and to justify your choice.

Box 6.10 Examples of research sampling strategies

Teaching staff from twelve departments in three different faculties (Social Sciences, Arts and Science) were invited to participate in this study in the autumn of 2001. The departments were selected to reflect a broad variety in characteristics such as field, size and culture . . . In all, 52 members of teaching staff took part in 11 focus group discussions. The participants were chosen by departmental self-selection, based on our request that they represent broadly all categories of teaching staff and be individuals who are actively involved in teaching new students.

(Lahteenoja and Pirttila-Backman 2005: 643–4)

This study examines a number of journalistic articles in magazines, tabloids, newspapers and other publications covering the YCC [Your Concept Car] project. In October 2003, 272 articles and press clippings that addressed the YCC project had been registered. In order to get attention from potential and existing female clients, the public relations strategy was to aim for coverage in journals and magazines outside the narrow range of motor journals. Women's magazines and daily newspapers were, for instance, also targeted . . . The total body of text comprised 9987 column centimetres and 181 pictures . . . Most of the 272 articles and press clippings were briefly examined, and those published in languages we neither read nor understand, such as Arabic and Polish, were not integrated into the analysis. Most of these press clippings were more or less based on the information in the press release and reported the facts in neutral terms. Twenty of the articles that were based on interviews with the team members or contained some additional journalistic material, such as commentaries or additional remarks, were selected and carefully reviewed. The 20 documents constituted the textual corpus of the study . . .

(Styhre et al. 2005: 557–8)

We have gathered data on this daily reality of work from workplaces of two kinds: two technology enterprises and municipal youth centres. The data from the technology enterprises were collected by observing collaborative work situations and interviewing a total of 18 design and development engineers; and the data on municipal youth work by observing and audio taping weekly team meetings of youth workers in three municipal youth centres.

(Collin and Valleala 2005: 403)

Recording your progress

As we noted in Chapter 4, meticulousness is an important skill for the researcher to develop. This is as true during the data collection phase of your research as it is when you are reading. There are three key aspects to recording the process of data collection: keeping notes on the progress of your project, keeping your data secure, and chasing up.

> See also the section on **Recording your reading** in Chapter 4.

Keeping notes

To record, and reflect upon, your progress during this phase, you will need to keep notes in some form. These notes may deal with your plans, how they change in practice, your reactions, what you read, what you think, significant things that people say to you, and what you discover.

You do have considerable flexibility about how you keep records of the progress of your research project. Here are some alternatives:

• *Research diaries.* An ideal way of keeping a record of what you are doing, feeling and thinking throughout the research project as it happens.

> See the section in Chapter 2 on **Keeping your research diary**.

• *Boxes or files.* Keep all the material you are collecting in a number of boxes, one for each subject or chapter.
• *Coloured paper and Post-it notes.* Some people find these a helpful, even fun, way of organizing their records.
• *Computers.* You may input your thoughts, records and references directly on to a computer. Software is available to help extract, arrange and index materials. Remember to keep a back-up copy and to print out an up-to-date version every so often.

> See the section in Chapter 5 on **Using computers**.

• *Card indexes.* These can be particularly useful for keeping details of references, organized by author or subject.

Some examples of the alternative strategies developed by actual small-scale social science researchers for keeping research records are included in Box 6.11.

Box 6.11 Keeping research records

William decided that he would keep all his material according to its relevance to particular chapters of his thesis. He made this decision after a few months of his research, when he was feeling overwhelmed and directionless. Putting material into chapter files helped him gain a sense of progress and control, although he recognized that he would subsequently move material between files.

Jez decided that she would not use cards as the basis of her bibliographic index, as they would not be easily transportable. Instead, she bought a notebook with alphabetic sections and used this to record her growing literature. It provided her with a manageable resource which she subsequently typed on to her laptop.

Mary wanted to store the different types of material she was collecting according to type. She therefore used A4 box files, which were categorized in terms of literature reviews, interview transcripts, respondents' completed diaries and tape recordings.

Vena was going to do most of her literature research online, using electronic databases and journals. Her supervisor recommended that she learn to use RefWorks (http://www.refworks.com/) before she began.

Hint: However you decide to keep a record of your research in progress, it is very sensible to keep at least two copies of your records, each in a different place. Spare yourself the heartache of lost and irreplaceable files.

Keeping your data secure

In addition to being concerned with ensuring anonymity for your research respondents, a broader ethical, and indeed legal, issue is that of confidentiality of data storage. In the UK, the Data Protection Act 1998, which came into force in March 2000, covers personal data stored in both electronic and manual form. This means that any data kept in a structured filing system is subject to the Act. The Act sets out a number of principles for the storage of personal information, which include that it is fairly and lawfully processed; is adequate, relevant and not excessive; accurate and up to date; is secured and is not transferred to other countries without adequate protection. While there are certain exemptions for university staff and students conducting research, the Act does point up the importance of ensuring that your systems of record keeping are compliant. Box 6.12 provides a checklist.

Box 6.12   Keeping your data safely stored

1   Do you have a statement of consent from your research respondents or providers of any other information for the uses to which you will put your data? This will include sharing data with co-researchers and with supervisors.

2   Have you ensured that there is adequate protection for your stored data? For example:

- Do you have an adequate password (minimum of eight characters, mixture of upper- and lower-case letters and numbers)?
- Do you change your password regularly?
- Do you avoid indiscriminate surfing and opening documents from untrusted sources?
- Do you have appropriate anti-virus software installed on your computer?
- For manually stored data, is this kept in locked cabinets?

Details of the Data Protection Act 1998 can be found on the Office of Public Sector Information website at http://www.opsi.gov.uk/acts/acts1998/ukpga_19980029_en_1

Chasing up

The other aspect to being meticulous is chasing up your own progress, and the responses that you are expecting from others. Your research plans may look fine on paper, and you may have allowed plenty of time for collecting data, but you cannot expect other people to be as enthusiastic about, and committed to, your research as you are yourself. You may not be able to readily access all of the documents that interest you. Not everybody will readily grant your requests for interviews. You may be denied access to some of the events or settings which you wish to observe. The response rate to your questionnaire survey may be disappointing.

What can you do about this? There are two kinds of responses, which can be used in conjunction. On the one hand, you may need to be realistic and flexible about your expectations for collecting data. You don't need a 100 per cent response rate; you don't need to read every last word written on your subject area; perhaps it doesn't matter if you don't interview every member of the management team or observe every meeting. You can get a great deal of information without experiencing everything, and even then you'll probably never have time to analyse it all.

On the other hand, you can increase your response rate significantly by keeping tabs on your progress and assiduously following up your respondents. Possible strategies here might include:

- sending reminder letters to potential survey respondents who have not replied by your initial deadline;
- telephoning unwilling interviewees on a number of occasions;
- making yourself amenable to the librarian or custodian of the documents which you wish to get access to;
- maintaining regular contacts with the key people, or gatekeepers, for your research.

The ups and downs of data collection

The process of collecting data may be quite a lengthy and demanding part of your research project. It may be a part which you particularly enjoy, or you may dislike it intensely. Either way, however, you are likely to encounter ups and downs during the process. There may be days when you really enjoy yourself, when you discover something interesting, or when somebody says something which casts your whole project in a new and exciting light. There will also be days when you can barely force yourself to do the necessary work, when you just go through the motions, or when you begin to doubt where it is all leading. Things will go wrong, and you will have to find ways of coping.

This section identifies two of the most common 'downs' encountered when collecting data – loneliness and obsessiveness – and suggests how you might counter them. It then offers some positive thoughts about how you might ensure that you get more enjoyment out of data collection. Finally, the issue of when to stop collecting data is discussed.

Loneliness

It is a truth universally acknowledged that a PhD student in their first year will spend most of that year sitting in a library wondering what on earth they should be doing. They will then spend the next two or more years wishing they had put that year to better use. Unfortunately nobody ever warns you about this. In fact the Wasted First Year is just one of many PhD hazards that nobody ever warns you about – followed by loneliness, poverty, and tutors who think that it is their responsibility to ensure that you suffer as much as they did.

(Zuram, n.d.)

This is not the best advert for undertaking research is it? However, all researchers, even those who are involved in group research, have to learn how to cope with working alone. For some it may be enjoyable, but for others it can be stressful. It is, however, an essential part of research, since it is you who has to decide at the end about the meaning of what you are doing. It will affect you even if you are working on a project close to your heart and with people you can relate to comfortably.

Loneliness is, therefore, inevitable, and is particularly prevalent during the process of data collection. Alan Sillitoe once wrote a book entitled *The Loneliness of the Long Distance Runner*, but there is little to compare with the feelings of the lone researcher, particularly if they are conducting a lengthy piece of research. Indeed, under the banner headline 'The loneliness of the long distance learner', the *Times Higher Education Supplement* (17 January 2003) reported one student describing her experience of research in the following terms:

> It feels like a marathon, but you haven't been given a map or a watch. Everybody is told to run a different route, so they are all disappearing in different directions. I hear the occasional cheer as somebody finishes but I am just running. Somehow, I'm supposed to know where to go and when I am finished. When you start, you can explain to people at parties what you are doing, but in your second year you find yourself repeating what you said a year ago. You can't explain what interests you at the time because they need the introduction from the first year, and by the time you have finished that, the conversation has moved on. You are very much alone and sometimes it is difficult to convince yourself you have an audience. It is just you and your supervisor.

A particular form of isolation is common if you are carrying out fieldwork. In such cases, you will commonly be both an insider, having been accepted by the individuals, groups or institutions you are researching, and an outsider. However well you are accepted, you will still not be one of them. You may become a member of their group for a time, but you will simultaneously be operating as an external observer and analyst of the group's activities. The dual roles of stranger and colleague, of insider and outsider, can be difficult to manage and sustain psychologically (this can also occur if you are researching in your own workplace).

Your loneliness will be magnified if you have no one sympathetic with whom you can discuss your progress and problems. This will be particularly so if your supervisor, manager or colleagues are unhelpful, or if you are conducting an obscure, sensitive or challenging piece of research. This is why it is so important to spend time, when beginning your research, on developing your support networks.

> You may like to refer back to the section on **Sharing responsibility** in Chapter 5.

The other way to combat loneliness is to compartmentalize your research, to give it a certain time and space in your life, but no more, making sure that you leave opportunities for you to maintain and engage in some of your other interests.

Obsessiveness

The problem of obsessiveness may be closely related to that of feeling alone, particularly if you are carrying out your research project on your own. Research may be both an intensely stimulating and a very demanding experience. Whether you are conducting it on a part-time or full-time basis, it can take over your life, so beware! It may come to take up every spare moment that you have. You may want to talk about nothing else. You may be unable to wait to get back into the library, or for your next interview, observation or experiment. Research can get into your dreams!

This is likely, however, to cause you problems with your family, friends and colleagues, even with those who have been most ardent and reliable in supporting your research work. It can also be damaging to your research, as you can lose your understanding of the broader context for your work. The phrase 'going native' is used to describe a particularly severe form of research obsessiveness. It originated in an anthropological context, but has a more general application as well. The researcher who has gone native has become so immersed in the subject of their research that they are unable to separate their interest from those of their research subjects. They have lost the distance, strangeness or disassociation which is usually so important for the researcher.

Most researchers probably get obsessive about their research at one time or another. This may actually be useful or essential, for example if you are under pressure towards the end of the project to get it written up and finished on time. More generally, though, obsessiveness is to be guarded against. Three basic strategies which might help you are:

- Planning and scheduling your research from the start, and revising your plans regularly throughout the project so as to keep the work required feasible. This should make it less likely that you will need to devote a disproportionate amount of your time to the research at any one point, and hence reduce the likelihood of your becoming obsessive.

> You may find it useful to look again at the sections on **Managing time** and **Mapping your project** in Chapter 5.

- Instructing a friend, relative or colleague to take on the responsibility for identifying when you become obsessive, telling you so and distracting you from your research. This will need to be someone you both trust and respect, and who is capable of putting up with your possibly terse response.
- Developing and using a network of fellow researchers, so that you can share your progress and concerns, take an interest in the work of others, and get support in this way.

> The section in Chapter 5 on **Sharing responsibility** suggests how you might go about networking and seeking support.

How to enjoy data collection

As the previous discussion indicates, doing research can become fascinating and all-absorbing. The process of collecting data has its attractions as well as its drawbacks. So how might you enable yourself to enjoy data collection more?

One obvious strategy is to focus on a topic, or a methodology or a group of research subjects which you find of particular interest.

> The section in Chapter 2 on **Choosing a topic** suggests how you might go about this.

There will probably be times, however, when the attraction of your project, and in particular the data collection involved, pales a little, regardless of how interesting it is or how well motivated you are.

Another strategy is to deliberately combine the process of collecting data with other activities which give you pleasure. These might include, for example, visiting friends, tea shops (our favourite), football grounds, book-shops or other places of interest.

Take pleasure in your progress and achievements, and try not to be too down-hearted when you experience setbacks. Allow yourself little rewards along the way. You'll miss it when it's over!

When to stop collecting data

You may find great pleasure in data collection, particularly if it takes you away from your everyday world into an arena which you find interesting or attractive. You may doubt that you have collected sufficient data for the purposes of your research, and continue to search for further information to confirm, complement or deny your understanding. You may wish to delay beginning the analysis and writing up of your research findings.

However, unless you have an open-ended schedule and as many resources as you need for your research, it is critically important that you stop collecting data at a certain point or time. You should have drawn up a schedule or time-table, and will have allocated only so much time to the data collection process. Even allowing for some leeway, this period cannot be indefinitely extended if you are to complete within a reasonable time.

There is another issue here, however. In small-scale research, you cannot expect to collect all the data you might like. No social research project, in a more general sense, is ever going to provide the last, definitive word on any topic. The purpose of small-scale research is likely to be a mixture of practical application, illumination, self-directed learning and research training. You should not, therefore, place yourself under enormous pressure to produce the 'perfect' piece of work. So:

- Keep to your schedule as much as possible.
- Collect only sufficient data, allowing particularly for the time and facilities which you will have available for analysing it.
- Move on to analysing your data as soon as you have collected sufficient.

Summary

Having read this chapter, you should:

- have an appreciation of the complex access and ethical issues involved in doing social research;
- be aware of how you might go about sampling and selecting cases to research;
- be aware of the importance of keeping accurate, systematic and confidential records;
- be better prepared to cope with the ups and downs of data collection.

Exercises

6.1 Who or what do you want to research? Who are the key individuals, gate-keepers or stakeholders that you need to get permission from? How much of your respondents' time will you need? Is this reasonable? What potential problems do you anticipate with regard to access? Are there any rules about recording informed consent with which you will have to comply?

6.2 Identify the sampling strategy, or strategies, you plan to adopt for your research project. Justify this choice, and explore the merits of other strategies.

Further reading

In this section, we list a limited selection of books that are of particular relevance to the topics discussed in this chapter, together with an indication of their contents.

Best, S. and Krueger, B. (2004) *Internet Data Collection*. Thousand Oaks, CA: Sage.
  Covers the different stages of the data collection process, including sampling, instrument design and administration, drawing particular attention to the potential dangers and particular conventions of the internet.
Campbell, A. (2007) *An Ethical Approach to Practitioner Research: Dealing with issues and dilemmas in action research*. London: Routledge.
  Focused mainly on action research in educational settings, but also considering legal, nursing and social care.
Gregory, I. (2003) *Ethics in Research*. London: Continuum.
  Short text covering consent, confidentiality and related issues.
Hallowell, N., Lawton, J. and Gregory, S. (eds) (2005) *Reflections on Research: The realities of doing research in the social sciences*. Maidenhead: Open University Press.
  Forty-three contributors offer reflections on the place of emotions, self, others, control and ethics in research.
Israel, M. and Hay, I. (2006) *Research Ethics for Social Scientists*. London: Sage.
  Seeks to demonstrate the value of thinking carefully about ethics, show why the present regulatory regimes have emerged, and show how regulators and researchers can work together.
Lee-Treweek, G. and Linkogle, S. (eds) (2000) *Danger in the Field: Risk and ethics in social research*. New York: Routledge.
  Uses researchers' reflexive accounts of encounters with physical, emotional, ethical and professional danger.
Mauthner, M., Birch, M., Jessop, J. and Miller, T. (2002) *Ethics in Qualitative Research*. London: Sage.
  Addresses both theoretical and practical aspects of ethics, including discussion of access, informed consent, negotiating participation and tensions in researching as a professional.
Oliver, P. (2003) *The Student's Guide to Research Ethics*. Maidenhead: Open University Press.
  Using case studies, covers ethics throughout the research process, including discussion of consent, confidentiality and dissemination.
Richards, L. (2005) *Handling Qualitative Data: A practical guide*. London: Sage.

A practical guide, focusing on the development of skills in the collection and analysis of qualitative data.

Rossman, G. and Rallis, S. (2003) *Learning in the Field: An introduction to qualitative research*, 2nd edition. Thousand Oaks, CA: Sage.

Uses student characters and three themes – research is a learning process, research can and should be useful, and the researcher needs a clear vision – to help readers grasp the issues.

Swann, J. and Pratt, J. (eds) (2003) *Educational Research in Practice: Making sense of methodology*. London: Continuum.

Experienced practitioners address a common set of questions about their research: what they do, why they do it, its methodological basis and perceived outcomes.

Walford, G. (2001) *Doing Qualitative Educational Research: A personal guide to the research process*. London: Continuum.

Seeks to get below the surface of research by reflecting upon the trials and tribulations, and problems and promises, of conducting research in the field.

7

Collecting data

Introduction

All research involves the collection and analysis of data, whether through reading, observation, measurement, asking questions, or a combination of these or other strategies. The data collected during and for research may, however, vary considerably in their characteristics. For example:

- Data may be numerical, or may consist of words, or may be a combination of the two.
- Data may be neither numbers nor words, but consist of, for example, pictures or artefacts.
- Data may be 'original', in the sense that you have collected information never before collected; or may be 'secondary', already put together by somebody else, but reused, probably in a different way, by you.
- Data may consist of responses to a questionnaire or interview transcriptions, notes or other records of observations or experiments, documents and materials, or all of these things.

The purpose of this chapter is to guide you through the processes involved in data collection. The chapter is organized around the following themes and issues:

- **Applying techniques for collecting data**. The different methods which you may use for your research.

- **Documents**. Using written, online, archived and visual materials as a basis for your research.
- **Interviews**. Questioning or discussing issues with your sample.
- **Observations**. Collecting data through watching or engaging in activities.
- **Questionnaires**. Gathering information through written questions.
- **Mixed methodologies**. Combining approaches.

Applying techniques for collecting data

Approaches and techniques

In Chapter 3, we identified a series of research families, approaches and techniques. The four approaches – action research, case studies, experiments and surveys – provide alternative, though not necessarily mutually exclusive, frameworks for thinking about and planning research projects. They were considered separately in Chapter 3. In this chapter, we focus on the four main techniques, or methods for producing data, which were identified: documents, interviews, observation and questionnaires.

Before doing so, however, we will revisit the discussion of the two research families or dichotomies we identified in Chapter 3 – fieldwork or deskwork, and qualitative or quantitative – and consider how these relate to the four techniques. In a final section, at the end of the chapter, the use of mixed research methodologies (i.e. qualitative *and* quantitative) will be examined.

> You might like to take another look at Chapter 3 at this point, particularly the section on **Families, approaches and techniques**.

In the field or at the desk?

The first days in the field are often seen as the most challenging and emotionally awkward. Meeting any new group of people in an environment which they already inhabit can be uncomfortable and embarrassing, but it can be particularly so where those being met are to be research 'subjects' and do not fully understand the nature of ethnographic research. Yet the first days of research are also often seen as particularly exciting, for so much of what is experienced and observed is new to the researcher. Indeed, the researcher is often overwhelmed by the amount of new information that it is necessary to take in.

(Walford 2001: 53)

For many social science researchers, particularly perhaps in anthropology, geography and sociology, the collection of data involves fieldwork. Having refined their research projects, developed their questions and methods, the researchers then 'go into the field' to collect data directly through observation and/or questioning. For such researchers and disciplines, fieldwork has a considerable mystique and associated traditions.

In other cases, and commonly in disciplines such as economics and psychology, fieldwork as such may be unusual. Much research in these subjects is done using pre-existing data, or data which can be collected, perhaps experimentally, within one's employing institution.

You don't have to do fieldwork to be a researcher, even in those disciplines where it is common. You may choose to, if you enjoy it, if your research topic demands it, or if it is expected of you. Or you may, for equally valid reasons, choose not to do fieldwork, but to base your research within the library, office or laboratory. With the expansion of online data sets and archives it is becoming even more possible to undertake research without ever leaving your room or house.

Qualitative or quantitative?

[Q]uantitative research is thought to be more concerned with the deductive testing of hypotheses and theories, whereas qualitative research is more concerned with exploring a topic, and with inductively generating hypotheses and theories. While this is often true, these stereotypes can be overdone.

(Punch 2005: 235)

As we argued in Chapter 3 (see particularly Box 3.5), the distinction between qualitative and quantitative research can be exaggerated. While most research projects will emphasize either qualitative or quantitative approaches, it is difficult to imagine research that is wholly quantitative or wholly qualitative in its approach. Indeed, as the discussion in the final section of this chapter (**Mixed methodologies**) makes clear, it is becoming more common to explicitly combine qualitative and quantitative approaches, taking advantage of the strengths that each has to offer in combination.

The close relationship between qualitative and quantitative forms of research is evident when it is realized that the four main techniques for collecting data – documents, interviews, observations and questionnaires – which we consider in the next four sections of this chapter, can each involve either (or both) qualitative and quantitative elements. Documents may consist largely of words (e.g. policy statements) or numbers (e.g. statistical reports). Interviews may be open-ended conversations or used to collect facts (e.g. how long have you lived here?) or information that will be numerically coded (e.g. if there was an election tomorrow, who would you vote for?).

Similarly, observations may be organized in a quantitative (e.g. counting traffic) or qualitative (e.g. making notes on behaviour in a doctor's waiting room) fashion. And, while questionnaires are strongly associated with the collection of quantitative data through the use of multiple-choice questions and pre-coded responses, they may also include (or be entirely composed of) open-ended questions.

Documents

All, or virtually all, research projects involve, to a greater or lesser extent, the use and analysis of documents. Researchers are expected to read, understand and critically analyse the writings of others, whether fellow researchers, practitioners or policy-makers. Considerable attention has, therefore, already been given to the techniques of reading for research.

> See Chapter 4, particularly the section on **Good enough reading**, and Chapter 10, especially the section on **How to criticize**.

For some research projects, however, the focus of data collection is wholly, or almost entirely, on documents of various kinds and this is our focus here. They might, for example:

- be library-based, aimed at producing a critical synopsis of an existing area of research writing;
- be computer-based, consisting largely of the analysis of previously collected data sets;
- be work-based, drawing on materials produced within an organization;
- have a policy focus, examining materials relevant to a particular set of policy decisions;
- have a historical orientation, making use of available archival and other surviving documentary evidence.

Using documents can be a relatively unobtrusive form of research, one which does not necessarily require you to approach respondents first hand. Rather, as much family history research testifies, you can trace their steps through the documents that they have left behind. While unobtrusive methods do not rely solely on documents – they can also, for example, involve searching dustbins (garbology), looking at gravestones or monuments, and examining graffiti (Lee 2000) – there is no doubt that documents are an invaluable methodological tool. Some examples of research projects which have made considerable use of documents are summarized in Box 7.1.

Box 7.1 Examples of the use of documents in research

- Mason (1999) interviewed families about their *wills* as part of a research project into family networks and relationships. Questions about who is and who is not listed as a beneficiary can shed light on how stepfamilies view family ties.
- Nixon (2000) examined the *web pages* and *newspaper* reports of a small group of Australian schoolchildren who had been noted for their advanced information technology skills. Her analysis illustrated how their learning was conducted outside of formal school environments, and how this was related to issues of national identity and the commodification of these children's lives.
- Tight (2000) analysed a year's worth of the *Times Higher Education Supplement* to discover what images of the higher education world it presented. He found varied images of the sector, ranging from one in crisis to one where employment opportunities were plentiful.
- Payne et al. (2004) studied two years' output of four 'mainstream' and one 'specialist' British sociological journals, together with the papers presented at one British Sociological Association annual conference. They were interested in which research methods were being used, concluding that there was a need for more quantitative work.
- Arber and Ginn (1995) used *General Household Survey* data to explore the relationship between informal care and paid work. They found that it is the norm to be in paid work and also be providing informal care.

Researchers who base their studies on documents may make considerable use of secondary data; that is, data which has already been collected, and possibly also analysed, by somebody else. The most common forms of secondary data are official statistics collected by governments and government agencies. However, the potential for secondary analysis of qualitative data is increasingly being realized.

For example, the ESRC National Strategy for Data Resources in the Social Sciences is concerned with developing and maintaining a robust data infrastructure that addresses UK research priorities. In addition, the growth of online resources, including census and archival materials, data sets from national surveys and longitudinal studies, is enabling researchers to draw on multiple sources in innovative ways. Box 7.2 provides an example of such research, where the researcher accessed archived transcripts from a number of previous community studies, together with data from the Mass Observation directives of 1939 and 1995. While you will see that this was a large-scale study, the list of sources consulted does give an indication of what is available and ready for secondary analysis. The point here is that there are research questions that can be answered without needing to collect new data, and that

Box 7.2 Using multiple secondary sources

Savage (2008) reports on a study of 'Histories, Belongings, Communities', which was concerned with people's sense of belonging to the places where they live. The study accessed previously deposited transcripts of interviews and other documentation produced by sociologists in the 1950s and 1960s who were researching issues of community. Many of these are available from the Economic and Social Data Service (ESDS) Qualidata site (http://www.essex.ac.uk/qualidata/). Savage also consulted the Mass Observation archives (http://www.massobs.org.uk), where two relevant questions had been asked in 1939 and 1995. The list of sources that Savage consulted was:

1950–1953: Family and Social Network: Roles, Norms and External Relationships in Ordinary Urban Families, Elizabeth Boot, interview notes and interview summaries of 17 London households with your children (QDD/Bott)

1961–1962: Affluent Worker Collection, Goldthorpe et al., household interviews with 227 workers in Luton (QDD/Affluentworker)

1962–1970: Brian Jackson Collection, including interviews for Education and the Working Class and interviews and supporting documentation for Working Class Community

1966–1968: Metropolitan Village Survey, Ray Pahl, documentary sources on three villages in Hertfordshire (QDD/Pahl3)

1961: Three Hertfordshire Village Survey, Ray Pahl, 331 questionnaires on social and spatial mobility (QDD/Pahl2)

1964–1965: Lifestyles and Patterns of Mobility in Hertfordshire Commuter Villages (QDD/Pahl5)

1965–1967: Managers and their Wives: A Study of Career and Family Relationships in the Middle Class, Ray Pahl, 172 questionnaires with managerial husbands and their wives and supporting documents (QDD/Pahl4)

1968–1970: Orientation to Work and Industrial Behaviour of Shipbuilding Workers on Tyneside, 338 interview questionnaires with male shipyard workers, 15 observation field notes (QDD/Brown1)

Mass Observation: 1939 and 1995 directives, University of Sussex

there is a wealth of data ready and waiting for further analysis. As the examples in Boxes 7.1 and 7.2 indicate, secondary analysis can give fresh insights into data, and ready-made data sets or archives do provide extremely valuable and cost-efficient resources for researchers. Box 7.3 provides further examples of online and other archives.

Box 7.3 UK documentary sources for research

Government surveys

A full list is available from http://www.statistics.gov.uk/ which has an online service. Try also the UK Data Archive (http://www.data-archive.ac.uk/) which houses 5,000 computer readable data sets for research and teaching purposes. Comprehensive online information and links to access data are available for each data set. Searching and browsing information about data, including user guides and documentation, is free and does not require registration. You do need to register if you wish to access raw data. The site also provides access to European databases.

Examples of the data sets included are: the British Crime Survey/Scottish Crime Survey; British Social Attitudes Survey/Northern Ireland Social Attitudes Survey/Scottish Social Attitudes Survey/North Ireland Life and Times Survey/Young People's Social Attitudes; Family Expenditure Survey/Northern Ireland Family Expenditure Survey; National Food Survey; United Kingdom Time Use Survey; the Census of Employment; the Census of Population; the Labour Force Survey; the General Household Survey.

Government legislation

Government White Papers and legislative documents are important sources for policy research. The websites of key government departments offer search facilities and information on the latest policy initiatives.

- Directory of government departments, executive agencies, non-departmental government bodies, local councils and devolved governments: http://www.direct.gov.uk/en/DI1/Directories/
- Department for Health: http://www.doh.gov.uk/
- Department for Work and Pensions: http://www.dwp.gov.uk/
- Department for Children, Schools and Families: http://www.dcsf.gov.uk/
- Department for Culture, Media and Sport: http://www.culture.gov.uk/

Longitudinal Studies

There are relevant longitudinal studies including both quantitative and qualitative data. For example: the 1970 British Cohort Study; the British Household Panel Survey; the English Longitudinal Study of Ageing; the Families and Children Study; the Longitudinal Study of Young People in England; the Millennium Cohort Study; the National Child Development Study.

Go to the Centre for Longitudinal Studies, Institute of Education, University of London (http://www.cls.ioe.ac.uk/) for the 1958 National Child Development

Study (NCDS), the 1970 British Cohort Study (BCS70), and the Millennium Cohort Study (MCS).

These studies involve multiple surveys of large numbers of individuals from birth and throughout their lives. They have collected information on education and employment, family and parenting, physical and mental health, and social attitudes. Because they are longitudinal studies that follow the same groups of people throughout their lives, they show how histories of health, wealth, education, family and employment are interwoven for individuals, vary between them and affect outcomes and achievements in later life. Through comparing the different generations, we can chart social change and start to untangle the reasons behind it. Findings from the studies have contributed to debates and inquiries in a number of policy areas over the past half-century, including: education and equality of opportunity; poverty and social exclusion; gender differences in pay and employment; social class differences in health; changing family structures; and anti-social behaviour.

ESRC Timescapes, University of Leeds (http://www.timescapes.leeds.ac.uk/), is a major qualitative longitudinal study funded by the ESRC with a focus on how personal and family relationships develop and change over time. The emphasis is on relationships with significant others: parents, grandparents, siblings, children, partners, friends and lovers. Timescapes uses a method of 'walking along with' people to document their lives as well as in-depth interviews, oral narratives, photographs and other visual documents.

Historical records

Research into most aspects of social history (including political and business history) relies on archives.

- The National Register of Archives: http://www.nra.nationalarchives.gov.uk
- ARCHON is the principal information gateway for UK archivists and users of manuscript sources for British history: http://www.archon. nationalarchives.gov.uk/archon/
- Mass Observation, University of Sussex: http://www.massobs.org.uk. The Mass Observation Archive specializes in material about everyday life in Britain. It contains papers generated by the original Mass Observation social research organization (1937 to early 1950s), and newer material collected continuously since 1981.
- Census data: http://www.census.ac.uk. The ESRC Census Programme provides a one-stop gateway to data and support services which allow users and researchers in the UK to access the 1971, 1981, 1991 and 2001 censuses. It also provides access to other important census-related resources. Try also the Cathie Marsh Centre for Census and Survey Research (CCSR) at Manchester University (http://www.ccsr.ac.uk/).

Media documents

Newspapers, magazines, television and radio all have websites that can provide interesting sources of data and useful material for research analysis. Websites of newspapers internationally can be found at http://library. uncg.edu/news/. These documents are useful for analysis of job and other advertisements, the letters pages, personal columns, obituaries and wedding announcements as well as the news pages.

Personal documents

Internet home pages of individuals have been used very creatively for research (see Nixon 2000). More generally, however, researchers will have to rely on paper-based sources. These include diaries, letters, wills and photographs.

International organizations

Comparative information on other countries, and on international policies and programmes, may be found on the websites of international organizations, such as the World Bank (http://www.worldbank.org/), World Health Organization, International Labor Office and the Organization for Economic Co-operation and Development (http://www.oecd.org/).

For further examples of secondary data sets available online, see the section in Chapter 4 on **Using the internet**, in particular Box 4.5.

However, there are several cautions that have to be borne in mind in analysing secondary data. The questions you need to ask of any existing document are:

- What were the conditions of its production? For example, why, and when, was the document produced/written and for whom?
- If you are using statistical data sets, have the variables changed over time? For example 'ethnicity' was not recorded in the British census until 1991. This means that you cannot undertake some forms of analysis.
- If you are using statistical data sets, have the indicators used to measure variables changed? For example, the measurement of unemployment has undergone many changes in the past two decades. This impacts on any comparative or historical analyses that you might seek to make.

Health warning:
Statistics don't fall out of the skies. Like words – of which they are of course an extension – they are constructed by human beings influenced by culture and the predispositions and governing ideas of the organisations and groups within which people work. Statistical methodologies are not timeless creations. They are the current expression of society's attempts to interpret, represent and analyse information about economic and social (and other) conditions. As the years pass they change – not just because there may be technical *advances* but because professional, cultural, political *and* technical conventions change in terms of *retreat* as well as advance . . . Every student of social science . . . needs to be grounded in how information about social conditions is acquired. Statistics form a substantial part of such information. Acquiring information is much more than looking up handbooks of statistics. We have to become self-conscious about the process of selection.

(Townsend 1996: 26, emphasis in original)

Exercise 7.1 invites you to consider the reasons for using secondary data. Try it, whether the use of documents forms a major part of your research project or not. You may like to compare your own suggestions with those given in Box 7.4. You may conclude from this both that you cannot really avoid the use of secondary data to some extent, and that it is legitimate and interesting to base your research project entirely upon such data.

Box 7.4 Reasons for using secondary data

1   Because collecting primary data is difficult, time-consuming and expensive.
2   Because you can never have enough data.
3   Because it makes sense to use it if the data you want already exists in some form.
4   Because it may shed light on, or complement, the primary data you have collected.
5   Because it may confirm, modify or contradict your findings.
6   Because it allows you to focus your attention on analysis and interpretation.
7   Because you cannot conduct a research study in isolation from what has already been done.
8   Because more data is collected than is ever used.

Interviews

The unstructured interview has been variously described as naturalistic, autobiographical, in-depth, narrative or non-directive. Whatever the label used, the informal interview is modelled on the conversation and, like the conversation, is a social event with, in this instance, two participants. As a social event it has its own set of interactional rules which may be more or less explicit, more or less recognised by the participants. In addition to its generally social character, there are several ways in which the interview constitutes a learning process. At the level of this process, participants can discover, uncover or generate the rules by which they are playing this particular game. The interviewer can become more adept at interviewing, in general, in terms of the strategies which are appropriate for eliciting responses, and in particular, in our case, in enabling people to talk about the sensitive topic of sexuality, and thus to disclose more about themselves.

(Holland and Ramazanoglu 1994: 135)

The interview method involves questioning or discussing issues with people. It can be a very useful technique for collecting data which would likely not be accessible using techniques such as observation or questionnaires. Many variations on the interview method are possible: some of the main options are summarized in Box 7.5. Of particular note is the growth of internet and focus group interviews.

Box 7.5 Alternative interview techniques

- Interviews may take place face to face or at a distance, e.g. over the telephone or by email.
- They may take place at the interviewee's or interviewer's home or place of work, in the street or on some other, 'neutral' ground.
- At one extreme, the interview may be tightly structured, with a set of questions requiring specific answers (cf. questionnaires), or it may be very open ended, taking the form of a discussion. In the latter case, the purpose of the interviewer may be simply to facilitate the subject's talking at length. Semi-structured interviews lie between these two positions.
- Different forms of questioning may be practised during the interview. In addition to survey questioning, Dillon identified classroom, courtroom and clinical questioning, as well as the domains of personnel interviewing, criminal interrogation and journalistic interviewing (Dillon 1990).
- Prompts, such as photographs, can be useful for stimulating discussion.

- Interviews may involve just two individuals, the researcher and the interviewee, or they may be group events (often referred to as focus groups), involving more than one subject and/or more than one interviewer.
- The interviewee may, or may not, be given advance warning of the topics or issues to be discussed. This briefing might be very detailed to allow the subject to gather together any necessary information.
- The interview may be recorded in a variety of ways. It may be taped, and possibly later transcribed by an audio-typist. The interviewer may take notes, during or after the interview, or, where there is more than one interviewer, one might take notes while the other conducted the interview.
- Interviews may be followed up in a variety of ways. A transcript could be sent to the subject for comment. Further questions might subsequently be sent to the subject in writing. A whole series of interviews could be held over a period of time, building upon each other or exploring changing views and experiences.

Box 7.6 Pros and cons of focus groups

Pros

- The group members can challenge the researcher's agenda. It may be a more empowering experience for those interviewed.
- Diverse and different views may be generated. The discussion allows for an analysis of how meanings are made, negotiated and challenged.
- It may feel a safer experience for some people who prefer to discuss issues within a group rather than individually.
- The discussion may lead to unanticipated findings because of the ways in which the discussion itself generates thoughts and feelings.

Cons

- How to document the data in such a way that you are sure who has said what.
- The group dynamics may silence or exaggerate particular views.
- The economics of interviewing several people at one time may be outweighed by the higher level of organizational effort required to ensure all can participate.
- How do you deal with issues of confidentiality?

Box 7.7 Examples of using interviews in research

For his MA dissertation, Shu-Ming wanted to interview his ex-colleagues working in Taiwan about their experiences of mentoring. He drew up a sample and, using email, sent each of them a brief outline of his topic, its purposes and some details of how he planned to conduct the research, including the amount of time it would require of respondents and the broader timescale within which he was operating. His colleagues responded very positively, but there was an immediate problem. They were unfamiliar with the concept of mentoring, and so Shu-Ming's early work with them was to explain what he had understood about mentoring from studying in England. These initial interviews developed more into online tutorials than an exchange between peers, but the data that was produced was extremely useful in highlighting the culturally specific meanings of mentoring. Using this data, Shu-Ming's dissertation was refocused so that it explored the implications of online learning and research in the context of these culturally specific meanings. As a result, later interviews were conducted with his interviewees about their changing understandings and knowledge of mentoring.

Hollway and Jefferson (2000) used interviews to explore fear of crime with those whom they describe as 'defended subjects'. These are people who will protect themselves against any anxieties arising from the information provided in a research context. For example, defended subjects may not hear the questions in the same ways as other interviewees, and they may not know why they experience or feel things in the ways they do. They may invest in particular discourses to protect vulnerable aspects of themselves, and unconscious motivations may disguise the meanings of some of their feelings and actions. Hollway and Jefferson illustrate how early interview approaches were disappointing, but they argue that the problem 'went deeper than a few mistakes, which all interviewers make – through tiredness, lapses of concentration, a clumsily worded question or tapping into unknown (and unknowable) sensitivities' (p. 30). In consequence, they argue that a biographical-interpretive method was more appropriate than traditional interview approaches. This method has four principles: use open questions, elicit stories, avoid 'why' questions and follow respondents' ordering and phrasing. In addition, Hollway and Johnson argue that in their research the use of free association was an important adaptation of the biographical-interpretive method.

In our research study, an array of outside experts had approved a research protocol which outlined that eight focus groups would take place over a twelve-month period: each group would involve between eight and ten users. The project's full-time research assistant spent considerable time at the gym making links with service users with a view to recruiting

> participants to the first focus group. Although payment of expenses was offered to participants, recruitment proved difficult. Many users were unwilling to take part in a focus group, and half of those who agreed to take part failed to attend on the day. The research assistant for the project felt that she had developed a good relationship with users, so in the end, we began to ask direct questions about what prevented them from joining focus groups.
>
> (Truman 2003: para. 39)

Focus groups offer the opportunity to interview a number of people at the same time, and to use the interaction within the group as a source of further insight. Exercise 7.2 invites you to consider a number of practical issues you might face in conducting focus groups. Box 7.6 outlines their major advantages and disadvantages.

Through the use of email, the internet offers a relatively cheap way of conducting interviews at a distance. Of course, internet systems allow for both individual and group interviews to be conducted as, through asynchronous conferencing, you can arrange for several people to be online simultaneously.

Some contrasting examples of the use of the interview method for research are given in Box 7.7.

If you have decided to carry out a number of interviews for your research project, one of the basic decisions you will have to take is whether to record the interview or to take notes. In practice, of course, you may not have much choice, if, for example, you cannot afford or get access to an audio or digital (or even visual) recorder. If you do decide to record, you may find that some of your interviewees refuse you permission to do so, so you should practise note-taking (during and/or after the interview) whatever your plans.

Each of these strategies has associated advantages and disadvantages:

- Using an audio or digital recorder means that you need only concentrate on the process of the interview. You can focus your attention on the interviewee, give appropriate eye contact and non-verbal communication. You will have a verbatim record of the whole interview.
- Recording may, however, make respondents anxious, and less likely to reveal confidential information.
- Recorders have a habit of not working properly from time to time, and there can be awkward pauses when you start, stop or change tapes. Recordings also take a long time to transcribe and analyse.
- Note-taking gives you an instant record of the key points of an interview. You do not need to acquire an audio or digital recorder, and do not need to worry about initial sorting, categorizing and analysing of the data collected.
- However, note-taking can also be distracting, for both interviewee and interviewer. Putting pen to paper may lead interviewees to think that they have said something significant. Conversely, when you don't make a note,

they may think that you find their comments unimportant. You may not realize, until later on or after the interview is finished, the significance of a comment you didn't note in detail.

• Concentrating on asking questions, listening to the responses *and* taking notes is a complex process, and you will not get a complete verbatim record. If you leave taking notes until after the interview, you are likely to forget important details.

If you do decide to record your interviews, bear in mind that the most expensive recorder is not necessarily the best. A solid, second-hand and relatively cheap tape recorder may be a sound investment. The key qualities are that it is not too large or heavy, that it can work off batteries as well as the mains, and that it can record quiet talkers when there is a lot of background noise. The availability of good quality play-back equipment may also be an issue for you. If you are listening to or watching recorded material, and taking notes on the content, then a foot-operated on/off button can be invaluable.

Health warning: Interview tapes take a great deal of time to transcribe and analyse. Tizard and Hughes (1991) made recordings of children at school and at home to study how they learnt. Each hour of the home tapes, which included a lot of talk, took 12 hours to transcribe and a further 5 hours to check and add context. The transcripts of the home tapes averaged 60 typed A4 pages.

Another key issue in carrying out interviews, as well as other forms of questioning such as questionnaires, is how best to ask potentially sensitive questions. These may include, for example, the age of your respondents, their ethnic group, marital status, income, social class and educational level. Exercise 7.3 invites you to consider this problem. Some possible answers are given in Box 7.8. Compare them with your suggestions, and try them out in practice to see how well they work.

Hint: Instead of asking all of your questions directly and verbally, you could make some use of prompt cards, particularly for sensitive questions, and ask your interviewee to point to the answer.

Observations

Doing participant observation research is riddled with dilemmas. As an observer/researcher I did not want my presence to affect the group dynamics I was attempting to study. But as a participant – a volunteer – I often

---

Box 7.8 Different ways of asking sensitive questions

About age:
- ask for year of birth
- or the year when they left school
- or how old their first child is
- or when they are due to retire

About ethnic group:
- ask them to select from a range of options
- or to write it down for you
- or ask them how they would like you to describe their ethnic group
- or make an assessment yourself

About income:
- ask them if they could afford to buy a new car or house
- or whether they would regard their income as above average, average or below average
- or which of a number of income bands they come in

---

found it impossible to avoid being drawn into relationships with members of Proteus [a creative workshop for people with learning difficulties], thereby changing the context of my research. I tried to do the 'right thing' for my research participants, even if this was at odds with my research. In Gail's case, I did not want to 'control' or 'contain' her (as had happened to her during most of her earlier life living in institutions), I merely wanted to prevent her from being ostracized from the group. In doing what I saw as the right thing, I often found I had to compromise my research role.

(Hallowell et al. 2005: 61)

How people see and understand their surroundings will no doubt play a part in the ways in which they behave, they act and interact with others, and in the ways their actions are perceived by others. Observation is an extremely handy tool for researchers in this regard. It can allow researchers to understand much more about what goes on in complex real-world situations than they can ever discover simply by asking questions of those who experience them (no matter how probing the questions may be), and by looking only at what is said about them in questionnaires and interviews.

(Wilkinson and Birmingham 2003: 117)

Box 7.9 Examples of the use of observation in research

[W]e resolved to concentrate as much as possible on studying positive aspects of human interaction. With this new focus, we were now no longer obliged to seek out violent pubs, but could spend time in pleasant ones . . . We could observe ordinary, law-abiding people doing their shopping, instead of interviewing security guards and store detectives about the activities of shoplifters and vandals. We went to nightclubs to study flirting rather than fighting. When I noticed some unusually sociable and courteous interaction among the crowds at a racecourse, I immediately began what turned out to be three years of research on the factors influencing the good behaviour of racegoers. We also conducted research on celebration, cyber-dating, summer holidays, embarrassment, corporate hospitality, van drivers, risk taking, the London Marathon, sex, mobile-phone gossip and the relationship between tea-drinking and DIY (this last dealing with burning social issues such as 'how many cups of tea does it take the average Englishman to put up a shelf?').

(Fox 2004: 5–6)

That night I learned something very important about scaboos [Special Care Baby Units or SCBUs] and, indeed, other front-line medical situations – day and night are quite different. There are fewer people around, and the atmosphere is much more relaxed. Unless there are major emergencies people have more time to sit and talk. Professional boundaries become much weaker. There are no visitors. A lot of coffee gets drunk. Home life and all sorts of issues beyond the scaboo are discussed. I quickly found that some of the conversations that had not happened during my daytime visits were easy to have at night. And so I became a night worker. Sometimes there were emergencies and occasionally babies died. When these things had happened during the day, screens were drawn and I felt I should keep out of the way. At night the nurses and doctors seemed to feel I should share all they had to do. Later on I began to stay over the shift changes and resumed my daytime visits. Luckily, what seemed to have become a changed role persisted into the daylight hours. Finally, I had become a participant in the life of the SCBU, not just an observer.

(Hallowell et al. 2005: 83)

The observation method involves the researcher in watching, recording and analysing events of interest. Two examples of its use are given in Box 7.9.

As the quotations and examples given indicate, a range of different approaches are possible in observation studies:

- The events may be recorded, either at the time or subsequently, by the researcher, or they may be recorded mechanically (including through photographs).
- The observation may be structured in terms of a predetermined framework, or may be relatively open.
- The observer may also be a participant in the events being studied, or may act solely as a 'disinterested' observer.

These differences are analogous to those already noted for interviews. There are, of course, many other details which need to be considered before you begin your observations. Box 7.10 outlines some of the key questions.

Box 7.10 Issues in observation

1   Are the times at which you carry out your observations relevant?
2   Do you need to devise an observational schedule or determine pre-coded categories? If so, you might like to test these out in a pilot observation before they are finalized.
3   If the answer to the last question was negative, how are you going to organize your data recording?
4   Is it important to you to try to record 'everything', or will you be much more selective?
5   Are your age, sex, ethnicity, dress or other characteristics likely to affect your observations?
6   How artificial is the setting? How visible are you as the observer? Does this matter?
7   Is observation enough, or will you need to participate and/or use other means of data collection?
8   Are there any situations to which you cannot get access but where observation may be important? How can you get 'off the road' or 'backstage'?
9   If you are going to participate more directly in the events you will be observing, how are you going to balance the demands of participation and observation? Again, you should find some practice beneficial here.

Using observation as a method of collecting data – whether or not you also act as a participant in the events you are observing – is, like interviewing, potentially very time consuming. The time absorbed occurs not just during the observation, but afterwards as well, when you come to interpret and analyse what you have recorded. Pre-categorizing and structuring your observations can reduce the time commitment dramatically, though at the risk of losing both detail and flexibility.

At one extreme, where the researcher's focus is on a limited number of specific events, and with noting or measuring participants' responses to certain stimuli, the observational technique shades into the experimental approach. At another, where the observer is a key and active participant in the events being studied, it shades into action research.

Questionnaires

Questionnaires are one of the most widely used social research techniques. The idea of formulating precise written questions, for those whose opinions or experience you are interested in, seems such an obvious strategy for finding the answers to the issues that interest you. But, as anyone who has tried to put a questionnaire together will tell you – and then tried again to interpret the responses – it is not as simple as it might seem. Box 7.11 summarizes two examples of the use of questionnaires in social research, and, in doing so, begins to suggest some of the potential difficulties in devising and using questionnaires.

There are a number of different ways in which questionnaires can be administered. They can be sent by post to the intended respondents, who are then expected to complete and return them themselves (preferably, if you want them to respond, using a reply-paid envelope). They can be administered over the telephone or face to face, in the latter case becoming much like a highly structured interview. They can be sent over the internet.

Each of these methods has advantages and disadvantages. Face-to-face surveys may get a better response rate, but are more time consuming for the researcher. Postal and email surveys are likely to have lower response rates, and possibly poorer answers because the respondent has no one available to answer any queries; but they may allow a larger number of people to be surveyed.

Just as questionnaires can be administered by different means, so there are a variety of ways in which questions can be asked. Box 7.12 illustrates seven basic question types: quantity or information, category, list or multiple choice, scale, ranking, complex grid or table, and open-ended. These types may be combined in various ways to give questions of increasing complexity.

As the examples given so far may have suggested, there are a number of issues to be considered when wording questions for survey purposes. While there is no such thing as the ideal questionnaire, some basic guidelines regarding question wording are given in Box 7.13. Box 7.14 adds to these with some suggestions on how questionnaires might best be laid out and presented.

If you follow these guidelines, you should be able to produce a competent questionnaire, though you are unlikely to produce a foolproof one. There will always be at least one question which proves to be inadequate or which brings an indignant response. You would be well advised, as with the use of any research technique, to pilot your questionnaire before you carry out the full survey, and to modify your questions in the light of the responses you receive.

Box 7.11 Examples of the use of questionnaires in research

To answer our specific research questions on the use of GAs [graphic accents], we developed a three-condition survey study that we planned to conduct via the Internet. To that end, we drew on traditional methods of questionnaire design . . . Our survey instrument contained extensive formatting to maximize clarity in the electronic environment. Each questionnaire element included (a) response scales with each item so that it would not be necessary for end users to scroll up and down if they wished to refer to the scales, (b) response boxes aligned on the left margin to minimize keystrokes, and (c) graphic rules and white space for maximum readability. We then set about pretesting the questionnaire with friends and acquaintances. To our surprise, even though these particular respondents knew us and supported our project, they were either unwilling or unable to complete the questionnaire and return it. It was clear that data collection through e-mail potentially could stall our project . . . We therefore suspected that the low response to our preliminary questionnaire might be, at least in part, the result of its length. Our instrument consisted of 42 stimulus items, which were constituted of 12,860 characters and formatted to 384 lines. This translated to 19 screens on a desktop computer.

(Witmer et al. 1999: 145–8)

In developing the questionnaire, the first requirement was to identify the potential range of specialist industry knowledge that may be of benefit to the auditor. Thus, the instrument included areas that have been noted in the literature, professional standards of prior research as being potentially important knowledge for industry specialist auditors. To ensure other important knowledge items that were not listed in the questionnaire would nonetheless be identified, participants were provided with an opportunity to add additional knowledge items to the end of each knowledge category. Based on the literature review and categorisations used in the standards, six broad knowledge categories, capturing 29 knowledge items, were constructed.

(Simnett and Wright 2005: 91)

Box 7.12 Types of survey questions

1 Quantity or information

In which year did you enrol on the part-time degree? _____

2 Category

Have you ever been, or are you now, involved almost full-time in domestic duties (i.e. as a housewife/househusband)?

Yes (currently) ☐   Yes (in the past) ☐   Never ☐

3 List or multiple choice

Do you view the money spent on your higher education as any of the following?

a luxury ☐   an investment ☐   a necessity ☐

a gamble ☐   a burden ☐   a right ☐

none of these ☐

4 Scale

How would you describe your parents' attitude to higher education at that time? Please tick one of the options below:

very positive	positive	mixed/ neutral	negative	very negative	not sure
☐	☐	☐	☐	☐	☐

5 Ranking

What do you see as the main purpose(s) of your degree study? Please rank all those relevant in order from 1 downwards:

personal development ☐   career advancement ☐

subject interest ☐   recreation ☐

fulfil ambition ☐   keeping stimulated ☐

other (please write) _____

6 Complex grid or table

How would you rank the benefits of your degree study for each of the following? Please rank each item:

for:	very positive	positive	neutral	negative	very negative	not sure
you						
your family						
your employer						
the country						
your community						
your friends						

7 Open-ended

We would like to hear from you if you have any further comments.

_____

_____

_____

Box 7.13 Hints on wording questions

- Try to avoid questions which are ambiguous or imprecise, or which assume specialist knowledge on the part of the respondent.
- Remember that questions which ask respondents to recall events or feelings that occurred long ago may be answered with a lesser degree of accuracy.
- Two or three simple questions are usually better than one very complex one.
- Try not to draft questions which presume a particular answer, or lead the respondent on, but allow for all possible responses.
- Avoid too many questions which are couched in negative terms; though in some cases, such as when you are asking a series of attitude questions, it can be useful to mix positive and negative questions.
- Remember that hypothetical questions, beyond the experience of the respondent, are likely to attract a less accurate response.
- Avoid questions which may be offensive, and couch sensitive questions in a way and in a place (e.g. at the end of the questionnaire) such that they are not likely to affect your overall response rate.
- Do not ask too many open-ended questions: they take too much time to answer properly, and too much time to analyse.
- If asking questions in a different language, have them translated from English, and then back-translated into English, to ensure accuracy of translation.

Box 7.14 Hints on questionnaire layout and presentation

- Questionnaires should be typed or printed, clearly and attractively laid out, using a type size which is legible.
- If you are administering your questionnaires by post or email, you should enclose a covering letter identifying yourself and describing the purposes of your survey, and providing a contact address or telephone number.
- If you are administering your questionnaires face to face, or over the telephone, you should introduce yourself first, give a contact address or telephone number if requested, and be prepared to answer questions about your survey.
- If the questions you are asking are at all sensitive, and this will be the case for almost any questionnaire, you should start by assuring your respondents of the confidentiality of their individual replies.
- Make sure any instructions you give on how the respondent is expected to answer the questions are clear.

- It is usually better to keep the kind of response expected – ticking, circling or writing in – constant.
- It is desirable that the length of the questionnaire is kept within reasonable limits, but at the same time it is better to space questions well so that the questionnaire does not appear cramped.
- If the questionnaire is lengthy or complicated, and you are expecting a substantial number of replies, you should think about coding the answers in advance on the questionnaire to speed up data input.
- Remember to thank your respondents at the end of the questionnaire, and to invite their further comments and questions.

Mixed methodologies

It is common for researchers to use more than one method of data collection. This is even more likely if you are carrying out your research project as part of a group, rather than on your own. As well as collectively having more resources, you and the other members of the group will probably also bring a range of skills and interests to the project, and may effectively agree to 'carve up' the work between you.

Yet even individual researchers can mix methods. Thus, your main method may, for example, be a questionnaire survey, or a set of interviews, or a series of observations, but this is likely to be complemented, at the very least, by some documentary analysis to enable you to explore the relevant research or policy literature. Most research projects in the social sciences are, therefore, in a general sense, multi-method.

There are, however, good reasons for deliberately seeking to use more than one method in the main body of your research. You may follow up a survey with some interviews, in order to get a more detailed perspective on some of the issues raised. The telling anecdote may be much more revealing and influential than almost any amount of figures. You might follow the reverse process, using interviews to identify the key issues, which you would then use to ask questions about in your survey. You might complement interviews or observations within an institution with the analysis of available documents, in order to compare written and spoken versions (or what people say they do and what they actually do).

Where two or more methods are used in this way, to try to verify the validity of the information being collected, the process is referred to as triangulation. This kind of approach should be carefully considered if your resources allow. Box 7.15 suggests eleven ways in which qualitative and quantitative research approaches may be productively combined, while Box 7.16 gives two examples of research projects where mixed methods have been applied.

Box 7.15 Eleven ways to combine qualitative and quantitative research

1 *Logic of triangulation*. The findings from one type of study can be checked against the findings deriving from the other type. For example, the results of a qualitative investigation might be checked against a quantitative study.

2 *Qualitative research facilitates quantitative research*. Qualitative research may: help to provide background information on context and subjects; act as a source of hypotheses; and aid scale construction.

3 *Quantitative research facilitates qualitative research*. Usually, this means quantitative research helping with the choice of subjects for a qualitative investigation.

4 *Quantitative and qualitative research are combined in order to provide a general picture*. Quantitative research may be employed to plug the gaps in a qualitative study that arise because, for example, the researcher cannot be in more than one place at any one time. Alternatively, it may be that not all issues are amenable solely to a quantitative investigation or solely to a qualitative one.

5 *Structure and process*. Quantitative research is especially efficient at getting at the 'structural' features of social life, while qualitative studies are usually stronger in terms of 'processual' aspects.

6 *Researchers' and subjects' perspectives*. Quantitative research is usually driven by the researcher's concerns, whereas qualitative research takes the subject's perspective as the point of departure.

7 *Problem of generality*. The addition of some quantitative evidence may help generalizability.

8 *Qualitative research may facilitate the interpretation of relationships between variables*. Quantitative research readily allows the researcher to establish relationships among variables, but is often weak when it comes to exploring the reasons for those relationships. A qualitative study can be used to help explain the factors underlying the broad relationships.

9 *Relationship between macro and micro levels*. Employing both quantitative and qualitative research may provide a means of bridging the macro–micro gulf. Quantitative research can often tap large-scale, structural features of social life, while qualitative research tends to address small-scale behavioural aspects.

10 *Stage in the research process*. Quantitative and qualitative research may be appropriate to different stages of a longitudinal study.

11 *Hybrids*. When qualitative research is conducted within a quasi-experimental (i.e. quantitative) research design.

(*Source*: Adapted from Punch 2005: 241–2)

Box 7.16 Two examples of mixed method research

In order to explore and collect data concerning facets likely to lead to teacher satisfaction or dissatisfaction in schools a focus group of seven teachers was constituted. The focus group included teachers from both the primary and secondary sectors, at varying levels of seniority within their careers, placed in an environment where they felt comfortable with self-disclosure. Teacher discussion within the focus group phase yielded forty possible facets which encompassed organizational values, organizational climate, managerial processes, teaching and learning and self-realisation . . . All forty facets . . . were included in a survey instrument created in the form of a questionnaire to be distributed to schools . . . together with an explanatory letter.

(Rhodes et al. 2004: 69)

The choice to undertake qualitative interviews in the context of a case study seemed an obvious one given our objective of listening to working people and asking about their experiences as learners. Given the enormous range of occupations and work settings in the public sector, the survey was seen as essential to provide a wider profile of the workforce. The case studies involved semi-structured interviews with corporate managers and trainers and union branch representatives. This was complemented by more intensive observation of particular departments . . . the case studies in effect became ethnographies of a number of departments or units. The survey was conducted in one local authority and one health service trust. It was a self-completion postal survey which aimed to gain a picture of the educational and competence profile of the workforce, including details of recent employment-related training and educational participation. Four departments were chosen from each organization for the survey on the basis of having a large proportion of 'unskilled' workers.

(Munro et al. 2004: 292–3)

Summary

Having read this chapter, you should:

- better understand the different ways in which the use of documents, interviews, observations and questionnaires could contribute to your research project;
- be aware of the advantages and disadvantages of these different techniques for collecting data;

- appreciate when and why it might make sense to combine qualitative and quantitative methods for data collection.

Exercises

7.1 How will, or might, you use secondary data in your research project? What are the advantages and disadvantages of doing so?

7.2 You are facilitating a focus group discussion. How do you deal with the following: (a) two members of the group begin an argument; (b) one member of the group dominates the conversation; (c) a few members of the group get up to help themselves to refreshments, and begin a conversation in a corner of the room; (d) the group runs out of steam after 15 minutes, and seems to have exhausted their thoughts on the topic; (e) one member of the group never speaks.

7.3 In a face-to-face interview, how would you ask a stranger about their age, ethnic group, marital status, sexuality, income, social class and educational level? What could you do to help ensure the accuracy of their response?

Further reading

In this section, we list a limited selection of books that are of particular relevance to the topics discussed in this chapter, together with an indication of their contents.

Angrosino, M. (2007) *Doing Ethnographic and Observational Research.* Thousand Oaks, CA: Sage.
Includes discussion of the selection of cases, observation and interviewing, recording data and ethical issues.

Arksey, H. and Knight, P. (1999) *Interviewing for Social Scientists: An introductory resource with examples.* London: Sage.
This text covers the whole process of interview-based research, from design through practice to transcription, analysis and reporting. Different approaches to interviewing, specialized contexts, and ethical issues are also given attention.

Barbour, R. (2008) *Doing Focus Groups.* London: Sage.
Offers practical advice on planning and organizing successful focus groups, their advantages and limitations, and effective methods for collecting and analysing data.

Brophy, S., Snooks, H. and Griffiths, L. (2008) *Small-Scale Evaluation in Health: A practical guide.* London: Sage.

Considers how to plan an evaluation, research governance and ethics, understanding data, interpreting findings and writing a report.

Czaya, R. and Blair, J. (2005) *Designing Surveys: A guide to decisions and procedures*, 2nd edition. London: Sage.

Written for first time researchers, this book is a guide to undertaking a survey. It includes sections on data collection, designing a questionnaire and sampling.

Fink, A. (2008) *How to Conduct Surveys: A step-by-step guide*, 4th edition. Thousand Oaks, CA: Sage.

Considers how to organize data for analysis, create reports and present them using computers, human subjects protection, and the use of the internet and email.

Fox, M., Martin, P. and Green, G. (2007) *Doing Practitioner Research*. London: Sage.

Focuses on helping practitioners conduct research in their own organizations, with attention given to the best methods for doing this effectively and sensitively.

Gillham, B. (2008) *Developing a Questionnaire*, 2nd edition. London: Continuum.

Discusses how, why and when to use questionnaires, how to analyse data and present results, and how to relate questionnaires to other forms of research.

Gillham, B. (2008) *Observation Techniques: Structured to unstructured*. London: Continuum.

Covers understanding the value of observation, setting up the observation, and using structured and unstructured techniques.

James, N. and Busher, H. (2009) *Online Interviewing*. London: Sage.

Aims to offer a short, accessible and highly practical introduction to designing and conducting online interviews in qualitative research.

Keats, D. M. (2000) *Interviewing: A practical guide for students and professionals*. Buckingham: Open University Press.

Considers the structure and process of interviews, their use in research and other settings, and the particular issues involved in interviewing children, adolescents, the aged, people with disabilities, and people from different cultural backgrounds.

King, N. and Horrocks, C. (2009) *Interviews in Qualitative Research*. London: Sage.

The philosophy and theory underlying interview methods, how to design and carry them out, group and remote interviewing, reflexivity and ethics.

Krueger, R. and Casey, M. (2009) *Focus Groups: A practical guide for applied research*, 4th edition. Thousand Oaks, CA: Sage.

Aims to cut through the theory and gives hand-on advice to those who are seeking to conduct a focus group.

Kvale, S. (2008) *Doing Interviews*. London: Sage.

Covers both the theoretical background and the practical aspects of the interview process, incorporating discussion of the wide variety of methods in interview-based research and the different approaches to reading the data.

Kvale, S. and Brinkmann, S. (2008) *InterViews: Learning the craft of qualitative research interviewing*, 2nd edition. London: Sage.
Covers narrative, discursive and conversational analyses, interviewing as a social practice, harmonious and confrontational interviews.

O Dochartaigh, N. (2002) *The Internet Research Handbook: A practical guide for students and researchers in the social sciences*. London: Sage.
Aims to set out best practice in the use of the internet as a mainstream research resource.

Prior, L. (2003) *Using Documents in Social Research*. London: Sage.
Covers the nature of documents, documents in organizational settings, making meaning of documents, and using documents as evidence.

Puchta, C. and Potter, J. (2004) *Focus Group Practice*. London: Sage.
Relates the practice of focus group moderation to underlying theory.

Rubin, H. and Rubin, I. (2004) *Qualitative Interviewing: The art of hearing data*, 2nd edition. Thousand Oaks, CA: Sage.
Considers how choice of topic influences question wording, and how the questions asked influence the findings.

Sapsford, R. (2006) *Survey Research*, 2nd edition. London: Sage.
Multivariate analysis techniques, constructing scales to measure attitudes or personality, using internet materials.

Sapsford, R. and Jupp, V. (eds) (2006) *Data Collection and Analysis*, 2nd edition. London: Sage.
An overview of issues in research design, data collection and analysis for both quantitative and qualitative approaches. The most common methods are covered, including observation, questioning, databases and documents, along with statistical and multivariate analysis, and documentary and textual analysis.

Seale, C. (1999) *The Quality of Qualitative Research*. London: Sage.
Discusses the evaluation of qualitative research, and provides guidance on the collection of good quality data and its thoughtful analysis. Chapters examine issues such as contradiction, generalization, reliability and reflexivity.

Wengraf, T. (2001) *Qualitative Research Interviewing: Biographic narrative and semi-structured methods*. London: Sage.
Organized in six parts, covering: concepts and approaches, strategies for getting the right materials, contact management, working the materials, comparison of cases, writing up.

Wilkinson, D. and Birmingham, P. (2003) *Using Research Instruments: A guide for researchers*. London: RoutledgeFalmer.
Six chapters cover questionnaires, interviews, content analysis, focus groups, observation, and the things people say and do.

8

Preparing to analyse data

Introduction • The shape of your data • The nature of data • Managing your data • Computer-based data management and analysis • The process of analysis • Summary • Exercises • Further reading

Introduction

We hope that you are reading this chapter well before you have finished collecting your research data. You are likely, after all, to begin analysing your data before you have collected it all, possibly starting as soon as you have some data to work on. Analysis is an ongoing process which may occur throughout your research, with earlier analysis informing later data collection. Research is, as we have said a number of times in this book, a messy business, and the stages and processes involved do not simply follow one after the other.

> You might like to refer back at this point to the section on **Getting a flavour of possibilities** in Chapter 1.

You would probably be best advised to look through this chapter, and the following one, before you finally decide how you are going to focus your study, and what kinds of approaches and techniques you will apply. It makes sense to have some understanding of the kinds of data analysis you might engage in, and how the kinds of data you collect will affect and limit this, before you commit yourself to a particular project.

The purpose of this chapter is to help you get your data into shape, and to discuss the process of analysing data. We start from those unsure, initial feelings, which are so common to both novice and more experienced researchers, of having an overwhelming or chaotic collection of research data. Chapter 9 then examines the techniques involved in analysing documents, interviews, observations and questionnaires.

This chapter is organized in terms of the following themes:

- **The shape of your data.** The condition which your research data are in, and the facilities you have available to analyse them.
- **The nature of data.** What research data are, the meaning of numbers and words.
- **Managing your data.** Coding, reducing and summarizing your raw data.
- **Computer-based data management and analysis.** Using software packages with quantitative and qualitative data.
- **The process of analysis.** Thinking about and planning your analysis.

Hint: If you feel traumatized or terrorized by the process of analysing the data you have collected, you might like to think of it as analogous to cooking. What and how you cook depends on your taste, skills and the resources you have available. You may like your food simple and freshly prepared, or carefully blended over a long period, or fast and processed. You may mix the ingredients together using a recipe, or based on previous experience, or you may buy a packet already prepared. You may use a range of tools in your cooking, from a simple knife or spoon through to an expensive food processor. You may be preparing food just for yourself or for a banquet. See if you can find further parallels as you cook your data!

The shape of your data

Two basic issues affecting your whole approach to data analysis are considered in this section:

- The condition of your data.
- Where, and with what facilities, you are able to analyse them.

Order or chaos?

You will probably spend a considerable amount of time collecting your research data, and – unless you are relying entirely on secondary data sources with which you are already familiar – the shape of the data collection that you end up with will almost certainly be rather different from the way you had envisaged it when you started. While your plans for data collection may have seemed very methodical, the data you have actually collected may initially appear to be anything but. They may seem more chaotic than ordered (see Box 8.1).

Box 8.1 Ordered or chaotic data?

Appearance of order	Appearance of chaos
Neat notebooks	Odd notes
Card indexes	Scraps of paper
Sorted piles of questionnaires	Baskets of cuttings
Colour-coded folders	Bulging or empty files
Labelled, transcribed tapes	Jotted down quotes
Highlighted photocopies	Half-remembered references
Clear plan and schedule	Back of an envelope
Computer database	Illegible handwriting

Whether your data appear ordered or chaotic depends in part on your preferences, and in part upon your perceptions: one person's chaos may be another's order. The real issue is what works well for you. So long as you know where to find what you want or need to find, that's OK. If you are new to the process of research, you may be finding this out as you go along. There is no single 'right' strategy for carrying out research, or for ordering and analysing data. Much of what is said in this book can be taken to indicate a preference for planning, structure and order, but these qualities may be conceived of very differently in practice.

The condition your data are in will undoubtedly change during the process of analysis. However poor, ill-organized or inadequate you may think they are at the beginning, you are likely to find strengths in them as you proceed. Similarly, even if you start from the position that you have all the data you need, you are likely to recognize deficiencies as you get into the depths of analysis.

Data analysis is about moving from chaos to order, and from order to chaos. Data which seem under control are likely to become somewhat more disorganized, at least for a while; whereas some semblance of order will be found, or imposed upon, even the most chaotic collection. Your data may, at times during the process of analysis, appear to be both messy and structured. Areas where you think that your data add to an understanding of the topic you are researching may be seen as ordered, whereas areas in which your work has raised more questions than answers (the normal pattern) may appear as more chaotic.

Where to analyse, and with what?

The resources you have available for your research, and how you might tailor your research plans to them, have already been considered elsewhere in this book.

> You might like to have another look at the sections on **Choosing a topic** in Chapter 2, and **Using computers** in Chapter 5.

Obviously, you are restricted in how, where and when you carry out your data analysis by the available resources. There are, however, practical issues concerned with the place, space and time in which you do your analysis which are worth further consideration. For example:

- Do you prefer working at a desk or in an armchair?
- Will you want to spread your work over a floor or a wall?
- Do you like to work with paper and pen (or pencil)? Or straight on to a computer screen?
- Does your analysis require extensive dedicated periods of time, or can it be done in smaller chunks? Or are there elements of both?
- Can you do your analysis in one place, or will it require visits to a number of separate facilities?

Clearly, your answers to these and related questions will help to determine how you go about analysing your data. You will need to reconcile your preferences with what is feasible, and with the nature of the data you have collected.

The nature of data

The data you have collected are likely to be in a number of forms, though it is perfectly possible to carry out interesting and valid research with just one form of data. Your data might include, for example, completed questionnaires, interview transcripts, notes on readings or observations, measurements of behaviour, internet materials, policy documents, academic articles, charts, diagrams and photographs. Some may be in digital form. Now might be a good point to take some time to remind yourself about the nature of your data, the amount you have, where they have come from and how they have been produced.

Boxes 8.2 and 8.3 include a variety of examples of different sorts of quantitative and qualitative data to remind you of some of the possibilities.

Box 8.2 Examples of quantitative data

Order	No. of responses	Factor
1	113	Higher pay
2	73	Feeling valued by stakeholders in education
3	70	Desire to help children learn
4	64	Less administration
5	59	More non-contact time for planning and preparation
6	51	More support with pupil discipline issues
7	49	A reduction in overall work load
8	48	Good working relations with managers and other staff
9	41	Good prospects of career advancement
10	35	Smaller class sizes

(*Source*: Rhodes et al. 2004: 74)

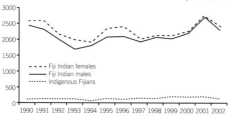

(*Source*: Chandra 2004: 185)

Profile of Returnees

Start	Finish	University	Course	College in NZ?	Scholarship	Work in NZ	PR	Twin Program
1959	1963	VUW	BA/MA (Geog)	N	Y	N	N	N
1965	1966	VUW	Accounting	N	Y	N	N	N
1963	1967	Canterbury	BE/BSc/MA (Chemical Engineering)	N	Y	N	N	N
1964	1967	Canterbury	Economics & Agriculture	N	Y	N	N	N
1961	1967	Canterbury and Otago	B.Sc & PGDip Statistics	N	Y	N	N	N
1961	1969	Canterbury	B.E./1/2 M.E.	N	Y	N	N	N
1970	1973	VUW	BA (Hons:Psychology)	N	Y	N	N	N
1974	1977	VUW	BA (History and Ed)/Hons (Ed)	N	Y	N	N	N
1988	1991	VUW	BA (Eng & Pol)/Hons (Engl Lit.)	N	N	N	N	N

(*Source*: Butcher 2004: 280)

Factor Analysis of Predictors of Identification with the Employing Organization

Predictor	Organizational attributes	Relationship with management	Relationship with colleagues	Positive distinctiveness
	Factor Loadings			
Providing opportunities to creatively solve problems	.86	.18	.12	.23
Keeping up to date with changes in IT	.82	.15	.01	.24
Providing career advancement opportunities	.81	.18	.11	.28
Doing high-quality work	.77	.28	.00	.24
Providing a work environment that is free of politics	.77	.16	.11	.01
I trust that this person will advance my best interests when decisions which affect me are made.	.27	.88	.16	.23
I have trust and confidence in that X employee regarding his/her general fairness.	.29	.88	.11	.21
I feel free to discuss the problems and difficulties in my job with that X employee.	.18	.87	.15	.18

(*Source*: Chattopadhyay 2005: 69)

Box 8.3 Examples of qualitative data

Chapter 6

1 We recommend to the Government that it should have a long term strategic aim of responding to increased demand for higher education, much of which we expect to be at sub-degree level; and that to this end, the cap on full-time undergraduate places should be lifted over the next two to three years and the cap on full-time sub-degree places should be lifted immediately.

Chapter 7

2 We recommend to the Government and the Funding Bodies that, when allocating funds for the expansion of higher education, they give priority to those institutions which can demonstrate a commitment to widening participation, and have in place a participation strategy, a mechanism for monitoring progress, and provision for review by the governing body of achievement.

(*Source*: National Committee of Inquiry into Higher Education 1997: 42)

Cris: I remember playing dress up and I got to be the princess and you had to be the prince, you were the older sister and you had to be the prince.

Kathy: I remember that; that was a lot of fun. I remember I hated the way Mom used to always make me wear pink and you always got the blue dress.

Cris: I always hated dressing up like that anyway. Regardless of what it looked like.

Kathy: It was kind of cute.

Cris: It was so uncomfortable.

(*Source*: Davis and Salkin 2005)

Principle	Explanation	Foundational citations
1 Reformation of the professor– student relationship	A feminist pedagogy offers the professor and the students new relational roles. Individuals involved in the learning experience share knowledge and thus enact the teaching role as well as acquire knowledge and thus enact the learner role (Parry 1996).	Bowker and Dunkin 1992, Bell 1993, Bright 1993, Shrewsbury 1993, Foss and Griffin 1995, Christie 1997, Scering 1997, Stanovsky 1997
2 Empowerment	To empower a student is to enact 'a participatory, democratic process in which at least some power is shared' (Shrewsbury 1993: 9). The professor can acknowledge power as evaluator and grader, while also redefining the teaching role from knowledge leader to 'activation of multiple perspectives' (Scering 1997: 66).	Bright 1993, Shrewsbury 1993, Woodbridge 1994, Chapman 1997, Scering 1997, Middlecamp and Subramaniam 1999

(*Source*: Webb et al. 2004: 425)

(*Source*: Bagnoli 2004: 11)

The qualitative/quantitative divide

Among these different kinds of data we may recognize a basic distinction between the quantitative (i.e. numbers) and the qualitative (i.e. words and everything else). This distinction has a major influence on how data may be analysed, and also reflects the varied 'traditions', philosophies and practices of different social science disciplines or sub-disciplines. You are almost certain to have examples of both types among your data, though either the qualitative or the quantitative may predominate.

> You may wish to refer back to the sections on **Which method is best?** and **Families, approaches and techniques** in Chapter 3.

However, the distinction between words and numbers is not as precise as it may appear to be at first sight. Both offer representations of what we as individuals perceive of as our 'reality'. It may be that qualitative data offer more detail about the subject under consideration, whereas quantitative data appear to provide more precision, but both give only a partial description. Neither are 'facts' in anything but a subjective sense. The accuracy of the representation is also likely to be reduced further during the research process, as we attempt to summarize or draw out key points from the vastness of the data available.

The quantitative and qualitative also have a tendency to shade into each other, such that it is rare to find reports of research which do not include both numbers and words. Qualitative data may be quantified, and quantitative data qualified. For example, it is common practice in analysing surveys to assign, sometimes arbitrarily, numerical values to qualitative data, such as, 'successful' (1), 'unsuccessful' (2).

Researchers who adopt an explicitly qualitative stance can find themselves giving prominence to numbers. Thus, if you conduct your research entirely through interviews, and analyse the results by searching for similarities and differences in the interview records, you are quite likely to end up using numbers or expressions of quantity in your writing: e.g. 'all of the interviewees', 'most of the respondents', 'half of the women I spoke to'. On the other hand, if you base your study wholly on numerical data, you will still introduce qualitative factors in your analysis, as in discussing the relative worth of different data sources, and in interpreting what your results mean for practice.

The next two subsections aim to make these points clearer. You may want to skip one or other of them if you are already familiar with quantitative or qualitative approaches.

What do numbers mean?

Exercise 8.1 asks you to examine the examples of quantitative data included in Box 8.2. Box 8.2 does not, of course, include examples of all the different kinds or uses of numbers which you might come across in the course of your research, but it does contain some of the most common. If you have carried out a survey or experiment as part of your research, you are quite likely to have produced figures not unlike some of them. These may include, for example:

- direct measurements, or what might be called 'raw' or 'real' numbers;
- categories, where responses have been coded or assigned a numerical value;
- percentages, a measure of proportion;
- averages, which summarize a series of measurements.

The second question posed in Exercise 8.1 highlights a key point about quantitative data (and data in general), namely that they might tell you a lot if you only knew how they were arrived at and how to interpret them. Every data source needs to be interrogated as to its representativeness, reliability and accuracy. Researchers ideally need to know by whom the data were produced, for what purpose and in what ways. Numbers, by their very seeming precision, can hide their manufacture, imprecision and subjectivity. These issues are considered further in the section on **Interpretation** in Chapter 9.

The third question posed in the exercise indicates that, once you are presented with a set of quantitative data, you can usually start to do other, quantitative or qualitative things, with it. You may have found yourself calculating averages, or thinking that one item was bigger or smaller than another, or of the same value. If you have sufficient information, you can calculate percentages from raw data, or produce the raw data from the percentages reported.

The quantitative data presented, whether you have produced them yourself or obtained them from a secondary source, are usually only the starting point of the analysis. In carrying out an analysis, the researcher inevitably gets further and further away from the original, or 'real', data, producing more and more highly refined abstractions. You need to be able to trace the routes taken in this process, whether they are your own or another researcher's.

What do words mean?

Exercise 8.2, in a way analogous to the previous one, asks you to examine the examples of qualitative data included in Box 8.3. As in the case of Box 8.2, Box 8.3 does not include examples of all possible forms or types of words (or other forms of representation). It is restricted to English language sources for a start. Nevertheless, we can recognize from the examples given some of the most common forms of written data, including:

- directly written words, and spoken words which have been transcribed either directly or in the form in which they were reported;
- written notes, put together during, soon after or long after the events which they purport to describe;

- carefully considered written words, intended for publication and broad circulation, and those not published and meant for a smaller and more ephemeral distribution.

Within these examples, we can recognize different levels of abstraction. Notes clearly only offer a partial summary of events, focusing on those aspects which the person making the notes felt to be most significant at the time for their own purposes (and could remember). Documents are usually released only after a process of drafting and redrafting, and may be as interesting for what they don't say as for what they do say, as well as for how they say it.

Even direct speech is selective, however: spoken only after the speaker has thought for a longer or shorter period about what they might say; and determined in part by what the speaker thinks the listener might want to hear. It also, when compared with written English, betrays the effects of improvization in its punctuation, stumblings, repetitions and pauses. Again, as with quantitative data, there is a need to interrogate the sources and to ask where the speakers or writers are coming from and why.

This brief discussion suggests that some analysis has already occurred in all of the examples given. Anything which you, as a researcher, may do to data in the course of your analysis will further refine and select from the words given. Thus, you may choose (as we have) particular quotes or phrases as significant or illustrative, and will almost certainly in the end effectively ignore the great bulk of the written texts available.

As you will probably have noted by now, this subsection and the preceding one, on the meanings of numbers and words, are very similar in format and approach. We have taken this approach for two main reasons:

- The processes involved in analysing these forms of data are broadly analogous.
- Neither form of data is intrinsically better, more accurate or 'real'; rather, each has to be assessed, analysed and used on its own merits.

Having assembled your data for analysis, the next stage is normally a managerial one. This typically involves sorting, coding, reducing or summarizing the data from its original form, and getting it into a shape better suitable to analysis and reportage. These techniques are the subject of the next section.

Managing your data

You might well find yourself, 6 months before the end of your study, with an alpine collection of information that might require a week just to read over carefully. A chronic problem of qualitative research is that it is done chiefly with words, not with numbers. Words are fatter than numbers and usually have multiple meanings . . . Numbers are usually less ambiguous and can be processed more economically. Small wonder, then, that many researchers prefer working with numbers alone or getting the words they collected translated into numbers as quickly as possible. We argue that although words may be more unwieldy than numbers, they can render more meaning than numbers alone and should be hung onto throughout data analysis.

(Miles and Huberman 1994: 56)

You will probably have collected a substantial amount of data for the purposes of your research project. But your data in their raw state do not constitute the results of your research. You would be unlikely, for example, to simply bind together transcripts of all the interviews you have undertaken, or of all the questionnaires you have had returned, or of all the notes you have taken, and present that as your report or dissertation. That would be too long and too demanding for your readers, and it would lack insight and significance. The business of analysing the data you have collected, therefore, really involves two closely related processes:

- Managing your data, by reducing its size and scope, so that you can report upon it adequately and usefully.
- Analysing your managed set of data, by abtracting from it and drawing attention to what you feel is of particular importance or significance.

The first of these processes is considered in this section and the next one; the second process in the following chapter, Chapter 9. Each process is essential to research.

Hint: Some of the tasks involved in analysing data are very basic and repetitive. Save these for when you are unable to do, or do not feel like doing, anything more demanding.

You may choose to manage your data in a whole series of related ways. Some of these you will already be familiar with, whether you realize it or not. Thus, the techniques described in Chapter 4, **Reading for research**, are all about management, and are used by many social science researchers. Those described in Box 8.4 are analogous, and also overlap to a considerable extent. You will probably use all of them in your own analysis.

All of the techniques outlined in Box 8.4 – coding, annotating, labelling, selection, summary – may be applied to a range of types of data, both qualitative and quantitative. All of them also result, though perhaps not initially, in a reduction in the quantity of the data which you have available for analysis.

Box 8.4 Techniques for managing data

Coding. The process by which items or groups of data are assigned codes. These may be used to simplify and standardize the data for analytical purposes, as when characteristics like sex, marital status or occupation are replaced by numbers (e.g. replacing 'male' by '1', 'female' by '2'). Or the process may involve some reduction in the quantity of the data, as when ages, locations or attitudes are categorized into a limited number of groups, with each group then assigned its own numerical identity (e.g. categorizing ages as 'under 21', '21–64' and '65 and over', and then replacing these by '1', '2' and '3' respectively).

Annotating. The process by which written (or perhaps audio or visual) material is altered by the addition of notes or comments. On books or papers, annotations may take the forms of marginal notes, or (if you own the text or copy) underlining or highlighting the text itself. The process may draw attention to what you consider to be the more significant sections, perhaps for later abstraction and quotation. Or it may serve as part of your continuing debate with your texts, a means to refine and progress your ideas further.

Labelling. Where you have an analytical scheme in mind, or are developing one, you may go through materials such as interviews or policy documents and label passages or statements with significant words (e.g. 'mother', 'conservative', 'career break', 'introvert'). These labels can then serve to direct your further analysis. A fine distinction might be drawn between the related processes of labelling and annotation, in that labelling smacks of stereotyping, of having your ideas or prejudices worked out in advance, whereas annotating seems more open or flexible.

Selection. A key process in the management of data, through which interesting, significant, unusual or representative items are chosen to illustrate your arguments. This may take the form, for example, of one member of a group, one institution, one answer to a survey, one particular quotation, one text, or a number of such selections. The point is that you are choosing, for a variety of reasons, which examples of your data collection to emphasize and discuss. There is always a good deal of subjectivity involved in such a process.

Summary. The process where, rather than choose one or more examples from a larger body of data, you opt to produce a reduced version, precis or synopsis of the whole data set. This would probably aim to retain something of the variability of the original data collected, while saying something about the generality and/or typical cases.

Note: All of these techniques may be carried out, for qualitative or quantitative data, using available software as well as manually (see Box 8.5). The names given here to the techniques are often used in interchangeable ways.

This is essential if you are going to be able to carry out a manageable analysis. All are subjective to a greater or lesser degree, and all involve the loss of some information. Given the same data set, different researchers would proceed with its management in somewhat different ways, leading to different forms of analysis and different results. That is why, if you are involved in a group research project, it can be relatively easy for each person to submit a different report.

Computer-based data management and analysis

It may be that your research project is sufficiently small-scale for you not to need to use sophisticated, computer-based software packages to manage and analyse your data. Or you may have made a conscious choice not to use them: much analysis can, after all, be done manually, and you may prefer to do yours in this way. However, even if you have collected a relatively modest amount of data – say, a few dozen questionnaires, or half a dozen interviews, or the records of twenty observations – there is still much to be said for computer-based analysis. Once your data have been input into the computer, computer-based analysis is much quicker and more accurate than anything you might do manually. If you're not sure, Box 8.5 may help you to make up your mind.

If, then, you are considering using a software package to help you manage and analyse your data, you will find it worthwhile to explore the various possibilities before committing yourself. The sooner you start doing this, the better.

> **Hint:** Doing a research project provides you with a splendid opportunity to learn about what some of these software packages can do. It is much more difficult to learn about them in the abstract, without any real data or any real purpose for analysing them.

Software packages designed to carry out quantitative analysis are much better established than those for qualitative analysis. The most widely available quantitative package in university social science departments is probably SPSS (Statistical Package for Social Sciences). There are, however, other common quantitative data analysis packages, such as Minitab; while many spreadsheet and database packages also support the simpler forms of quantitative analysis.

SPSS enables you to input raw data, to modify and reorganize them once they have been input, and to carry out a wide range of simple, statistical and multivariate analyses. These range from listing the frequencies of different responses and calculating means, through cross-tabulation, correlation and regression analyses, analyses of variance and covariance, to cluster and factor

---

Box 8.5 Is it worth putting it on a computer?

	Pro	Con
General	Speed of processing data Enables flexible handling of large quantities of data Your data is held in a form which enables you to return repeatedly to find things, and to try out different ideas May impress people	Requires access to expensive technology Can exclude others from the analysis process May require time to learn to use program You will usually need some human help to get started with a new program You will know the data less well than if you analyse it by hand May create an illusion of accuracy!
Quantitative analysis	Ability to return to calculations and re-calculate easily if changes are made Can draw graphs directly from the data Better control for human error, though you still have to get the data entry right	If you lack experience, it can lead to feeling you have 'lost control'
Qualitative analysis	Enables handling of large quantities of qualitative data Easy to re-code data when you change the categories you want to use, encouraging a flexible approach	Requires a lot of text to be typed into the computer

(*Source*: Laws et al. 2003: 380)

---

analysis. In the UK, the Economic and Social Research Council (ESRC) has a website (http://tramss.data-archive.ac.uk), which offers online training for those interested in statistical data analysis.

See also the section in Chapter 9 on **Analysing questionnaires**.

If your data are primarily qualitative, the choice of a software package to manage and analyse them may not seem so straightforward. Box 8.6 outlines some of the questions to bear in mind. Another ESRC website, CAQDAS (http://caqdas.soc.surrey.ac.uk) provides a key site for information and knowledge about the software (e.g. ATLAS.ti, NVivo) that is being developed to facilitate qualitative data analysis, with links to software developers and demonstrations. CAQDAS also provides transcription guidelines.

Box 8.6 Issues to consider when choosing data management packages for qualitative research

---

- What kind(s) and amount of data do you have, and how do you want to handle it?
- What is your preferred style of working?
- Do you primarily want better access to your data and good note/memo making tools?
- What is your theoretical approach to analysis and how well developed is it at the outset?
- Do you have a well defined methodology?
- Do you want a simple to use software which will mainly help you manage *your* thinking and *thematic* coding?
- Are you more concerned with the *language*, the terminology used in the data, the comparison and occurrence of words and phrases across cases or between different variables?
- Do you want both thematic and quantitative content information from the data?
- Do you want a multiplicity of tools (not quite so simple) enabling many ways of handling and interrogating data?
- How much time do you have to 'learn' the software?
- How much analysis time has been built into the project?
- Are you working individually on the project or as part of a team?
- Is this just one phase of a larger project – do you already have quantitative data?
- Is there a package – and peer support – already available at your institution or place of work?

(*Source*: Lewins and Silver 2009: 6–7)

The process of analysis

Analysis can be a fearful word for the novice small-scale researcher. You will probably have started your research project with some preconceptions of what you would find. You have now collected a great deal of data on your topic, and have got them into a shape for analysis. But how do you get from the vast array of words and numbers that you have collected or produced to a seemingly neat set of conclusions or recommendations? What is this process called analysis? Exercise 8.3 asks you to think about its nature and meaning.

In doing Exercise 8.3, did you refer to terms like concept, explanation, theory and understanding? These, together with synonymous and related terms, are at the heart of the process of analysis. Put simply:

- *Concepts* are abstract or general ideas, which are important to how we think about particular subjects or issues.
- *Theories* are suppositions which explain, or seek to explain something.
- *Explanations* are statements which seek to make something intelligible, about why things are the way they are.
- *Understanding* is our perception of the meaning of something, in this case the subject area, the issues and/or the research questions under consideration.

Analysis is about the search for explanation and understanding, in the course of which concepts and theories will likely be advanced, considered and developed. You will find a great deal, and much more detailed, discussion of these and related ideas in some of the books listed in the **Further reading** section at the end of this chapter.

> **Remember**: Analysis is meant to be a rigorous process, using data that have been carefully produced and managed. In the end, however, what you produce from them is your own 'document', an attempt to persuade your readers of your own interpretation.

Summary

Having read this chapter, you should:

- have an appreciation of the different forms of data, and the kinds of analysis appropriate to them;
- be aware of the interleaving processes of data management, analysis and interpretation which are involved in making sense of your data collection.

Exercises

8.1 Box 8.2 contains some examples of quantitative data. What kinds of numbers are included? How do you think they were collected or produced? What might you do with or say about these numbers?

8.2 Box 8.3 contains some examples of qualitative data. What kinds of words are included? How do you think they were collected or produced? What might you do with or say about these words?

8.3   What do you understand by the term 'analysis'? Try to write an explanatory definition in your own words. You probably won't find it very helpful to turn to a dictionary, as these tend to give only brief definitions and do not have a research focus.

Further reading

In this section, we list a selection of books that are of particular relevance to the topics discussed in this chapter, together with an indication of their contents.

Bazeley, P. and Richards, L. (2000) *The NVivo Qualitative Project Book*. London: Sage.
How to use qualitative data analysis software. Includes demonstration software on a CD-ROM.

Coxon, A. P. M. (1999) *Sorting Data: Collection and analysis*. Thousand Oaks, CA: Sage.
Part of an extensive series of short books on 'quantitative applications in the social sciences'. Includes chapters on the collection, description and comparison, and analysis of free sorting data.

Gahan, C. and Hannibal, M. (1998) *Doing Qualitative Research Using QSR NUD*IST*. London: Sage.
A practical guide to using the NUD*IST package for the analysis of unstructured data such as text from interviews, historical or legal documents, or non-textual material such as videotapes.

Gibbs, G. (2002) *Qualitative Data Analysis: Explorations with NVivo*. Buckingham: Open University Press.
Chapters cover data preparation, coding, memos and attributes, searching for text, developing an analytic scheme, visualizing the data and communicating.

Gorard, S. (2006) *Using Everyday Numbers Effectively in Research*. London: Continuum.
This book illustrates how numbers can be used routinely and successfully for research purposes, without engaging with complex statistics.

Lewins, A. and Silver, C. (2007) *Using Software in Qualitative Research: A step-by-step guide*. London: Sage.
The authors work on the Computer Assisted Qualitative Data Analysis (CAQDAS) project at the University of Surrey. This book aims to help the reader to choose the most appropriate package for their specific needs and to get the most out of the software once they are using it.

Richards, L. (2009) *Handling Qualitative Data: A practical guide*, 2nd edition. London: Sage.

Covers the processes of making, meeting, sorting, coding, documenting and exploring qualitative data, and smoothly integrating software use, and discusses the main challenges that readers are likely to encounter.

Vaus, D. de (2002) *Analyzing Social Science Data: Fifty key problems in data analysis*. London: Sage.

A substantial text organized in seven parts: data preparation, variable preparation, data reduction, generalization, single-variable analysis, two-variable analysis, multivariate analysis.

9

Analysing your data

Introduction

Chapter 8 should have got you thinking about the kind of data you have collected, and what you might do with it. This chapter focuses on the nitty gritty business of analysing your data. This can seem to be the most difficult part of research: after all, once you've got started and got a framework for your research, reading about it and collecting data can become fairly repetitive activities. But, now, what do you do with all of this data that you have carefully collected, saved and sorted?

That is what we look at in this chapter. By the time you have finished it, and sorted out the analysis of your data, we aim to have got you to a position where you can begin to write up your results and conclusions.

The chapter is organized in terms of the following themes:

- **Analytical strategies**. How you work with your data.
- **Analysing documents**. How to make sense of your notes.
- **Analysing interviews**. How to make sense of your transcripts.
- **Analysing observations**. How to make sense of your records.
- **Analysing questionnaires**. How to make sense of your replies.
- **Interpretation**. How to understand and contextualize the results of your analyses.

Analytical strategies

As the discussion in the previous chapter should have made clear, the process(es) of analysis – whether for qualitative data, quantitative data, or a mixture of the two – are, at a generic level, fairly similar. Through techniques such as coding, annotating, labelling, selection and summary, the researcher manipulates and substantially reduces the size of the data set, drawing particular attention to pieces or aspects of data (i.e. findings) that are felt to be of 'significance'.

The strategies which underlie these processes, however, may seem to be quite different, depending upon the view you take on how knowledge is generated. The most common distinction made here is that between those researchers who take a positivist or post-positivist approach, and those who adopt an interpretivist, critical or even postmodern stance (see the discussion in Chapter 3, and particularly Box 3.1). The former are likely to start their research with an idea, or hypothesis, and then collect data in order to explore or test this. This is the classic scientific, or hypothetico-deductive, method. The latter, by contrast, are more likely to start from an interest in a particular topic, and gather data to see what light it sheds on the topic. This is a more inductive strategy, as practised by researchers who apply the precepts of grounded theory or other forms of thematic analysis. While the former strategy may be seen as starting from a theory (which may then be revised), the latter will, at least hopefully, lead to the development of theory.

As with most distinctions in the social sciences, however, this dichotomy is not as clear cut as it might seem. It is difficult to imagine any researcher starting a project without any idea of what they might find (or, at least, what they might like to find): we all have preconceptions. Research rarely moves seamlessly from a clear set of hypotheses or research questions to a set of answers; more typically, the questions are later adjusted to fit the answers you have come up with. And all researchers are, or should be, concerned, at least to some extent, with issues of significance, generalizability, reliability and validity (see the discussion in this chapter on **Interpretation**, particularly Box 9.13).

So, again, we would encourage you to resist too easy a division of research into qualitative or quantitative, deductive or inductive, positivist or interpretivist. And we would emphasize that each of the four key techniques for data collection that we have identified – documents, interviews, observations and questionnaires – may be used from either or both of these perspectives.

Analysing documents

> Documents . . . do not simply reflect, but also construct social reality and versions of events. The search for documents' 'meaning' continues, but with researchers also exercising 'suspicion'. It is not then assumed that documents are neutral artefacts which independently report social reality, or that analysis must be rooted in that nebulous concept, common-sense reasoning. Documents are now viewed as media through which social power is expressed. They are approached in terms of the cultural context in which they were written and may be viewed 'as attempts at persuasion'.
>
> (May 2001: 183)

As we have already indicated, documentary analysis is akin to the processes gone through in reading for research purposes.

See Chapter 4, especially the section on **Good enough reading** and Box 4.9; the section in Chapter 7 on **Documents**; and Chapter 10, particularly the section on **How to criticize**.

Documentary analysis involves the careful consideration of a range of related questions. These have been summarized in Box 9.1. Some examples of the process of analysing documents are given in Box 9.2.

Box 9.1 Issues in documentary analysis

For each document you are analysing, ask yourself:

- Who is the author?
- What is their position?
- What are their biases?
- Where and when was the document produced?
- Why was the document produced?
- How was it produced? Who for?
- In what context was the document produced?
- What are its underlying assumptions?
- What does the document say, and not say?
- How is the argument presented?
- How well supported and convincing is its argument?
- How does this document relate to previous ones?
- How does this document relate to later ones?
- What do other sources have to say about it?

Box 9.2 Examples of documentary analysis

The original analysis of Summerland [the fire at the Summerland Leisure Centre in the Isle of Man] was based upon data drawn entirely from the official public inquiry into the incident . . . I worked paragraph by paragraph through this report, as I did for all of the accident reports published between 1965 and 1975. I asked, for each paragraph, what names or 'labels for ideas' I needed to identify those elements, events or notions which were of interest to me in my broad and initially very unfocused concern to develop a theory of disaster preconditions. I then recorded each name or concept label on the top of a 5″ by 8″ file card, together with a note of the source paragraph, and added further paragraph references to the card as I encountered additional instances of the concept identified. Eventually for my whole study I ended up with 182 of these cards, which had to be sifted, sorted and juggled into a coherent theoretical model. I produced general definitions for each of the categories which recurred, looking for causal and other links and moved gradually towards a theoretical pattern which helped to explain the range of data which I had about accidents.

(Turner 1994: 198)

Tight (2003) studied 406 articles published in 17 specialist higher education journals in the year 2000, and 284 books that were in print in that year, restricting his sample to non-North American sources and to English-language publications. These materials were analysed in terms of the themes or issues they addressed (eight key themes were identified), the methods and/or methodologies they employed (again eight categories), the levels on which they focused (seven categories), and the characteristics of their authors.

Two key points come out of the list of issues in Box 9.1 and the examples given in Box 9.2:

- Documents, whatever their nature (statistics or words, official or unofficial, public or private), cannot be taken at face value. They are artificial and partial accounts, which need to be critically assessed for research purposes.
- Much of the significance and interest in documents is revealed when they are considered in relation to each other. We develop our understanding of the ideas, issues and policies with which documents deal through a comparative analysis.

If you doubt these points, try Exercise 9.1.

Documentary analysis proceeds by abstracting from each document those elements which we consider to be important or relevant, and by grouping together these findings, or setting them alongside others which we believe to be related. What you see or read in documents will be a product of your viewpoint, discipline or focus.

Like social research in general, documentary analysis may proceed by quantitative or qualitative means, or a combination of both. A common quantitative approach is content analysis, which is outlined in Box 9.3. An alternative, qualitative strategy, discourse analysis – commonly also used for the analysis of conversations and interviews – is outlined in the next section in Box 9.5.

Box 9.3 Content analysis

[C]ontent analysis . . . comprises three stages: stating the research problem, retrieving the text and employing sampling methods and interpretation and analysis. This focus considers the frequency with which certain words or particular phrases occur in the text as a means of identifying its characteristics . . . Words or phrases in the document are transformed into numbers. The number of times in which a word occurs in the text is taken as an indicator of its significance . . .

In considering the problems of a quantitative count . . . [five issues are raised]. First, this method considers product and says little of process . . . Second, an empiricist problem is raised for it deals only with information which can be measured and standardized and for this reason considers only data which can be simplified into categories. Third, in this pre-occupation, it reproduces the meanings used by authors in the first instance, as opposed to subjecting them to critical analysis . . . Fourth, from an ethnomethodological perspective, it fails to understand the common-sense context of their production and interpretation as part of the methods by which people make sense of their social world. Fifth, it assumes that the audiences who receive the methods must translate it as the analyst does. By default, it therefore negates the idea that a text is open to a number of possible readings.

(May 2001: 191–2)

Analysing interviews

Working with a long transcript – on average of 60 pages – and various pages of field notes is not an easy task . . . In addition to the volume of data produced, focus group transcripts have multiple meanings and several different interpretations. Moreover, researchers have different assumptions and principles of analysis – about systematicity, verification, accessibility and so on. It is therefore important that the analysis is as

focused as possible: key or primary questions are of the utmost importance for analysis, some questions do not deserve analysis at the same
level, while others may be eliminated, as they simply set the background
for discussion.

(Litosseliti 2003: 91)

Three examples of the process of analysing interviews are given in Box 9.4.
These examples usefully illustrate both some of the different approaches possible, and some of the commonalities, in the analysis of interview data.

Box 9.4 Examples of interview analysis

Explicitation of the data

This explicitation process has five 'steps' or phases, which are:

1 Bracketing and phenomenological reduction.
2 Delineating units of meaning.
3 Clustering of units of meaning to form themes.
4 Summarizing each interview, validating and where necessary modifying it.
5 Extracting general and unique themes from all the interviews and making
a composite summary.

(Groenewald 2004)

Thematic analysis

1 *Familiarizing yourself with your data*. Transcribing data (if necessary),
reading and re-reading the data, noting down initial ideas.
2 *Generating initial codes*. Coding interesting features of the data in a systematic fashion across the entire data set, collating data relevant to each
code.
3 *Searching for themes*. Collating codes into potential themes, gathering all
data relevant to each potential theme.
4 *Reviewing themes*. Checking if the themes work in relation to the coded
extracts (Level 1) and the entire data set (Level 2), generating a thematic
'map' of the analysis.
5 *Defining and naming themes*. Ongoing analysis to refine the specifics of
each theme, and the overall story the analysis tells, generating clear definitions and names for each theme.
6 *Producing the report*. The final opportunity for analysis. Selection of vivid,
compelling extract examples, final analysis of selected extracts, relating
back of the analysis to the research question and literature, producing a
scholarly report of the analysis.

(Braun and Clarke 2006: 87)

An orderly person spreads out her interview records in the garden

Hester was working on the records of the interviews she had carried out with a sample of students. Each record contained her typed-up shorthand notes made during the interview, and a summary of the student's background. Each consisted of several pages, including direct quotations. She first went through the interview notes, analysing them 'question by question'. This meant having all of the records spread out at once. She wanted her analysis to be both 'professional' and 'scientific', without losing the personal touch. She preferred an orderly approach: 'I tried breaking up all of the scripts, question by question. I sat with the scripts and got out my pad, and went through each script and each question and noted down the similarities and dissimilarities. First of all I looked for common themes, and then I went through each script again noting which themes had come up'.

The first two of these examples involve more experienced researchers. The first applied an established methodology developed within the phenomenological tradition, explicitation, organized in five stages. This could be carried out by individual researchers, alone, comparatively or together. The second, developed by qualitative psychologists, sets out a particular strategy towards thematic analysis. Like most methods of qualitative data analysis, both explicitation and thematic analysis work by steadily extracting from the data collected a series of themes.

The third example in Box 9.4 involved a novice researcher who was not consciously following any particular approach to the analysis of the data she had collected. Nevertheless, the account of her analysis shows strong similarities to the other examples (if you would like to tease out these similarities and differences further, try Exercise 9.2). The examination of interview transcripts question by question, and the comparison of the answers to specific questions given by a range of interviewees, is also analogous to the general approach to documentary analysis outlined in the previous section.

There are, of course, other approaches to the analysis of interviews. You may not produce a transcript, but analyse the recordings direct. You may not have recorded the interviews, but be working from your notes. You may input your data to a computer and use a software programme for analysis (see the section in Chapter 8 on **Computer-based data management and analysis**). You might use a particular strategy for your analysis, such as explicitation, thematic analysis or critical discourse analysis (see Box 9.5 – discourse analysis might also be employed in analysing documents). The process of looking for significant statements, and comparing what was said in different interviews, will, however, be similar.

Box 9.5 Critical discourse analysis

- Views a prevailing social order as historically situated and therefore relative, socially constructed and changeable.
- Views a prevailing social order and social processes as constituted and sustained less by the will of individuals than by the pervasiveness of particular constructions or versions of reality – often referred to as discourses.
- Views discourse as coloured by and productive of ideology.
- Views power in society not so much as imposed on individual subjects as an inevitable *effect* of a way particular discursive configurations or arrangements privilege the status and positions of some people over others.
- Views human subjectivity as at least in part constructed or inscribed by discourse, and discourse as manifested in the various ways people *are* and *enact* the sorts of people they are.
- Views reality as textually and intertextually mediated via verbal and non-verbal language systems, and texts as sites for both the inculcation and the contestation of discourses.
- Views the systematic analysis and interpretation of texts as potentially revelatory of ways in which discourses consolidate power and colonize human subjects through often covert position calls.

(*Source*: Locke 2004: 1–2)

Analysing observations

A small sales and marketing team from a shoe manufacturing company was sent on a tour of the Pacific region to assess market potential. The marketing manager received two early reports. One read: 'The majority of the population are not wearing shoes: excellent marketing opportunity!' The other read: 'Most of the people do not wear shoes: poor marketing opportunity.'

As this (apocryphal) anecdote suggests, it is possible for two people to analyse the same observation data and come to very different, indeed diametrically opposed, conclusions. It is also possible, as the examples of observational studies given in Box 9.6 and in Chapter 7 indicate, to focus on either a more quantitative or a more qualitative form of analysis.

You might like to refer back to Box 7.9 at this point.

A number of key points may be made about the analysis of observations in social science research:

- Quantified forms of observation lend themselves to fairly routinized forms

---

Box 9.6 Examples of observation analysis

The first stage of analysis involved transcribing and importing each episode of observation into the QSR NUD*IST program. The transcriptions were read and re-read to form impressions of emerging themes and categories. A set of analytic categories were identified: inverted comma criticism, direct criticism and indirect criticism. In the second stage, data were quantified by counting instances which showed palliative care nurses doing criticism of other professionals who worked outside their organizations, for example, GPs [general practitioners] and hospital doctors. Key phrases spoken by palliative care nurses were identified. The number of times when collective pronouns 'they' or 'them' appeared in talk were counted and the number of times hospital doctors or general practitioners occurred in the nurses' talk was also counted. The constant comparative method helped to reveal systematic differences or similarities in doing criticism in each of the three palliative care settings. It also helped to identify how palliative care nurses constituted their own, their patients and other professionals' moral character. Application of the tools of CA [conversation analysis] helped to deepen analysis so as to reveal and make visible participants' local activities in palliative care nurses' talk.

(Li 2005: 1953)

[D]ata were obtained from 7 months of participant observation conducted in a university-affiliated government hospital in Tel Aviv where alternative practitioners were working with hospitalized patients. Observations were supplemented by informal interviews with biomedical and alternative practitioners working together in the hospital.

(Mizrachi and Shuval 2005: 1652)

---

of data collection and analysis, which can be very powerful in getting across particular issues in tabular or diagrammatic form.

• The collection and analysis of observation data, as with that of other research techniques, occur as much in parallel as in sequence.
• Observation, again like other research techniques, is very often used in conjunction with other methods, both to contextualize and to extend the analysis being carried out.

The studies briefly reported in Box 9.6 make clear one further point about the analysis of observation data, namely that it is selective. This is, however, true of all social research. While this may seem more or less obvious in any particular example, and indeed may be made manifest by the researchers concerned, these characteristics are present in other research projects as well. Being selective and, indeed, partisan is inevitable in research, and it is healthy to recognize and discuss this within your project report or dissertation.

Analysing questionnaires

Some examples of the process of analysing questionnaires are given in Box 9.7.

Box 9.7 Examples of questionnaire analysis

Research on livelihoods and land use patterns in southern Belize used semi-structured questionnaires to generate qualitative and quantitative data from about 100 respondents in three villages. The data was analysed by hand because the team had no computer, and also both members of the research team could do the work together. Tables were drawn up on paper to contain the answers to each question. All the data was then entered onto these sheets and added up accordingly. Questions included, for example, enquiries about problems faced in agricultural production, producing a range of answers around: limited markets for specific products, lack of credit, and limited access to land in some places.

(Laws et al. 2003: 381)

A sample of 7318 rating forms from the Universidad del Pais Vasco (UPV) . . . and another sample of 90,905 rating forms from the Universidad Autonoma de Madrid (UAM) were analysed. In both cases, students filled out a rating form [questionnaire] for each teacher from whom they received classes . . . Both questionnaires shared a focus on teacher performance in lecturing . . . The rating form applied at the UPV included 50 items. Sixteen items were dropped for these analyses, because they reflect the dimensions of fulfilment of teachers' formal duties and exercises, as well as those items with a non-response rate higher than 10%. The overall rating items were also dropped from the analyses, as we considered that they would favour unidimensional solutions . . . Applying the same criteria, we analysed 13 of the 17 items in the UAM rating form . . . The statistical analysis was carried out by means of the structural equations model (confirmatory factor analysis, CFA) of the AMOS software and of similarity structure analysis (SSA) non-parametric multidimensional scaling.

(Apodaca and Grad 2005: 733–4)

The data collected by questionnaires may, of course, be either qualitative or quantitative. Alternative strategies for analysing qualitative data have been suggested and discussed in the preceding sections. Questionnaires do, however, lend themselves more to quantitative forms of analysis. This is partly because they are designed to collect mainly discrete items of information, either numbers or words which can be coded and represented as numbers. This emphasis is also partly due to the larger scale of many questionnaire surveys, and their common focus on representation, which encourages a numerical or quasi-numerical summary of the results.

The discussion in this section focuses, therefore, on quantitative forms of analysis. This necessarily calls for some consideration of statistics, which is a term that some readers may find very offputting or threatening. Quantitative analysis may be used, however, at a number of levels, and the simplest of these may be the most useful in your case (see Box 9.8).

Box 9.8 Levels of quantitative analysis

Descriptive statistics

Variable frequencies, averages, ranges

Inferential statistics

Assessing the significance of your data and results

Simple interrelationships

Cross-tabulation or correlation between two variables

Multivariate analysis

Studying the linkages between more than two variables

Many small-scale research studies which use questionnaires as a form of data collection will not need to go beyond the use of descriptive statistics and the exploration of the interrelationships between pairs of variables (using, for example, cross-tabulations). It will be adequate to say that so many respondents (either the number or the proportion of the total) answered given questions in a certain way; and that the answers given to particular questions appear to be related. Such an analysis will make wide use of proportions and percentages, and of the various measures of central tendency ('averages') and of dispersion ('ranges') (see Box 9.9).

Box 9.9 Descriptive statistics

For nominal or ordinal data

- Proportions
- Percentages
- Ratios

For interval or ratio data

Measures of central tendency:

- Mean: total sum of values divided by the number of cases
- Median: the value of the middle case
- Mode: the most frequently occurring value

Measures of dispersion:

- Range: the difference between the highest and lowest values
- Standard deviation: the square root of the mean of the squared deviations from the mean

---

You may, however, wish or need to go beyond this level of analysis, and make use of inferential statistics or multivariate methods of analysis. There are dozens of inferential statistics available: three commonly used examples are outlined in Box 9.10. The functions of these statistics vary, but they are typically used to compare the measurements you have collected from your sample for a particular variable with another sample or a population, in order that a judgement may be made on how similar or dissimilar they are. It is important to note that all of these inferential statistics make certain assumptions both about the nature of your data (see Box 9.11) and about how they were collected, and should not be used if these assumptions do not hold.

Multivariate methods of analysis may be used to explore the interrelationships among three or more variables simultaneously. Commonly used examples of these are outlined in Box 9.12. While you do not need to have an extensive mathematical knowledge to apply these techniques, as they are all available as part of computer software packages, you should at least have an understanding of their principles and purposes.

See also the section in Chapter 8 on **Computer-based data management and analysis**.

Box 9.10 Examples of inferential statistics

Chi-square

Function: to compare sets of values
Assumptions: random sampling, nominal data

Kolmogorov–Smirnov

Function: to compare two samples
Assumptions: random sampling, ordinal data

Student's *t*-test

Function: (a) single-sample test of mean; (b) two-sample test of means
Assumptions: random sampling, interval data, normal distribution

Box 9.11 Types of quantitative data

Nominal

Numerical values are assigned to categories as codes. For example, in coding a questionnaire for computer analysis, the response 'male' might be coded as 1, and 'female' as 2. No mathematical operations can be performed on the resulting codes. No ordering is implied.

Ordinal

Numerical values are assigned in accordance with a qualitative scale. For example, in coding a questionnaire, the responses 'very satisfactory', 'satisfactory', 'neither satisfactory nor unsatisfactory', 'unsatisfactory' and 'very unsatisfactory' are coded 5, 4, 3, 2 and 1 respectively. The ordering of the responses is retained in the coding.

Interval

Measurements are made on a quantitative scale, in which the differences between points are consistently of the same size but the base point is arbitrary. For example, dates. The year AD 2000 occurs 1500 years after the year AD 500. The ordering of, and distance between, values is given. Addition and subtraction can be used, but not multiplication or division.

Ratio

Measurements are made on a quantitative scale, in which the differences between points are consistently of the same size and there is a 'true zero'. For example, people's ages, countries' populations. All basic mathematical operations – addition, subtraction, multiplication and division – may be applied.

Box 9.12 Commonly used multivariate analysis techniques

Correlation analysis

Measures the degree and direction of relationships between variables.

Regression analysis

Fits a model to a data set, enabling the prediction of the value of one (dependent) variable in terms of one or more other (independent) variables.

Analysis of variance (ANOVA)

Measures how independent variables interact with each other and impact upon the dependent variable. *Multivariate analysis of variance (MANOVA)* is used where there is more than one dependent variable.

Cluster analysis

Groups cases together into clusters on the basis of their similarity in terms of the variables measured.

Factor analysis

Reduces a large number of variables to a limited number of factors, so that the underlying relationships within the data may be more easily assessed.

Discriminant analysis

Enables discrimination between groups on the basis of predictive variables.

One key point to be aware of when carrying out quantitative analyses is the question of causality. One of the purposes of analysis, we have argued, is to seek explanation and understanding. We would like to be able to say that something is so because of something else. However, just because two variables of which you have measurements appear to be related, this does not mean that they are. Statistical associations between two variables may be a matter of chance, or due to the effect of some third variable. In order to demonstrate causality, you also have to find, or at least suggest, a mechanism linking the variables together.

Interpretation

> After presenting a lecture on the book's findings, I was approached by a member of the public who quietly and authoritatively explained:
> 'It's all bollocks, no offence mind, but it's bollocks. You make us all like fucking wallies, they must be them dopey ones who fuck up everything, but us no. Like me, I'm a face, East End face. I own two houses. I'm her landlord, yeah, the student she pays me rent. I could pull up £250k if I had to. I'm a face. No offence, but all these people in this book they must be fucking backward. I know a good champagne, Bollinger I always drink. I'm not the only one, there's lots like me, all my mates we're all like it, all got a few bob. The Pakis they come in, all this about capitalism and the docks, we moved out 'cos the Pakis. That's why we all vote for Maggie, fucking Labour won't let you buy your Council house. We got money all of us.'
> D.H.: 'Have you read the final section in the chapter on entrepreneurship?'
> 'No, I just had a look at some of her notes, all these silly fucking stories so I thought I'd come and front you with it.'
>
> (Hobbs 1993: 60–1)

Interpretation is the process by which you put your own meaning on the data you have collected and analysed, and compare that meaning with those advanced by others.

Your own perspective

We have emphasized at a number of places in this book how important it is to recognize, and make explicit, your own role and position within your research. This is partly about asserting ownership, and partly about recognizing the possible limitations, influences and biases of your own perspective. A critical element of the data analysis process is arriving at your own assessment of what the results mean, and how these relate to other relevant research and writing in your subject area. What do you think is significant? What do you think this suggests? Where and how do you think this kind of study might be developed further? These are the kinds of questions you should be asking yourself, and doing so, at least initially, without any direct reference to other authorities.

> **Hint**: Try explaining your research to a non-specialist again. See the section on **Focusing** in Chapter 2.

Distancing yourself from your data sources

At the same time as recognizing and asserting your own perspective on your data and its analysis, it is important to not get too embedded and bound up in this view. Researchers generally have a commitment to their projects, their methods, their data and their interpretations. It is healthy, therefore, to stand back for a time and attempt to view your research from the more dispassionate perspective of an outsider. Of course, it is impossible to do this in any absolute sense, given the personal commitment which any researcher makes to their research. But it is possible to achieve some distance, although the ways in which you might do this will probably vary. Possible strategies include:

- The management of your data, through the processes of coding, annotating, labelling and so on, as discussed earlier in Chapter 8, can reduce its immediacy and make it appear as if it has been put together by somebody else.
- Taking some time out, perhaps a week or two, before you come back to your analysis can increase the strangeness or foreign-ness of your data, and lead to a livelier interpretation (this is not a bad idea, if you have the time and are not afraid that you will lose your purchase, at any stage of your research).
- Analysing your data alongside a similar set may lead you to focus on the similarities and dissimilarities, rather than just on your own findings and interpretations.

Shared understandings

Having recognized, and begun to develop, your own perspective on what your research indicates, it becomes important to review these views in the light of those of others. To what extent do your findings, and your interpretation of them, agree or disagree with those of other authorities or researchers? Confirmatory or supportive results can be extremely useful in advancing general understanding. Such shared understandings can also be generated by, for example, reporting on your findings in a seminar, workshop, conference or paper, and debating with others their significance or interpretation.

How to handle different accounts

As well as recognizing and building upon shared understandings, you will also need to be able to accept and work from alternative perspectives. This can occur in at least two major ways: different accounts within your own data, and differences between your interpretations and those of others. Both are to be expected, welcomed and acknowledged. There is no reason, given our lack of comprehensive understanding of the world we live in, together with the varied perspectives held by different individuals, why our views and behaviours should always be common and shared. An important part of the interpretation of research is, therefore, the recognition of the diverging patterns within the data collected, and the attempted explanation of these. Similarly, you should not be unduly concerned if your findings appear to diverge from those of other researchers in your field; but you should look for reasons why this might be so, and/or argue the relevance of your interpretation against those of others.

The value of data that doesn't fit

The preceding discussion suggests the importance of the observation that doesn't fit your general interpretation, or 'the exception that proves the rule'. This saying may, of course, be taken at least two ways. One, the most literal reading, suggests that a single exception is a rogue piece of data which should be ignored. The other reading, perhaps the more relevant to the research process, would be that data which doesn't fit should not be ignored, but accepted, reported and cherished. It is not uncommon for accepted interpretations to be challenged and eventually demolished. Do not cast aside pieces of data which may be the basis for doing this!

What does it all mean?

Unless your interpretation is to be a one-off and wholly personal exercise, you will have to engage in a more general consideration of the relevance and usefulness of your work. Such a consideration will bring you into touch with four related concepts: significance, generalizability, reliability and validity. All competent researchers need to have an understanding of what these concepts mean, and need to be able to review and defend their own work in this light (see Box 9.13).

In the end, your interpretation of your findings is, however, limited by the methods you have used and the sample you have studied:

[S]ome of the seeming polarity in the debate around home-based work can be explained by the differing methodologies and sampling procedures. For instance, the evidence collected by local homeworking research projects, officers and campaigns on the incidence and persistence of extremely low-paid, arduous, manufacturing, home-based work in the UK had often only been possible after building of trust between project workers and

---

Box 9.13 Significance, generalizability, reliability and validity

Significance

The concept of significance has both a specific, statistical meaning and a more general, common-sense interpretation. In statistical parlance, it refers to the likelihood that a result derived from a sample could have been found by chance. The more significant a result, the more likely that it represents something genuine. In more general terms, significance has to do with how important a particular finding is judged to be.

Generalizability

The concept of generalizability, or representativeness, has particular relevance to small-scale research. It relates to whether your findings are likely to have broader applicability beyond the focus of your study. Thus, if you have carried out a detailed study of a specific institution, group or even individual, are your findings of any relevance beyond that institution, group or individual? Do they have anything to say about the behaviour or experience of other institutions, groups or individuals, and, if so, how do you know that this is the case?

Reliability

The concept of reliability has to do with how well you have carried out your research project. Have you carried it out in such a way that, if another researcher were to look into the same questions in the same setting, they would come up with essentially the same results (though not necessarily an identical interpretation). If so, then your work might be judged reliable.

Validity

Validity has to do with whether your methods, approaches and techniques actually relate to, or measure, the issues you have been exploring.

---

home-based workers . . . but because these surveys have been conducted largely in inner cities they have had little to say about non-manual homeworkers and whether the latter face particular problems.

(Phizacklea and Wolkowitz 1995: 19)

Small-scale research has its limitations, therefore, but is also able to make a significant contribution in under-studied areas.

Summary

Having read this chapter, you should:

- have an understanding of the different approaches which you might take to the analysis of documents, interviews, observations and questionnaires;
- be able to assess the significance, generalizability, reliability and validity of your research and findings.

Exercises

9.1 Take notes of a meeting you have to attend, or, if you rarely attend meet-ings, a television programme. After a few days, take a careful look at your notes. How full a summary are they? What has been left out, and why? What biases are there? Why are they organized in this particular way? What other documents would allow you to better assess the value of your notes?

9.2 Compare and contrast the three approaches to interview analysis out-lined in Box 9.4. What do you see as the key differences and similarities between these approaches. Which do you think would produce the most rigorous results, and why?

Further reading

In this section, we list a selection of books that are of particular relevance to the topics discussed in this chapter, together with an indication of their contents.

Argyrous, G. (2000) *Statistics for Social and Health Research, with a guide to SPSS*. London: Sage.
  The six sections of this comprehensive text cover univariate descriptive statistics, bivariate descriptive statistics, inferential statistics (for one sample, two or more independent samples, and two dependent samples), and multi-variate descriptive statistics.

Babbie, E. R. and Halley, F. (2005) *Adventures in Social Research: Data analysis using SPSS for Windows*, 5th edition. London: Pine Forge.
  Designed for students, this text introduces SPSS through Windows. The text includes activities to aid learning.

Banks, M. (2008) *Using Visual Data in Qualitative Research*. London: Sage.
Includes discussion of visual data produced by the researcher and by those under study. Aims to provide a comprehensive introduction to the practice of visually oriented research.

Blaiklie, N. (2003) *Analysing Quantitative Data: From description to explanation*. London: Sage.
Aims to demystify quantitative analysis and help the reader to overcome symbol phobia and figure blindness.

Bryman, A. and Cramer, D. (2008) *Quantitative Data Analysis with SPSS 14, 15 and 16*. London: Routledge.
Designed as a non-mathematical introduction for social scientists, explains the use of statistical tests in non-technical language.

Burn, A. and Parker, D. (2003) *Analysing Media Texts*. London: Continuum.
A variety of forms of texts and their analysis are explored in this book, including moving images, websites, computer games and interview data.

Connolly, P. (2007) *Quantitative Data Analysis in Education: A critical introduction using SPSS*. London: Routledge.
Sets out to be user-friendly, assuming no prior knowledge.

Fairclough, N. (2003) *Analysing Discourse: Textual analysis for social research*. London: Routledge.
Standard guide to these analytical techniques.

Field, A. (2005) *Discovering Statistics using SPSS for Windows: Advanced techniques for the beginner*, 2nd edition. London: Sage.
Covers data exploration, correlation and regression, logistic regression, comparing means, analysis of variance and factor analysis.

Fielding, J. L. and Gilbert, G. N. (2006) *Understanding Social Statistics*, 2nd edition. London: Sage.
The three sections of the book focus on preliminary issues (including the use of computers), univariate analysis (e.g. frequencies, percentages, measures of central tendency, the normal curve) and bivariate analysis (e.g. correlation and regression, sampling and inference, modelling data).

Foster, J. J. (2001) *Data Analysis using SPSS for Windows*, new edition. London: Sage.
Following an introductory overview of statistical analysis, twenty chapters set out what can be done with SPSS, illustrated stage by stage. Topics covered include *t*-tests, analysis of variance, correlation and regression, non-parametric techniques, reliability analysis and factor analysis.

Gibbs, G. (2008) *Analysing Qualitative Data*. London: Sage.
Includes chapters on the nature of qualitative analysis, thematic coding and categorizing, analysing biographies and narratives, analytic quality and ethics, and getting started with computer-assisted qualitative data analysis.

Hahn, C. (2008) *Doing Qualitative Research using your Computer: A practical guide*. London: Sage.
Sets out to 'walk' readers through the process of managing and streamlining

research projects, using commonly available Microsoft software applications such as Word, Access and Excel.

Hinde, A. (1998) *Demographic Methods*. London: Arnold.
Describes and explains the methods used to analyse population data. Covers basic methods as well as parity progression ratios, survival analysis and birth interval analysis.

Hinton, P. R. (2004) *Statistics Explained: A guide for social science students*, 2nd edition. London: Routledge.
Written for psychology and other social science students, this text takes the reader through the principles of statistical analysis. Contents include descriptive statistics, hypothesis testing, sampling, significance, variance, chi-square and using statistics programs on computers.

Howarth, D. (2000) *Discourse*. Buckingham: Open University Press.
A comprehensive overview of the different conceptions and methods of discourse analysis, and of the traditions of thinking (structuralist, post-structuralist, post-Marxist) from which these have emerged.

Hoyle, R. H. (ed.) (1999) *Statistical Strategies for Small Sample Research*. Thousand Oaks, CA: Sage.
The methods and issues considered include randomized designs, bootstrapping, categorical and non-parametric data, dynamic factor analysis and structural equation modelling.

Kinnear, P. and Gray, C. (2004) *SPSS 12 Made Simple*. London: Routledge.
Covers all the facilities available in SPSS, from creating and manipulating files through comparing averages to exploratory factor analysis.

Locke, T. (2004) *Critical Discourse Analysis*. London: Continuum.
This slim volume covers theory and practice, and the analysis of both print and oral texts.

Miller, R., Acton, C., Fullerton, D. and Maltby, J. (2002) *SPSS for Social Scientists*. Basingstoke: Palgrave Macmillan.
Covers hypothesis testing, cross-tabulation, analysis of variance, correlation and regression, factor analysis and log-linear analysis.

Pallant, J. (2001) *SPSS Survival Manual: A step by step guide to data analysis using SPSS*. Buckingham: Open University Press.
Text and screen illustrations take the reader through data preparation, preliminary analyses, and the use of a range of statistical techniques to explore relationships and compare groups.

Rapley, T. (2008) *Doing Conversation, Discourse and Document Analysis*. London: Sage.
Introduces the theory and practice of conversation, discourse and document analysis, demonstrating their usefulness in social science research.

Rugg, G. (2007) *Using Statistics: A gentle introduction*. Maidenhead: Open University Press.
Sets out to cover descriptive, inferential, parametric, non-parametric and multi-dimensional statistics in an accessible and relatively jargon-free manner.

Salkind, N. (2004) *Statistics for People who (think they) hate Statistics*, 2nd edition. Thousand Oaks, CA: Sage.
   Uses a conversational tone to guide the reader through simple and more advanced statistical techniques.
Silverman, D. (2006) *Interpreting Qualitative Data: Methods for analyzing talk, text and interaction*, 3rd edition. London: Sage.
   Chapters discuss ethnography and observation, interviews, texts, naturally occurring talk, visual images, ethics and writing your report.
Spicer, J. (2004) *Making Sense of Multivariate Data Analysis*. Thousand Oaks, CA: Sage.
   Discusses philosophy, theory and practice.
Wright, D. B. (2002) *First Steps in Statistics*. London: Sage.
   Chapters consider graphing, distributions, sampling and allocation, inference and confidence intervals, hypothesis testing, analysis of variance, regression and correlation, and contingency tables.

10

Writing up

Introduction

Research without writing is of little purpose. There are, of course, other ways of communicating your research and its findings, most notably through oral presentation, but writing them up remains of paramount importance in most areas of research. The research report, thesis or dissertation, the journal article, academic text and conference paper remain the major means by which researchers communicate with each other, and with other interested parties, across space and time. The rapid development of new information and computer technologies may have changed the speed and scope of such communication, but it has not altered the importance of writing as the means for communicating.

It is something of a contradiction or paradox, therefore, that many researchers, both novice and experienced, are extremely reluctant or fearful of committing their ideas to paper. This is perfectly understandable in the case of the new or relatively inexperienced researcher, who may have little idea of their potential readership or what might be expected of them. That it is common among more experienced researchers would seem to indicate a distaste for writing, partly due, no doubt, to a preference for other aspects of the research process, as well as a continuing lack of confidence in their abilities.

Writing up is not just a critical, but a continuing, part of the research process, which should start soon after the commencement of the research project, and continue to and beyond its completion. So don't be misled by this being the penultimate chapter: writing up begins as soon as you start thinking about and reading around your research.

The purposes of this chapter, then, are to encourage early and regular writing, to identify the different skills and issues involved in writing up research, and to build up confidence by confronting the concerns commonly encountered in writing up.

This chapter has the following sections:

- **Drafting and redrafting.** How to progress your writing up.
- **How to argue.** The organization and structure of your writing.
- **How to criticize.** Placing your work in the context of that of others.
- **Who am I writing for?** Writing appropriately for your audience.
- **Grammar, referencing and plagiarism.** Some hints and tips.
- **Using tables, diagrams and other illustrations.** When and when not to.
- **Panics.** Common worries encountered in writing up research.

Drafting and redrafting

The matter of format reveals in part the whole philosophy for the research paper. The keywords in this philosophy are organization, discipline and convention . . . in my experience, students tend to carry over into the realm of the research paper attitudes and aims, formed in the field of creative writing, that have no place in research . . . Organization is necessary for the efficient allocation of one's time and effort, and for the presentation of a paper whose internal structure is balanced and sound, and whose argument proceeds along logical lines. Discipline is central to the long labour of sifting authorities, and adding one's own critical comments only when these authorities have been fully assimilated. Conventions are vital in a context where one writes not for oneself, but for a critical public.

(Berry 2004: 3)

I realised that I was trying to ensure that my ideas were 'right', so that I could be sure when voicing them, and not expose myself to either undue praise or criticism. I despaired of achieving this, especially given some of the thorny, long-running questions in the area (such as whether men and women are *really* the same or different), and the many committed camps of theorists. I envied the makers of films such as 'Thelma and Louise', who seemed to be able to present multi-faceted explorations of gender-related issues without taking the mincing steps of academic debate. Happily I woke one morning with a revelatory insight – that I would never get it right, that seeking to do so was a futile waste of energy, that I should proceed with this 'truth' in mind and allow myself to be more playful in my explorations.

(Marshall 1995: 28–9, emphasis in original)

Writing up your research should start early and become a regular and continuing activity. It is also likely to be an iterative or cyclical process. That is, you will draft a section or chapter, then move on to some other activity, and return one or more times to redraft your original version. This is partly because as the totality of the research thesis or report takes shape, what you have written in subsequent sections affects what you wrote earlier and necessitates changes in it. It is also the case that as your research proceeds you find out more, read more, and change your mind about some things.

Two key skills here are, therefore: recognizing when you need to redraft your report or thesis, or part of it; and knowing when you have done enough drafting, and it is time to present your report or thesis, and then move on to something else. Writing up, like other aspects of research, is at root a set of pragmatic skills, honed through experience.

> The importance of recognizing when you have done enough is the subject of the next chapter, **Finishing off**.

How to recognize procrastination and what to do about it

But what do you do if you just don't know how or what to write, or you don't feel like writing? We have all, at one time or another, sat in front of a blank screen or sheet of paper. You may be suffering from any of the twenty forms of procrastination listed in Box 10.1, or from some other unmentioned version. At such times, the suggestion that you just start by writing anything seems trite and unhelpful. You might find some comfort and assistance in Box 10.2, which contains twenty practical suggestions for overcoming procrastination.

Whatever your reasons for procrastination, the basic advice has to be to do something, whatever works, to get you writing something, and preferably something which will be of use to you. What you write is unlikely to come out straight away as a polished and finished piece of work, however good and experienced at research writing you are. The point is to aim to produce some writing as regularly as you can, and then work from that. It is likely to get somewhat easier as you progress, though there will be more and less difficult times throughout.

Most of the problems and suggestions contained in Boxes 10.1 and 10.2 are dealt with, directly or indirectly, later in this chapter. The remainder of this section tackles three of the most common issues encountered in drafting and redrafting your writing.

Box 10.1 Twenty forms of procrastination

1   I just can't get started.
2   There are too many words to write.
3   There are too few words to play with.
4   I've never written an academic thesis before.
5   I've never written a work report before.
6   I'll do it tomorrow.
7   I'm not in the mood.
8   I'd rather be surfing.
9   It's too noisy to concentrate.
10   I can't type.
11   My computer has broken down.
12   It's all been done already.
13   What's the point?
14   The oven needs cleaning.
15   It's too difficult.
16   I'm no good at writing.
17   I've only got half an hour.
18   I wish I'd never started.
19   I don't feel very well.
20   The children will be home soon.

Box 10.2 Twenty suggestions for overcoming procrastination

1   Make notes on what you have read.
2   Make notes on interviews you have conducted.
3   Make notes on your last discussion with your supervisor or manager.
4   Draft your contents page.
5   Type out your references or bibliography.
6   Draft the structure for a section or chapter.
7   Type out the quotations you think you may use.
8   Note down the points you think you will refer to.
9   Set yourself a target for writing a given number of words each day, week or month.
10   Speak your ideas out aloud, tape record and then transcribe them.
11   Write anything so that you dirty your page or screen.
12   Work out how many words you will devote to each chapter, section or subsection.
13   Write up to your word limit, and then edit what you have written.
14   Give yourself a treat, but then come straight back.

15   Think about all the other times you procrastinated, and what you did about it then.
16   Don't allow yourself to do anything else until you have written something.
17   Give someone else the responsibility to oversee your writing.
18   Talk it through with somebody else.
19   Try writing at a different time of day, or time of the week.
20   Just write anything.

Editing and reworking your writing

Once you have written something – anything – the writing-up process becomes in part a process of rewriting what you have already written. You will need to rewrite in order to:

- bring in new material, ideas and thinking;
- reduce the length of what you have written;
- revise old sections to refer to newly drafted material;
- alter the structure of what you have written;
- respond to the suggestions made by your readers;
- remove any inadvertent repetitions.

Rewriting, or redrafting, can be a difficult skill to learn. You may find it helps to deliberately leave your drafts alone for a period of time, so as to render them unfamiliar. Box 10.3 offers some further suggestions for editing your work as an 'outsider'.

Box 10.3 Editing your work as an 'outsider'

- Does the piece of work have a central idea? Is this idea apparent for the reader or do you have to 'search' for it? Is it clear enough for you to restate in a different way?
- Does the piece of work raise any questions that it does not answer?
- Is there a sense of an 'argument' developing?
- Do points – both within and beyond paragraphs – seem to follow logically? Does the whole piece hang together?
- Why is a particular bit of information in the piece? What work is it doing for expressing the ideas of the assignment? (For example, is there too much 'chronology writing' at the expense of analysis?)
- Can you understand what is written? If not, can you see why? Does the use of subject terminology seem clear and confident?
- Does the introduction seem helpful as a signpost to the whole piece?
- Is there a sense of a satisfying ending?

- Does the ending in particular, as well as the piece as a whole, answer the question that has been set? How do you know? Has the writer referred to the question clearly and explicitly?

(*Source*: Adapted from Crème and Lea 1997: 125)

Redrafting is a normal event. It does not mean that your original draft is useless, merely that the writing process takes place over a period of time, during which you do what you can to make your report or thesis as effective as possible.

The process of redrafting is made a lot easier if you are using a computer. This will enable you to easily access those sections you wish to change or update, to move sections of text around, to make simple alterations through-out the text and to check your spelling. Your software may even produce a contents page and index for you. If you don't have access to a computer, or don't wish to use one, you will still need to do these kinds of things, but it will probably take a little longer.

One question often posed about redrafting is how often to do it. This depends partly on your own preferences and partly also on the length of your project in both time and words. The longer the project, the more likely that you are going to want to redraft at a number of stages, and your work is likely to benefit from this. For relatively small-scale projects, including those lasting less than one year, it may be best to first draft all of the chapters or sections individually, though not necessarily sequentially, and have a single redraft near to the end of the project. Either way, it is good practice to make notes on earlier drafts, as you go along, indicating where and how you intend to make changes.

> **Hint**: It's a good idea to meet with your supervisor, mentor or manager before (and after) you produce your final draft.

Writing to the appropriate length

The need to reduce the length of what you have written has already been mentioned as one of the reasons for redrafting material you have already drafted. You might also, though this is less likely, need to increase the length of what you have written.

Writing to the appropriate length is not easy. You may have a specific limit, perhaps both a maximum and a minimum, set on the number of words or pages which your report or thesis can comprise. Or you may have general guidance, or perhaps no guidance at all; in which case it could be a good idea to set your own limit, and then check this out with your likely readers.

There are two basic approaches which you can then adopt for writing to a given length:

- The **planned** approach, where you sketch out the contents of your report or thesis in some detail, allocate a given number of words or pages to each subsection, and then endeavour to keep to those lengths as you draft.
- The **slash and burn** approach, where you initially draft without reference to any length constraints, and then subsequently cut down or extend your drafts as necessary.

Whichever combination of these approaches you use – it is unlikely that you will be able to rely solely on the first approach – you will probably need to employ a range of simple techniques for getting your initial drafts to the appropriate length in the redrafting process.

To contract your writing, you might use any or all of the five techniques outlined in Box 10.4. These techniques avoid the use of artificial and self-defeating methods, such as reducing your print size, increasing the size of your page, or placing more material in appendices outside of the main text. All researchers have to engage in editing their work at some time; most have to do it repeatedly. It is both a courtesy to your readers – to reduce the amount of time they have to spend in getting to the nub of your argument – and a means of helping to ensure that you have more readers.

Box 10.4 How to contract your writing

---

1   Remove unnecessary, qualifying or repetitive words, and perhaps clauses, from sentences.
2   Summarize one or more sentences, perhaps whole paragraphs, in one sentence.
3   Delete references and quotations which are not essential to your discussion.
4   Replace lengthy descriptions by tables or charts where possible.
5   Remove whole sections, or perhaps even chapters, where these are not central to your argument.

The need to expand what you have written is a less obvious skill in writing up, but all researchers have to face it when they first begin to turn their outline into the finished report or thesis. It may also be necessary at a later stage when you, your supervisor or manager, detect imbalances or omissions in your work. You can't assume that your readers know all that you know, so there may be a need to put in more explanatory material. To expand your writing, you might use the five methods listed in Box 10.5.

Box 10.5 How to expand your writing

---

1   Look for more references and quotations on the subjects or issues which you are writing about.
2   Build individual sentences up into paragraphs by developing your argument.
3   Add new sections, or even chapters, of relevant material.
4   Integrate appendices within the main text.
5   Take more space to discuss your methodology, and how well it worked.

Coping with interruptions

[W]hen I came to write, there were very few material obstacles in my way. Writing was a reputable and harmless occupation. The family peace was not broken by the scratching of a pen. No demand was made upon the family purse ... You have only got to figure to yourselves a girl in a bedroom with a pen in her hand. She had only to move that pen from left to right – from ten o'clock to one.

(Woolf 1995: 1–2)

You may not be so fortunate! Most researchers, particularly those carrying out work-based projects and those who are studying part-time, have to learn to cope with interruptions. This can be particularly irritating when they occur during the process of writing up, since then the need for peace and quiet can seem to be particularly strong.

The obvious way of coping with this problem is to confine your writing to times and places when you are unlikely to be interrupted. Do it at lunch time, after working hours, when the children are at school or when they have gone to bed. Do it in a separate study, in a library, in a quiet room, away from home and work if necessary.

If these suggestions are impractical in your case, you might be best advised to do your writing up in a very planned way. That is, outline in considerable detail what you are going to write, so that you can then do it bit by bit or subsection by subsection. This way, you are less likely to lose the thread of what you are writing when you are interrupted, or, if you do, will need to spend less time to recover it.

Hint: When you stop writing for a period, write a note for yourself on what you planned to do next. Map out your plans several steps ahead if you can. This should be very useful in getting you back into writing quickly next time.

How to argue

Organization

Writing up your research, whether in the form of a work report or an academic thesis, requires particular skills and forms of organization. The extent to which you make use of these will vary depending on the size and scope of your research project.

However, in organizational terms, your report or thesis is likely to include, as a minimum:

1 An introduction at the beginning and a set of conclusions at the end. These may be supplemented, or perhaps replaced by, a summary and a series of recommendations, respectively.
2 A series of distinct sections or chapters, which may be further divided into subsections or sub-chapters. Each section or chapter may have its own introductory and concluding passages.
3 References to existing research and publications, possibly illuminated by selected quotations. A list of the material referred to will be included, probably at the end of the report or thesis, possibly in the form of a bibliography.

In addition, your report or thesis may include:

4 Tables, diagrams, charts and other forms of illustrations (the use of these is discussed in more detail later in this chapter).
5 A number of preliminary sections, such as a preface, abstract, dedication and acknowledgements; and/or supplementary sections, in the form of appendices.

> The use of preliminary sections and appendices is discussed in the section on **Added extras** in Chapter 11.

Argument

The above organizational elements are the bare bones of any research report or thesis. To put them together to make a successful and effective argument requires four things:

1 a context;
2 one or more themes;
3 some ordering; and
4 linkages.

You may like to refer back to the section in Chapter 2 on **Focusing**, which discusses related issues at an earlier stage of the research process.

Context

The context for your report or thesis, and for your research project as a whole, consists of your broader understanding of the area within which you are researching. This may operate at three levels:

- In terms of your disciplinary background: thus, if you are a sociologist, this will be sociology and sociological writings.
- In terms of your field of study: for example, the sociology of the family, transport economics, 16–19 educational policy.
- In terms of the methodology you are employing: for example, questionnaire surveys or participant observation.

Your report or thesis may not refer to all of these levels, but it is likely to include some reference to at least two of them if you are to provide an adequate contextualization of your study for your readers. This contextualization is likely to form an important part of the early sections or chapters of your work, with some reference back to it towards the end.

Themes

The themes of your report or thesis are the key issues, concepts or questions you identify as being of relevance and interest. These will both inform the research you undertake – so will be evident in your contextual discussion – and help to structure your analysis and findings. They are the aspects of your field of study or discipline to which your research is contributing. They could include, for example, development theory, gender relations at work, the spatial structure of the city, the effectiveness of different forms of staff training, or measures of monetary supply.

These themes are likely to be introduced early on in your report or thesis, forming part of its context. They will then be referred to throughout the main body your discussion, as the running thread holding it all together. A significant part of the concluding sections will probably be devoted to reflecting on what your research has told you about these themes, and how they might be explored further in future. Exercise 10.1 is designed to help you identify the context and themes for your writing.

Ordering

The ordering of your report or thesis relates to how you set out your argument in stages, and how you break it down into manageable chunks for the reader. We have already indicated some aspects of this ordering, by referring to the use of introductory and concluding sections, and suggesting an early contextualization and a later discussion and reflection. Some further suggestions as to what a typical academic thesis or work report might look like are given in the next subsection.

Linkages

Linkages – or signposting – have to do with how you aid the reader in finding their way through your report or thesis. They may take the form of regular references to the themes you have identified. They are also likely to be made apparent through cross-references between chapters, sections or pages. The aim is to present a coherent whole to the reader, however the report or thesis may be structured and organized. When done effectively, the reader should be able to quickly make sense of your work whichever page they start reading from.

What an academic thesis or work report might look like

Boxes 10.6 and 10.7 offer suggestions of what academic theses and work reports, based on a small-scale research project, might look like in terms of organization and structure.

Box 10.6 Possible forms for an academic thesis

A dissertation is far more than a passive record of your research and generally involves presenting an argument or point of view. In other words, it must 'say' something and be substantiated with reasoned argument and evidence. If you want it to be interesting as well as academically convincing, you will need to raise intriguing issues and discuss them, besides presenting your outcomes.

(Barnes 1995: 100)

The 'classic' dissertation structure is:

- contents
- abstract
- introduction (10% of words or space)
- review of the background literature (20%)
- design and methodology of the research (10%)

- implementation of the research (15%)
- presentation and analysis of data (15%)
- comment and critique of the outcomes or findings (20%)
- summary and conclusion (10%)
- references
- bibliography
- appendices

[A]cademics . . . say they enjoy innovative structures devised by their students, but they also warm very positively to this classic model.

(Barnes 1995: 130)

Box 10.7 Possible forms for a work report

Short report

- Title page
- Abstract/executive summary
- Introduction (what you did and why)
- Materials and methods (how you did it)
- Results (what you found out)
- Discussion (what the results mean)
- References

Long report

- Title page
- Abstract/executive summary
- Acknowledgements
- Table of contents
- Introduction
- Materials and methods
- Results
- Discussion
- Recommendations
- References
- Appendices

(*Source*: Hay et al. 2002: 88)

It should be emphasized at once that these are just examples, albeit common ones. The indications as to chapter or section titles, and as to the relative proportion of the overall report or thesis which they would comprise, are meant only as guidelines. There are many other, and much more innovative and interesting, ways of putting together a report or thesis. Every individual case is likely to differ, not least in terms of varying disciplinary practices, and of the titles and subtitles used. It would be excessively boring for the readers of research if all reports or theses were arranged in the same fashion.

> **Health warning**: Remember, though, to check on any regulations or expectations which may effect what your thesis or report should look like.

By comparison with academic theses, work reports tend to be briefer – otherwise they are never read – and to focus more clearly on the practical applications of the research undertaken. Research is rarely undertaken in the work setting just for the sake of it. However, as in the case of the academic thesis, the bulk of the work report is likely to be devoted to a discussion of the context for the research and of the results uncovered.

Three further differences may be noted. First, the work report is much less likely to include a separate section of references. Fewer works will typically be mentioned, and they will tend to be detailed in the text itself. Second, the work report is quite likely to be presented in terms of numbered sections and paragraphs, rather than chapters. Third, it may contain an executive summary at the beginning.

Exercise 10.2 invites you, in the light of these suggestions, to consider how you will organize your research report or thesis.

How to criticize

Where it is not explicit, criticism is implicit within research writing. Since you are always writing within the context of existing research and understanding, your research also constitutes your evaluation of others' work and beliefs. This is the essence of criticism: placing your work within the context of others'; acknowledging the deficiencies of that work, both yours and theirs; and then moving the debate forward.

> You may like to refer back to the section in Chapter 4 on **Good enough reading**, particularly Boxes 4.9 and 4.10.

Criticizing is not rubbishing

Criticizing others' research and writing does not mean rubbishing them. You may, in certain extreme cases, feel that this is justifiable, but it is unlikely to achieve much. By the same token, the blind acceptance of others' data, arguments and conclusions, just because they have been published, or because they are widely accepted, is ill advised. Even the most reputable authors may benefit from a little measured criticism.

Criticism is evaluation. It should be careful, considered and justified. It should also be even-handed, recognizing that you yourself are capable of error, and may change your mind in time. Anything may be criticized: underlying assumptions, arguments, methodologies, the accuracy of data collected, the interpretation of that data. You may also use your own research to critically assess others', where you feel these are in disagreement.

Criticism is about joining in a wider research debate with others you may never meet. Research is never perfect. It could always have been done differently or better. By joining in a critical debate, you can help to improve future research and understanding.

Using your sources

At the heart of critical writing is your use of your sources, your response to them and your written account of this. Much depends therefore on the reading you have undertaken, a theme dealt with in Chapter 4. Your sources cover more than just all of the published or unpublished materials which you may have accessed and studied in the course of your research project. They also include your broader engagement with ideas through discussion with others, as well as your own research data and your interpretation of this.

You should make full use of this range and variety of sources in your writing, where it is relevant to, or illustrative of, the argument you are putting forward. Thus, you will probably use selected sources:

- to build up the context for your own research, demonstrating existing thinking and practice;
- to exemplify and justify the methodology you adopted;
- to complement, or contrast with, your findings and interpretations.

You will likely have a mixture of positive and negative comments to make about these sources.

Establishing your argument

Do not, however, get swamped by your sources. Even if your aim is just to provide a synopsis of the literature, it is your argument and your interpretation that should be at the forefront of your writing. You need to control your sources, therefore, rather than have them control you. You will provide the summaries and the linkages; you will determine the order in which you introduce and comment on your sources; you will decide what else to add and how to progress the argument of your research.

This will involve establishing your voice and your argument early on in your report or thesis; maintaining it as the key thread running through your work; and returning to a fuller evaluation of it at relevant points.

Going back to the literature

As well as returning to your argument, it is also common to return to a discussion of existing research and understanding towards the end of your thesis or report. Having introduced and critically discussed a selection of this material early on, you can then relate it to your own research findings once these have been presented and discussed. You may wish to re-evaluate your earlier thinking and criticism at this point.

As this suggests, the whole process of criticism, like that of research as a whole, is cyclical and iterative. As a researcher, you are engaged in a continuing round of evaluation and re-evaluation.

Who am I writing for?

the researcher is also a narrator and an active producer of 'knowledge' in research . . . the researcher is also involved in writing his or her life, reflecting on experiences both within and outside the research context – both are also related. Here, there is the 'intellectual biography' of the researcher who not only 'translates' the experience of others but also writes and interprets their own life.

(Roberts 2002: 85–6)

Voice and style

When you start to write up your research, there are two related issues which you will need to address, whether explicitly or implicitly, early on. These are the issues of voice and style.

- **Style** relates to how you write up your research, which may be determined by the requirements of your audience, by your own predilections, or by a mixture of the two.
- **Voice** has to do with how you express yourself and tell the story of your research, and is something you are likely to develop further as you write and research.

It's a good idea to study a variety of examples of research writing to get some guidance on both the range of possibilities and how you might approach your own writing. Box 10.8 contains extracts from an article which deliberately

Box 10.8 Writing styles

Middleton's paper is written in two columns. It has been deliberately structured in this way to indicate the links between theory and 'lived reality' which can be generative of theoretical construction. It is also a response to, and demonstration of, postmodernist writing techniques. Middleton says 'This is an experimental piece of writing, which transgresses conventional academic forms in order to expose their constructedness.' An extract from the article is given below. The left-hand column is written in conventional academic form and is concerned to draw out the implications of 'postmodern theory for feminist pedagogy in education courses'. The right-hand column describes the 'location and circumstances in which the left hand column was written'.

TOWARDS A FEMINIST PEDAGOGY FOR TEACHER EDUCATION

Academic papers normally begin, as Dorothy Smith has described it,

from a position in the discourse as an ongoing process of formally organized interchange. We begin from a position within a determinate conceptual framework which is identified with the discipline . . . and by virtue of our training and of what it means to do the professional work in our discipline, we begin from outside ourselves, to locate problematics organized by the sociological, the psychological, the historical discourse (Smith, 1979: 146).

Postmodernism is becoming increasingly influential within feminist educational theory. Postmodernists have rejected the monolithic categories upon which previous feminisms have rested – 'the rationally autonomous individual' (liberalism); the 'essential feminine' (radical feminism); and the class-differentiated gender groups of Marxism. Post-modernist theories are based on a scepticism about the possibility or desirability of attempting to produce totalizing

INTERRUPTIONS

It is the last day of the Winter term. Tomorrow the August study break begins. Winter sun beckons me through my office window. I shall go home early – snatch this afternoon to write my proposal for AERA. I want to reflect on the experience of being a feminist academic writer – to write about the rhythms, and the fragmentations, of our lives. The harmonies, dissonances, and disruptions . . .

The phone shrieks. A breathless voice asks, "Dr Middleton – have you noted the change in date for the meeting of the Administrative Committee? It will now be at 9.00 on the first morning of the study break?" . . . I hadn't . . . The relevant agenda surfaces from the cascades of papers on my desk. I place it in my canvas carry bag and dig deeper under the piles of unopened brown envelopes for my copy of the conference paper instructions . . .

This office is seldom my space for academic writing. It is the place where I compose memoranda, file minutes of meetings, write letters in response to the contents of brown envelopes . . . It is also the space where I meet with students. I have made it as 'safe', as 'like home' as possible. The bureaucratic flooring is covered with a large rug – earth-colours -ochre red, gold, beige, black. There is an old armchair in one corner. The cream walls are hidden behind shelves of books. Above the smaller book-cases are pictures – a poster from Queensland; a batik from Kenya. Near the door is a sketch which my daughter, Kate, drew several years ago for a social studies project. Hippies – beads, flowers, banners . . . A 1960s protest march.

Like many of today's feminist teachers and writers I attended university during the 1960s and began paid work (in my case secondary school teaching) in the early 1970s – times of full employment and hope. Today, as an educator in the 1990s, I watch my students and my daughter moving into adulthood in times of economic recession and despair. The kinds of feminism and progressive educational theories which offered possibilities to my generation may seem to today's students irrelevant and quaint anachronisms. How can we, middle-aged and older teachers of women's studies

(*Source*: Middleton 1995: quotes from pp. 87 and 88, extract from p. 89)

counterposed two very different forms of writing. Exercise 10.3 invites you to reflect upon styles and voices in writing. Box 10.9 suggests some good reasons why you might want to experiment with alternative forms of writing.

Box 10.9 Alternative forms of writing

As more attention has been given to the connections between writing in the social sciences and writing in the humanities, there has been a growing interest in alternatives to 'traditional' forms of writing. There are some very good reasons why researchers may want to experiment with different writing styles:

- Engaging in experimental forms of writing allows the researcher to nurture her or his voice. This is important because it presents a counterbalance to a problem faced by many new, and established, researchers when they are overreliant on the voices of others. Experimental writing need not require citations. You are freed up to create your new knowledge without feeling that you have to know everything that has been written on the topic.
- Experimental forms of writing are explicit attempts to engage the emotions of the writer and the reader. This can be either positive or negative. For example, Richardson (1992) describes how writing her data as poems enabled her to engage with the subject of her research in a much more intensive and joyful way.
- Experimental forms of writing can give greater recognition to how readers create their own meanings. A common method for reporting research is one where the researcher's main aim is to guide the reader through the 'facts' of the research in a linear or cumulative way. The data is used as evidence of the findings. However, some researchers try to disrupt the idea that the researcher has all the knowledge. They want to leave more space for the reader to come to their own conclusions. Using different forms of writing is one way in which researchers try to do this. For example, the lines of a standard text are dense and often crammed on to the page. A short poem will have a much less cluttered appearance. The idea is that as the clutter diminishes, so the potential for thinking and feeling around, within, and through the words and lines grows. The point is to open up the potential for new and unexpected ways of knowing.

One of the key distinctions here is whether to write impersonally in the third person (e.g. 'it appears') or in the first person (e.g. 'I found'). Writing impersonally is standard for much research, and conveys an impression, whether justified or not, of considered and distanced objectivity. The first person comes across as more immediate, personal and committed, and does not deny any inherent subjectivity. Whether you use the first or third person will depend upon your discipline, your politics, your purpose and your audience. You may be able, or choose, to switch between them, perhaps confining your use of the first person to particular chapters or sections.

Representing reality

Another important factor to be borne in mind during your writing up is that you are in the process of fashioning and presenting a representation of reality. You are, in other words, telling a story, and need to be aware of the different techniques which you might make use of in so doing. Indeed, it has been suggested that constantly asking 'What's the main story here?' is a useful tool for data analysis (Strauss 1987: 35). Your research participants and sources may be seen as the characters in this story, and will need to be introduced and developed as they would be in a novel.

This is not to imply that your research has been made up, or is arbitrary or wholly subjective. You will likely have devoted a lot of time and consideration to collecting data, assessing its reliability, and then interpreting what you have found. Yet, however much work you have done, you are highly unlikely to have exhausted your research topic, and you will not be in a position to write the last word on it. You will have partial and incomplete information, and should be aware of its deficiencies as well as its strengths.

Different audiences and conventions

The different demands posed by writing up your research for your employer and for academic credit are discussed in the section on **How to argue** earlier in this chapter. Each of these approaches has its own varying set of conventions and particular styles, as well as similarities. Whichever you are writing, it is critical – as we repeatedly emphasize throughout this book – that you are aware of, and adhere to, any and all regulations or expectations concerning your writing up.

Safe and risky writing

Even if you take note of any and all regulations or expectations affecting your writing, there are still safer and riskier strategies for writing up. When in doubt, as when you are a novice researcher and you are unsure of the likely response to what you are writing, it is almost certainly in your best interests to adopt a safe strategy in writing up. If you are rather more experienced, think you are on to something, want to give yourself an extra challenge or simply can see no other way of doing it, you may choose to write up your research in a less standard and hence more risky fashion.

You might, for example, opt to write in the first person, and perhaps in an autobiographical style. You might use a chapter or section structure very different from those suggested in this book: perhaps organized in terms of the timeline of the research project. You might include poems or fictional elements in your report or thesis. You might present your work in terms of a dialogue or a play. All of these strategies can work very well, and can further illuminate the representational elements and issues involved in doing research. You would be well advised, though, to do some sounding out among your assessors or likely readers in advance.

What you want to avoid is a strong reaction against, or rejection of, your report or thesis purely on the basis of the way in which it has been written up and presented. You don't want to have to do it all again, reworking your writing to a more conventional or acceptable style. So don't take the risk unless you really have the freedom and know what you are doing.

Non-discriminatory writing

Beyond any formal regulations, there is now a general expectation that all writing will strive to be non-discriminatory. To do otherwise would make you likely to offend your readers, at the very least. You may actually be provided with, or recommended to, a style guide by your institution or employer. If not, the bibliography at the end of this chapter contains some helpful sources.

The basic principle involved is writing in a way that does not denegrate or exclude particular groups of people on the basis of what may be fairly arbitrary characteristics: such as sex, age, ethnic group, religion, physical and mental abilities or sexual orientation.

Being consistent

Above all, whatever audience you are writing for, it is important to be consistent in terms of style and organization. Switching between styles is usually confusing for all concerned, and hence inadvisable, except in exceptional or carefully handled circumstances. Thus, if you have written your thesis or report in the third person, and in a measured style, it is unwise suddenly to begin using the first person. The main exception to this is what you write in prefatory sections, such as a preface or acknowledgements, which lie outside of the main content of your thesis or report.

> The use of prefatory sections is discussed in the section on **Added extras** in Chapter 11.

Grammar, referencing and plagiarism

Two of the most common failings of written-up research – even of books like this one! – are errors in grammar, punctuation and spelling, and mistakes in referencing or in the bibliography. Hence, one of the easiest ways of making a good initial impression on your readers is to ensure, as far as possible, that your presentation is error free.

One thing you must avoid in writing up is, knowingly or unknowingly, committing the sin of plagiarism, or presenting other people's work as if it was your own. This has become more common with the development of the internet, and the increasing and easy availability of essays and publications online.

Grammar, punctuation and spelling

Many researchers, even experienced ones, have problems with grammar, punctuation and spelling when they are writing up. This is not unusual and should not be a cause for shame. Many of us may not have had a particularly good initial education, or were more interested in other matters at the time. For others, English is not their first language. However, once you begin to write up your research for consideration and assessment, as a report or as a thesis (and particularly if you are thinking of publishing some or all of it), your use of 'correct' grammar, punctuation and spelling becomes very important. Your readers are likely to be irritated, amused or put off by errors; consequently, errors will detract from your ability to get your ideas across.

There is not enough scope in a book of this nature to provide detailed guidance on this subject, but Box 10.10 suggests a number of general points to bear in mind.

Beyond this basic guidance, there are many useful publications which you could turn to. Some of these are listed in the bibliography.

Box 10.10 Some tips on grammar and punctuation

- Try to avoid long sentences. The sense of what you are saying gets lost, whereas a series of shorter, punchy sentences can advance the argument much better.
- Avoid one-sentence paragraphs. Paragraphs should contain a number of sentences on the same subject, and then lead on to the next paragraph, which will move the discussion on.
- Avoid beginning sentences with 'joining' words, such as 'but', 'and' or 'because'. These should normally be used to link clauses within sentences.
- Avoid incorporating lengthy lists of material in your text. Your writing should read as a flowing piece of text, not as a summary or precis. If you need lists, they are probably better placed separately from the main text in tables or figures.
- Understand and make use of the full range of standard punctuation forms, including, in particular, the colon (:), semi-colon (;), comma (,) and full stop (.).
- Use double and single quotation marks (" and ') consistently.

If you are writing up your research on a computer, you might want to make use of the facilities which much software has for checking your spelling and grammar, and for suggesting alternative words to use. These can be very useful for checking drafts, but remember that they will not recognize many specialist words or names, and, perhaps most importantly, that they will often use American English spelling.

> See the section in Chapter 5 on **Using computers**.

Referencing

One question you may face in writing up your research is whether to include a bibliography or just a set of references. The difference may be very small in practice:

- A set of references contains details of all the books, articles, reports and other works you have directly referred to in your thesis or report.
- A bibliography contains details of all, or a selection of, the books, articles, reports and other works of relevance you have consulted during your research, not all of which may be directly referred to in your text.

Whether you provide references or a bibliography may already have been determined for you. Alternatively, restrictions on the space you have available for writing up may lead you to limit yourself to just essential references or a select bibliography. In other cases, you will have to decide for yourself which is the more appropriate strategy. It is very unlikely, and probably inadvisable on grounds of space and repetition, that you will wish to include both references and a bibliography.

> **Hint**: Check your file of regulations and expectations, and follow the conventions of your discipline and institution.

Whichever you do use, you should make sure that you include full details of all the works you refer to, so that your readers can themselves track them down and examine them if they so wish. Box 10.11 provides guidance on referencing, based on the Harvard system – widely used throughout the social sciences and beyond – but check if your organization or university uses a different system.

> See also the section in Chapter 4 on **Recording your reading**, particularly Box 4.13.

Box 10.11 How to reference

Reference to a book

Covington, M. (1992) *Making the Grade: A self-worth perspective on motivation and school reform.* Cambridge: Cambridge University Press.

Reference to a chapter in an edited book

Weiner, G., Arnot, M. and David, M. (1997) 'Is the future female? Female success, male disadvantage and changing gender patterns in education', in A. Halsey, H. Lauder, P. Brown and A. Wells (eds) *Education, Economy, Culture and Society.* Oxford: Oxford University Press.

Reference to an article in a journal

Osler, A. and Morrison, M. (2002) Can race equality be inspected? Challenges for policy and practice raised by the OFSTED school inspection framework. *British Educational Research Journal*, 28: 327–38.

Reference to a government report

Department for Education and Employment (1992) *Choice and Diversity: A new framework for schools*, Cmnd 2021. London: HMSO.

Reference to material from the internet

Department for Education and Employment (2000) *Boys must Improve at the same rate as Girls – Blunkett.* Available from: http://www.dfee.gov.uk/pns/DisplayPN.cgi?pn_id=2000_0368

Reference to a newspaper article

Evans, A. (1996) Perils of ignoring our lost boys. *The Times Educational Supplement*, 28 June.

(*Source*: Adapted from Lancaster University 2005b: 26)

Plagiarism

Plagiarism most commonly occurs accidentally or unintentionally, when writers are unaware of the appropriate conventions for referencing other people's work. Whether it is accidental or deliberate, however, and particularly if you are submitting a piece of writing for credit or possible publication, you are likely to be severely penalized if you are found guilty of plagiarism. So be scrupulous when you quote, refer to or summarize someone else's work: Box 10.12 provides some general guidance.

Box 10.12 Plagiarism and how to avoid it

In plain English, plagiarism is cheating. This occurs when the work of others, either wholly or in part, is presented by you as your own work . . .

Naturally, in the course of presenting your own work, you will refer to the ideas, findings and explanations of others. Indeed, this is an expectation on our part which is encouraged as the standard road to academic improvement. But there is a clear distinction which you should always respect in your work:

it is one thing to make explicit reference to the work of others in your use of their work

it is something else again to use the work of others without any indication that this is what you are doing and so present others' work as your own

There is a well-defined procedure to ensure that you act in an academically honest way. You should conform to the recognised standards of good academic practice. What this means is that you should explicitly acknowledge the ownership of the theories, ideas, evidence that you discuss in your work. This is especially so in the case of quotation, i.e. when you quote phrases and/or sentences taken from the work of others.

(Lancaster University 2005b: 22)

Using tables, diagrams and other illustrations

It can be a good idea to include tables, diagrams and other illustrations in your research report or thesis, provided that these are both permitted and relevant. Such illustrations may serve to illuminate, break up, extend and confirm your writing. Their impact and intelligibility can be heightened further if you have access to a colour printer.

Tables may be used to summarize information, usually in a numerical format, and to indicate the relationships between the different variables under consideration. Diagrams, too, are useful for indicating relationships and structures: they can convey ideas much more effectively than lengthy textual explanations.

While tables and diagrams are the most common and popular means for illustrating research reports or theses, many other kinds of illustrations are used. Maps may be included to illustrate relative locations, and are common in geographical research. Graphs show relations between pairs of variables, as in the case of time series or correlations. Photographs also have their uses, particularly for observational or case studies. Line drawings can be employed in a similar fashion. In all cases, these illustrations may be reproduced or original to the research.

Hint: Many computer programs contain facilities for producing tables. See the section on **Computer-based data management and analysis** in Chapter 8.

The question then arises: when should you use such illustrations, and when are they better left out? Box 10.13 offers some general guidance.

Box 10.13 When to use illustrations

- Where the illustration replaces a substantial piece of text (i.e. a paragraph or more), use it, but do not keep the text as well.
- Where the illustration serves to make a point which would be difficult to make, justify or support otherwise, use it.
- Don't use the illustration if it is copyright and you do not have appropriate permission.
- Always refer to illustrations individually in the text. If you don't, there is no reason for the reader to examine them. They are there to be used as an essential part of your argument.
- In most cases, illustrations are better split up, and spread throughout the text close to where they are referred to. If they are gathered together, at the end of chapters or sections, or in an appendix, they are less likely to be consulted by the reader.
- Normally, the text should be the driving force of the research report or thesis. The reader will expect to encounter a near continuous text, interspersed with relevant illustrations. Large clutches of illustrations, or a text dominated by them, are likely to be offputting.
- Don't use the illustration unless it is clear, unambiguous and well reproduced.

Panics

The process of writing up, like many aspects of doing research, is likely to give rise to a number of common worries, particularly among relatively new researchers. We end this chapter, therefore, by considering four of the most common reasons for panics:

- If it's new to me, is it original?
- I've just discovered someone has written this before.
- It's all a load of rubbish.
- Conflicting advice.

If it's new to me, is it original?

See also the section in Chapter 1 on **Will I have anything new to say?**

The answer to the question as posed is, we would suggest, yes. Unless you have totally replicated somebody else's research, using the same literature, methodology, sample and analytical framework – a circumstance which is almost unimaginable unless you set out deliberately to do so – your research will be to some extent original.

You may have used the same methodology and analytical framework, and explored much the same literature, to study a different sample, and come up with much the same conclusions. This is still original research, however, in that you have used a different sample. It could also be very valuable, as replication research may confirm, deny or modify the conclusions of earlier studies.

Unless you are studying for a doctoral degree, trying to build up your research reputation, or are developing an invention for patenting, originality in research is unlikely to be that important. Highly original research is, as we said in Chapter 1, very unusual. So don't worry, and get on with your writing up.

I've just discovered someone has written this before

This is an observation quite often made by new researchers to their supervisors, mentors or managers, but it is never literally true. If it were, you would be guilty of some kind of amazing subconscious plagiarism. What is usually meant is that the researcher has just come across a book or article which makes many of the points their research has raised, or which has studied much the same issues or area. While it's preferable that the book or article has only been recently published, or has been difficult to get hold of, because this suggests that you have carried out a reasonably competent literature review, neither of these findings is cause for despair.

The most appropriate response is to add the book or article to your literature review, explain the circumstances of its discovery, critically assess its argument and then adjust your own report or thesis accordingly. It can actually be very useful to have a similar piece of research with which to confirm and contrast your own approach, argument and findings. It's also quite legitimate to start out with this deliberately in mind. While it may be disappointing to find that you are not first in the field, this is a common enough occurrence in research, and you are almost certain to find something in your own research project which adds to what has already been published.

It's all a load of rubbish

Again, this is a comment frequently made by researchers as they begin to engage with writing up. It usually means one or more of three things:

* you're bored;
* the writing up is not going as well as you think it might;
* you have become so familiar with a group of ideas and theories that they appear to you now to be no more than common sense.

These feelings strike all researchers at some time, and affect most of us with disturbing regularity.

There is no simple and foolproof response. You have to learn to find your own way around this problem, as it is endemic to research (and many other activities). You might, for example:

* take a break or give yourself a treat;
* seek somebody else's opinion on what you have written;
* remind yourself of how far you have travelled on your intellectual journey;
* use some of the suggestions given in the section on **Drafting and redrafting** earlier in this chapter.

Research and writing are, in part, about becoming more self-aware.

Conflicting advice

As a researcher, you are bound to encounter conflicting advice sooner or later, most probably sooner. This is because research is about conflict and uncertainty. We research to better understand our world. Because we do not currently fully understand our world (otherwise we would not be researching), it is likely that our developing understandings will be at least partially conflictual. This state of affairs is, to some extent, encouraged by the way research and research careers are structured. Put simply, one good strategy for getting ahead and being noticed as a researcher is to disagree with the findings of existing research.

Every time you submit your research work for consideration or assessment by more than one other person, you are likely to get more than one view: on your reading, on your methodology, on your findings, on your interpretation of those findings. This may occur even when you have only one adviser, since they are quite likely to disagree with your views and change their own. So you will get conflicting advice. And some people's advice will count for more than other's, because they are an authority or have influence over the progress of your research.

> The problems which power relations can cause are considered further in the section of Chapter 11 on **The process of assessment**.

Probably the best way to cope with this, if you find it unsettling, is to teach yourself to consider it as a strength. In your reading, you should already have come across conflicting views. You are adding to these through your research. Your advisers, and their conflicting views, are helping you to do so. They are giving you the opportunity to respond, in your drafting and redrafting, to some of the range of opinions of relevance to your area of research. The greater the range of the views you are exposed to as you are writing up, the better your report or thesis is likely to be, because it will have to have addressed many of the issues and questions which would otherwise have been raised only after it had been completed.

Conflicting advice is, therefore, to be welcomed, challenged and responded to.

Summary

Having read this chapter, you should:

- appreciate the need to begin writing as soon as possible, and to revisit and revise what you have drafted;
- understand what is meant by critical writing;
- have a greater awareness of who you are writing for, and the alternative writing styles and voices which may be open to you to use;
- have a clearer idea of the structure and organization of your research thesis or report.

Exercises

10.1 Note down the context and themes for your research report or thesis. Draw a diagram or chart to make the linkages between these clear. What does this suggest for the organization and argument of your writing?

10.2 Draw up a chart of how you propose to organize your argument, giving chapter or section titles and summary contents. How much space (or how many words) might you allocate to each of your chapters or sections?

10.3 What writing styles are you comfortable with, and practised at? How appropriate are they for your intended audience(s). Discuss your preferences with your mentor, supervisor and/or manager.

Further reading

In this section, we list a limited selection of books that are of particular relevance to the topics discussed in this chapter.

Berry, R. (2004) *The Research Project: How to write it*, 5th edition. London: Routledge.
 A concise guide to the elements of writing a dissertation, research project or paper. The chapters include discussions of using a library, the internet, preparing a bibliography, taking notes and composing the paper.

Crème, P. and Lea, M. R. (2008) *Writing at University: A guide for students*, 3rd edition. Maidenhead: Open University Press.
 Includes consideration of titles and key words, the role of reading in writing, organization and shaping, academic writing, and putting it all together on time.

Ely, M., Vinz, R., Downing, M. and Anzul, M. (1997) *On Writing Qualitative Research: Living by words*. London: Falmer Press.
 A comprehensive guide to, and analysis of, the processes of, and approaches to, writing. Successive chapters examine the purposes of writing, different narrative forms, analytic and interpretive modes of writing, negotiating, collaborating and responding, and the effects of writing on the writer and readers.

Groarke, L. and Tindale, C. (2004) *Good Reasoning Matters! A constructive approach to critical thinking*, 3rd edition. Oxford: Oxford University Press.
 Fifteen chapters with exercises address such themes as argument diagrams and components, definitions, bias, syllogisms and propositional logic.

Hartley, J. (2008) *Academic Writing and Publishing: A practical handbook*. London: Routledge.

Aims to show postgraduates and new academics (mainly in the social sciences) how to write and publish research articles.

Hertz, R. (ed.) (1997) *Reflexivity and Voice*. Thousand Oaks, CA: Sage.
Contemporary ethnographers grapple with the problems and new conventions of ethnographic writing. Chapters discuss communication problems in intensive care units, fieldwork strategies in cloistered and non-cloistered communities, gender and voice, writing, the limits of informants and interactive interviewing.

Holliday, A. (2002) *Doing and Writing Qualitative Research*. London: Sage.
How to plan, organize and structure qualitative research writing. Includes discussion of the use of identity, the avoidance of essentialist judgements, and the transfer of data to the text.

Lea, M. and Stierer, B. (eds) (2000) *Student Writing in Higher Education: New contexts*. Buckingham: Open University Press.
Focuses on research on student writing and its implications for, primarily, lecturers.

Lillis, T. (2001) *Student Writing: Access, regulation, desire*. London: Routledge.
Informed by UK and US research, argues for a perception of student writing as a social practice rather than a skill.

Murray, N. and Hughes, G. (2008) *Writing up Your University Assignments and Research Projects*. Maidenhead: Open University Press.
Chapters consider the key functions of academic writing, structuring writing, writing style, publishing and presenting, and the correct use of punctuation.

Murray, R. (2002) *How to Write a Thesis*. Buckingham: Open University Press.
Focuses on the development of writing skills and their use in the different stages of working on the thesis.

Murray, R. (2005) *Writing for Academic Journals*. Buckingham: Open University Press.
Which journals to target, how to develop your argument, drafting and redrafting, responding to reviewers' comments: these and related issues are covered in this book.

Murray, R. and Moore, S. (2006) *The Handbook of Academic Writing: A fresh approach*. Maidenhead: Open University Press.
Organized in three parts: defining and understanding academic writing; planning, running and participating in writers' retreats; redefining academic writing practices.

Oliver, P. (2008) *Writing Your Thesis*. London: Sage.
Designed to help postgraduate and research students with the process, preparation, writing and examination of their theses.

Pears, R. and Shields, G. (2005) *Cite Them Right: The essential guide to referencing and plagiarism*. Newcastle upon Tyne: Pear Tree Books.
Accessible guide, covering everything you could imagine ever wanting to cite, from books through journal articles and sacred texts to patents and musical scores.

Seely, J. (2004) *Oxford A–Z of Grammar and Punctuation*. Oxford: Oxford University Press.
Ever been accused of using a split infinitive, or of writing 'it's' when you should have written 'its'. This guide will help sort you out.

Soanes, C. and Ferguson, S. (2004) *Oxford A–Z of Spelling*. Oxford: Oxford University Press.
Over two thousand commonly misspelt words, with associated hints and tips.

Thomson, A. (2001) *Critical Reasoning: A practical introduction*, 2nd edition. London: Routledge.
Containing many exercises and summaries, this text deals with the identification of reasoning and assumptions, the evaluation of reasoning, and recognizing its implications.

Truss, L. (2003) *Eats, Shoots and Leaves: The zero tolerance approach to punctuation*. London: Profile Books.
Best-selling and amusing rant on the use and misuse of apostrophes, commas, dashes etc.

Winter, R., Sobiechowska, P. and Buck, A. (1999) *Professional Experiences and the Investigative Imagination: The art of reflective writing*. London: Routledge.
Explains and demonstrates how creative writing can be used successfully in the context of professional education.

Wolcott, H. (2009) *Writing Up Qualitative Research*, 3rd edition. Thousand Oaks, CA: Sage.
The style is conveyed by the chapter titles: on your mark, get going, keep going . . . getting published.

Woods, P. (1999) *Successful Writing for Qualitative Researchers*. London: Routledge.
Considers all aspects, including getting started, organizing your work, coping with problems and blockages, style and format, editing, writing alone and in a team, approaching publishers and getting published.

11

Finishing off

Introduction • Planning to finish? • The penultimate and final drafts •
Added extras • The process of assessment • What do I do now? •
Summary • Exercise • Further reading

Introduction

For the new researcher, and even many of those with considerable experience, finishing off can be as difficult as getting started. There is a common reluctance to let go, to present the completed work, and then to get on with something else. This is perfectly understandable, of course. If you have spent a long time on a particular task, and have gained something from it, you may not be aware that you have finished. You may be a perfectionist, or think that there is so much more that needs doing.

The purpose of this chapter, then, is to help you finish off your research project. We are assuming that you will be writing up your work for the consideration of others, in many cases for academic credit.

The chapter tackles the following issues:

- **Planning to finish?** Avoidable and unavoidable reasons for not finishing your research project on time.
- **The penultimate and final drafts.** Checking the presentation of your work.
- **Added extras.** When, and when not, to include prefaces or appendices.
- **The process of assessment.** What others may do with your thesis or report.
- **What do I do now?** Building on and looking beyond your research project.

Planning to finish?

There are just so many reasons – and there always have been – for not finishing off and handing in your report or thesis. If you doubt this, look at the list in Box 11.1. As you will see from the twenty suggestions made, some reasons are old and some are new.

Box 11.1 Twenty good reasons for not handing your report or thesis in on time

1 My computer crashed.
2 My car broke down.
3 My funder has refused to allow publication.
4 My mother has just died.
5 I've won the lottery.
6 My informants won't talk to me any more
7 My informants want to talk to me some more.
8 My supervisor won't talk to me.
9 I forgot the deadline.
10 I have too many other things to do.
11 It isn't finished yet.
12 There was a terrorist attack.
13 I've lost it.
14 It must have got lost in the post.
15 I got a (different) job.
16 I decided to get married/have a baby.
17 I haven't got enough data.
18 It isn't good enough.
19 I've not been very well.
20 The other members of my research group haven't finished their bits yet.

If you have been thinking ahead, however – that is, if you have read some or all of this book – you should be able to recognize that:

- some reasons are simply unavoidable: they are connected with life events over which you have no control;
- some reasons could have been avoided: if you had planned ahead, allowed yourself sufficient time and been strict with yourself;
- some reasons lie between the avoidable and the unavoidable: perhaps it's your bad luck that they cropped up, but you might also have anticipated something of this sort.

The message is that planning ahead is indispensable.

The penultimate and final drafts

Writing up your research project was the subject of Chapter 10. As part of that process, you will likely have drafted and redrafted the contents of your report or thesis a number of times. Here, our concern is with getting you from a full and near-final draft of your work – the penultimate draft – to the final draft itself. This is basically a matter of checking your presentation and of making any essential or desirable corrections before you run off, copy and bind the final version. This section provides a simple checklist of points you may need to address. They are summarized in Box 11.2.

Box 11.2 Checking your penultimate draft

---

1 Have you put the title, your name, the date and any other information required on the title page?
2 Are all the pages there?
3 Are they all numbered consecutively?
4 Are all of your chapters and/or sections numbered consecutively?
5 Have you checked for spelling and grammatical errors?
6 Have you allowed adequate margins, and double-spaced if required?
7 Are all the materials referred to in the text listed in the references or bibliography?
8 Have you provided full details for all of your references?
9 Have you checked your text against the regulations?

Checking the title page

What have you called your research report or thesis? Does this title accurately reflect the contents? You may have changed your topic or approach significantly since you began your research, so now could be a good time to revise your title as well if you have not already done so.

The issues involved in choosing a good title are also considered in the section on **What to do if you can't think of a topic** in Chapter 2.

Is your title too unwieldy? If it is to engage the reader, it should be relatively short and pithy. If you want to specifically locate your research, you might consider having a short title and a longer subtitle. The following book titles illustrate this approach:

Doing Cultural Studies: The story of the Sony Walkman
Paradise Dreamed: How utopian thinkers have changed the modern world
Never had it so Good: A history of Britain from Suez to the Beatles

This is, however, very much a matter of taste and style. If you've got a good, accurate, short title, don't feel that you have to embroider it.

The title is not the only thing to go on the title page. You should also add your name (it is surprising how commonly people forget to do this). If you have been involved in a piece of group research, you should already have agreed whose names are to appear on the title page, and in what form, but you may want to revisit and check this before you produce the final version.

You should also add the date, so that readers know when you wrote it, and perhaps your institution or job title, together with anything else you are required to include. For example, in some fields of research, it may be normal practice to acknowledge your sponsor or funder.

Most research reports or theses, unless they are very short, will usually also contain a contents page or pages. This should list your chapters or sections, together with the page or paragraph numbers where they start. Make sure that the titles and subtitles you list in your contents pages are the same as those in the main text, and that the page numbering is accurate.

Checking the contents

Are they all there? Are any pages, or is anything else, missing? Are they of the appropriate length (in terms of words and/or pages)?

Are all of the pages consecutively numbered? You may start your numbering with Arabic numerals (i.e. 1, 2, 3, etc.) from your title page, or you may opt to start the numbering on the first page of your first chapter or section, and either leave the title and contents pages, and any other prefatory material, unnumbered, or number them separately using Roman numerals (i, ii, iii, etc.). Unless you have specific guidance, do what you feel most comfortable with.

Are all of your chapters or sections (and perhaps also paragraphs) numbered consecutively? What about any tables, diagrams or figures? Are they all labelled and numbered appropriately?

Have you checked for spelling and grammatical errors? And how about readability and intelligibility? Here, you might find it useful to get a friend or relative, who need not know anything about the subject of your research, to read through your penultimate draft.

Is the layout as required or appropriate? Have you double-spaced? Have you left wide enough margins for binding, if your report or thesis is going to be bound? If you do not do this, you may find that part of your text, on the left-hand side of the page, either disappears when it is bound or becomes very difficult to read.

Checking the references

Are they all there? Are they in alphabetical order? You will probably have put together the penultimate draft over a period of time, so some sections or chapters, and their associated references or bibliographies, will have been put together well before others. In the process, it is possible that you may have forgotten to add some references, or that some may still be included which are no longer referred to in the text.

You should check two things at this stage:

- Have you provided all the details required for each individual reference, so that your readers can themselves trace them and read them if they so wish?

> If you are in doubt about referencing, see the sections on **Recording your reading** in Chapter 4 and **Grammar, referencing and plagiarism** in Chapter 10.

- Are all of the materials referred to in your text included in your references or bibliography? If you are listing just references rather than a wider bibliography, check also that there are no references listed which are not referred to in your text.

Checking the regulations

If you have been carrying out a research project for academic credit, there will, as has been pointed out a number of times in this book, be a set of regulations which you have to satisfy.

> You may like to refer back to the section in Chapter 2 on **Choosing a topic**.

Even if you are not producing a thesis for academic examination, there will probably still be a series of expectations you need to address.

You may think that you know the appropriate regulations by heart, and that you have been scrupulously following them throughout your research, but it is still a good idea to check them now. Similarly, you will probably find it useful to think about the expectations of those people who are going to read your thesis or report, and perhaps make a few amendments if this seems advisable. This important point is discussed in the section on **The process of assessment** later in this chapter.

Added extras

In addition to the basic components of almost any research report or dissertation – a title page, a contents page, a series of chapters or sections, a set of references or a bibliography – there are a number of additional or optional elements which you might wish to include. These could be acknowledgements, a preface, a dedication, an abstract and one or more appendices. The basic question to be addressed here is: do you really need any of these? On balance, if they are not required or necessary, we would recommend doing without all of them, for two related reasons.

First, they add to the length of your report or thesis. This may be a critical factor if you have a word or page limit, but should be an important consideration whatever your situation. Think of your readership, and of your own experience as a reader: do you really want your readers to have to wade through, and probably ignore, page after page of material at the beginning or end of your work? Second, if what is contained in this supplementary material is so important to your report or dissertation, shouldn't it be contained within the main body of the work itself, where it will be given proper attention?

However, there may be good reasons why you want or need to include one or more of these 'added extras'. Let us consider them individually.

Acknowledgements

The usual purpose of acknowledgements is to give credit to people or organizations who were particularly helpful to you in carrying out your research. In some cases, they may be used critically, as when those who have not been as helpful as you might have liked or expected are damned with faint praise; but that is probably best avoided.

Including a list of acknowledgements on a separate page at the front of your report or thesis can be a pleasant way of paying your dues. Those who might be mentioned could include your sponsor (mention of whom may be a mandatory requirement), supervisor, colleagues, family and friends, secretary or typist, copy editor, as well as any fellow researchers. The list might also include those who gave you access, and even your research subjects, but bear in mind any requirements of confidentiality here. You may, of course, wish (or have promised) to give copies of your report or dissertation to some of those you mention.

Prefaces

A preface is a form of writing which falls outside of the conventions of the main body of your text, and for that reason should not say anything which adds materially to the content of the main text. Prefaces are most typically used to say something about the author's personal experience of carrying out the research and writing it up. Where the research has been a group activity, a preface might locate the individual's work within the larger whole. Prefaces often include a list of acknowledgements at the end.

Dedications

Dedications are largely a matter of personal taste. They can be a nice way to ritualize the ending of a significant piece of work, and, at the same time, to link this to someone you respect or love. Thus, you might want to dedicate your report or dissertation to your partner or lover, to your children or parents. Alternatively, you might name it for someone who has been particularly influential or helpful to you in carrying out the research. The recipient of your dedication may be alive or dead, and you may never have met them. You might, though, at least in some cases, wish to check with them first before you put your dedication in print, or to send them a copy of the completed text.

Abstracts

Of all the added extras we have identified, an abstract is without doubt likely to be the most useful. It may also be a mandatory requirement. The executive summary, so beloved of business and commerce, may be seen as roughly equivalent. The function of the abstract or executive summary is to summarize the nature of your research project, its context, how it was carried out, and what its major findings were. Ideally, it should require no more than one page of text, and will typically be restricted to 200–300 words or less (i.e. no more than one page).

Abstracts are extremely useful to the potential reader, and for this reason are commonly published in specialist journals (now typically online) which publish nothing but abstracts. An abstract can help the potential reader decide quickly whether it is worth looking at a publication more closely. Many of your readers will likely do no more than look at the abstract, so it is important that you get it right.

Abstracts, or executive summaries, can also be helpful to the writer in forcing them to distil their wisdom as briefly as possible. This may then assist you in restructuring and putting together the final draft. They are, however, quite difficult to write well. You may find it useful to refer back to Chapter 4, particularly Exercise 4.3. If you would like or need some practice at writing abstracts, try Exercise 11.1.

Appendices

Researchers, and not just novice ones, are often tempted to include all kinds of material in the form of appendices at the end of their reports or dissertations. These may include copies of letters and questionnaires, transcripts of interviews, summaries of case studies, reproductions of institutional documents, and so forth.

While all of this material is, in some sense, relevant to your research, it is questionable whether you should aim to include any or all of it in your report. You are highly unlikely to be able to include all of the original material you have collected or generated during the course of your project. Much, therefore, has to be summarized or left out and, to a certain extent, taken on trust.

There are considerable advantages in minimizing, or omitting altogether, the use of appendices. It can be very irritating for the reader who is working their way through the main body of your text to be directed to one appendix after another for more details. Too often, the temptation will be not to bother, and the appendices you have so carefully put together will be ignored.

So, if you have to include some material which you have thought of putting in appendices, you might consider instead including this in the main body of your text. Or, alternatively, you might place your appendices at the end of the sections or chapters in which they are referred to, rather than at the end of your report or dissertation as a whole.

Remember to keep all of these added extras short and to the point!

The process of assessment

Once you have completed what you consider to be the final draft of your thesis or report, it is time to type or print it out; check again that everything is there and in the right order; make the requisite number of copies; get it bound or stapled together; and hand it to your supervisor, manager or readers.

If you have undertaken your research in an academic context, your dissertation or thesis will now be assessed by one or more examiners. The actual arrangements and regulations will vary from institution to institution, and depending upon the level of the course involved, so you will need to check these individually.

If you have been researching as part of your work role, or out of personal interest, your final report may not be assessed in an academic way, but it is still going to be read and 'judged' by others. The criteria on which this judgement is made may vary, but the process will be analogous to that which takes place in an academic setting.

There are several common issues which arise during this process:

- How will your work be received?
- What are the roles of your supervisor, examiner, manager, mentor, colleagues, funders or prospective publishers?
- What specific events are associated with the process of assessment?
- How do you cope with criticism, referral or rejection?

How will your work be received?

The period after you have completed your thesis or report can be one of considerable anti-climax. It may take months for the process of assessment to be completed. You may never receive any extended comments on your work. It can feel as if you have worked hard for a long time to no great purpose, as if no one is particularly interested in what you have done or what you have found, or as if everyone who is not indifferent is highly critical of what you have done. If doing research is a risky business, writing up that research for assessment makes these risks visible. To the individual participant, the whole process of assessment can seem to be an arbitrary and secret business.

It is natural to be concerned about how your work will be received, whether by your examiners, your colleagues, your family, the subjects of your research or other readers. There is a whole range of techniques which you might use in order to try to reduce any stress this may be causing you. There is relatively little you can do, however, to speed up the process, and you may need to exercise a considerable amount of patience and self-restraint. The middle of the process of assessment is probably not a good time to ask your supervisor or manager whether your work was good enough. It may be out of their hands, or they may not be in a position to tell you.

There are, though, plenty of things you can do once an initial assessment has been reached, and these are discussed in the sections which follow.

What are the roles of your supervisor, examiner, manager, mentor, colleagues, funders or prospective publishers?

Understanding the roles of those who may be involved in the process of assessment is an important, though usually avoided or overlooked, part of being a researcher. Two key aspects of these roles are not widely appreciated:

- The process of assessment can be as much an assessment of those doing the assessing as it is of the person(s) being assessed. The judgement of your assessors may be called into question, just as the quality of your work may be found wanting. So the process can be a stressful one for all concerned. Remember, research can be very threatening.
- The assessments of your report or thesis made by your assessors may not be consistent. They may be quite at liberty to disagree with each other, so the process of assessment may be largely about resolving those disagreements.

> You may find it useful to refer back to the discussion on conflicting advice in the section on **Panics** in Chapter 10.

While the assessment process may differ widely from institution to institution, and from case to case, there are certain features which tend to be common.

You should make it your business, if you do not already know, to find out as much as you can in advance about the practices affecting you.

If your thesis or dissertation is being assessed for academic credit, there should be considered and written regulations which apply to your case. Get hold of a copy and make sure that you understand them. While university and college practices vary, much also depends upon the level of degree you are studying for: e.g. first degree, masters degree, doctoral degree (see Box 11.3).

Box 11.3 Common academic assessment practices

The higher the level of qualification involved, the more likely are the following:

- Your assessment will no longer be largely a matter for the members of the department you have been studying in (internal examiners), but will involve a substantial input by academics from one or more other institutions (external examiners).
- Your academic supervisor will have less direct involvement in these processes.
- You will be assessed on your own, rather than at the same time as others who have been studying for the same qualification.
- The assessment will involve you in making a presentation to, and answering questions from, your examiners (this is considered further in the next subsection).
- Your work will be referred back for some further work, probably relatively minor in nature (this slightly worrying, but common, experience is considered further in the next but one subsection).

If your research report is being assessed in the work setting – as well as, or instead of, by a university or college – the process may be broadly analogous, but the emphases are likely to differ (see Box 11.4). However, assessment of research in the work setting is much less likely to be bound by regulations, or even established practices. It is, correspondingly, much more likely to focus on the practical changes or applications which might stem from your research.

What specific events are associated with the process of assessment?

The event most likely to be associated with the process of assessing a research report or thesis is some kind of presentation, perhaps a seminar if the research has been carried out in a work setting, or a viva if it has been completed for academic credit. In many, probably most, cases, however, particularly if you have been carrying out a relatively small-scale piece of research, or have not been studying for a research degree, there is unlikely to be a formal presentation involved. Unless you choose, and are able, to arrange one yourself, that is.

Box 11.4 Common work assessment practices

Depending on the size of your organization and the importance to it of the work you have been carrying out, as well as your own status within the organization, the process may involve:

- A simple report in writing to your immediate superior, or a substantial, glossy and widely circulated (at least internally) publication.
- A brief meeting with your immediate superior, a seminar to a section or group of managers, or a presentation to the board or to the leader of the whole organization.
- Little or no follow-up of the work itself, or a large-scale dissemination and retraining exercise.

Research presentations may have a number of related purposes. At the simplest level, they are about your having the opportunity to present your work to an audience in summary form, perhaps focusing upon your findings and conclusions, and the possible implications and applications of these. Beyond that, they are also concerned with giving you and your audience the opportunity to discuss your work together, perhaps with a particular emphasis on how it relates their own work and concerns. This also implies, of course, that you may be put on the defensive, criticized and challenged (the subject of the next subsection).

If your research has been carried out in a work setting, your presentation may involve close colleagues or superiors, those particularly concerned with your findings and in the best place to do something with them. There may be expectations that you use PowerPoint, and provide a handout and executive summary. The focus is likely to be on the extent to which your conclusions and recommendations fit with received wisdom and practices, or respond to particular felt needs or problems. There is likely to be less interest in how you actually did the research, and on any difficulties you may have encountered. The tenor of the meeting is likely to be fairly brisk and practical.

If, on the other hand, your research has been carried out for academic credit, then your viva, if you have one, will probably involve only two or three people. One of these may be your supervisor, but you may have met none of them before. However, you may, if you have prepared wisely, be familiar with their work, and have read and referred to some of it in your thesis (preferably not too critically). More advice on vivas is given in the references listed at the end of this chapter.

One common characteristic of most presentations, whether in academic or work settings, is that you are likely to be, and feel, on your own. This is unlikely to be the case, of course, if you have been involved in a piece of group research, though you may still feel alone when you come to present your bit. If this is going to bother you greatly, it may be worth investigating whether you can take some kind of supporter along with you (a friend, your supervisor, a colleague), even if they can take no direct part in the process. It's also a good idea to have a practice run, something your department, supervisor or manager may be happy to arrange for you.

Box 11.5 offers some general advice if you are going to present your research.

Box 11.5 What to do before presenting your research

Prepare as thoroughly as possible:

- Find out who is going to be there, what their interests and backgrounds are.
- Practise presenting the results of your research, using audio-visual aids if these are available and allowed.
- Keep up to date with what has happened in your research area in the period between finishing your report or thesis and its presentation.
- Read and reread your thesis or report so that you know it backwards, and can quickly find and respond to specific queries.
- Practise with a friend or colleague responding to questions of a friendly or unfriendly nature.
- Work out some questions which you would like to ask as part of the process.
- Be prepared to enjoy and get something out of your presentation, though you may also find it a draining and stressful procedure.
- Remember that you do have some measure of control: you know more about your particular piece of research than anyone else.
- Be prepared to defend and promote your work, while recognizing its limitations and deficiencies.

How do you cope with criticism, referral or rejection?

If your research project has been at all challenging and worthwhile, you are likely to meet with some criticism. You may also meet with referral, if you have carried out the work for academic credit, and possibly outright rejection. You may find these responses more or less difficult to cope with.

Criticism is, however, part of the process of doing research. Just as you have to be able, and are expected, to criticize other researchers and writers, so you have to be able to handle and respond to criticism of your own work. The most positive way of handling it is to see it as something which itself contributes to your research, potentially making it a better piece of work. Seen from that perspective, responding to criticism may have a number of typical stages (see Box 11.6).

If at all possible, do not be pressurized to respond instantly to criticism, even if it is presented verbally during your presentation. Take your time. Criticisms

---

Box 11.6 Responding to criticism

After recovering from any initial disappointment:

- Initially welcome and acknowledge the criticism.
- Evaluate the validity and implications of the criticism for your research.
- Compare each criticism with the other responses your work has engendered.
- Possibly modify your research findings or strategies.
- Make a considered response to the criticism.

---

may cause you to alter your report or thesis, usually to its benefit, but they can also be misguided.

Referral is a common response to research work carried out for academic credit. It means that your work is not judged to be quite up to scratch for the qualification you are seeking, but that you are being given a further opportunity to bring it up to scratch. As an alternative, and this is unusual, you might be offered a lower-level qualification than the one you were aiming for.

The modifications which your assessors suggest you make to your thesis will usually be fairly minor, but may be quite far-reaching. You should be given a specific timescale in which to make the corrections or amendments, fairly detailed guidance about what needs changing, and some further support from your supervisor during this process. Check the regulations, particularly those to do with appeals.

Let's make no bones about it. Referral is disappointing at best, depressing at worse. It places extra demands upon your time, and is likely to impose some additional costs. It is best avoided altogether, if at all possible, by making sure that you have done well enough before you submit your work for assessment. Even with the best intentions, however, this may not always be possible. You may have been poorly advised. You may have ignored the good advice you were given. Or you may have run out of time.

Referral can make you feel like giving up. It is probably best to think of it as a normal and common part of the academic assessment process, another hurdle to be cleared, which will have some benefits for you and your research, and which will lead on to the desired end of qualification. Having been once referred, you are relatively unlikely to be referred or rejected again, always provided that you carefully follow the guidance which you should be given on how to improve your report or thesis.

If your research report or thesis is rejected, however, things look rather gloomier. In an academic setting, you may be able to appeal if, for example, you believe your assessors have not reached their decision fairly, or have done so in ignorance of relevant facts. In a work setting, this is likely to be difficult unless you have recourse to other influential contacts within your organization. In extreme cases, recourse to the law may be a possibility. Bear in mind, however, that if your work has been rejected there are likely to be good reasons for this decision, even if you do not find them particularly palatable.

In the end, how you respond to rejection comes down to how committed you feel personally to the research you have carried out. You may be best advised to try to forget it and get on with the rest of your life. Or you could think in terms of dissemination and publication, or of further research (these are discussed in the next section).

What do I do now?

OK, you've finished! Your research project has been completed, written up, submitted and assessed. You are likely to feel at least two things. On the one hand, a great sense of relief and release, as if a great weight has been removed from your shoulders. On the other hand, a sense of loss, of a gaping whole in your life which will need filling in some way. What do you do now? The options are potentially limitless, restricted only by your resources, situation and imagination. Box 11.7 makes twenty more or less serious suggestions.

Box 11.7 Twenty things to do now that you've finished your research

1   Take a holiday.
2   Go to bed.
3   Stay in the sauna until you have forgotten it.
4   Celebrate with close family and friends.
5   Take the dog for more walks.
6   Try for promotion.
7   Organize seminars to disseminate your findings.
8   Plan what you are going to wear to your graduation.
9   Collect information about other courses of study or sources of research funding.
10 Read a good book.
11 Burn your books.
12 Go on a diet.
13 Give some time to your family.
14 Write up and publish your research.
15 Write to us about how you used this book.
16 Get another job.
17 Implement your findings.
18 Have another drink.
19 Get yourself a life.
20 Do some more research.

Three of the suggestions in Box 11.7 can be seen as part of the research process itself; namely:

- presentation;
- publication; and
- further research.

In other words, your research isn't really over when it's been written up and assessed. If it is of any potential interest or use to others, you owe it to yourself, your organization and the subjects of your research to disseminate it.

Presentation

Dissemination is the process by which you communicate your research report or thesis, its findings and recommendations, to other potentially interested parties. You might think about presenting your work:

- within your organization;
- to meetings where people from similar organizations gather;
- to your union branch;
- to professional associations;
- to a local adult education group;
- at national or international conferences.

There are also various different formats in which you might present your work: as a lecture (or series of lectures), as a seminar, as a workshop. Whichever format you adopt, however, you will need to give some thought (and practice) to how you present, particularly if you haven't done this kind of thing before.

Really confident presenters who have a lot to say can just sit or stand and talk for however long is needed or available; or, at least, they seem to be able to do so. Most of us, however, need props of one kind or another. The days of 'chalk and talk' seem now long gone, and even those who rely on a series of overhead (OHP) transparencies seem old-fashioned. The more dynamic can still work wonders with a flipchart and pens, scribbling down ideas and issues as they arise.

For most conferences and other forms of presentation, PowerPoint seems to have become the norm. You work out the structure and content of your presentation in advance, prepare a succession of screens and points, and then run through them in order as you present. PowerPoint can be less flexible than other means of presentation, unless you are adept with the software, and you are reliant on the technology working (don't assume that there will be technical support on hand). As you grow more confident, you can include sound or video clips, and digitized images, in your computer-assisted presentations.

Whatever form of presentation you adopt, then, planning and practice are clearly the keys. Run through the whole presentation a number of times, on your own or with family or friends, check how long it takes and how well it works, and modify accordingly.

You might also think about presenting in a written as well as a spoken form; that is, you may think about publication.

Publication

Publication, like dissemination in general, takes a variety of forms. It may be restricted to internal, and perhaps confidential, circulation within your organization or kindred bodies. It may be popular, professional or academic. It may be placed in mass-market newspapers or magazines, or in small circulation specialist journals. It may be in the form of a book, and may be self-published and distributed.

If you are interested in publishing your research, there are a number of general points to bear in mind:

- Think carefully about the audience for your research. What will they be interested in reading about, and how best might you present it?
- If you are looking to publish in a journal or magazine of some kind, examine a number of recent issues carefully to get a better idea of the kind of material they publish. Look at the length and structure of articles, their use of references and language. Are there recent articles you might respond to? Specific guidance is often given in journals, or on their websites. It may be a good idea to contact the editor for advice in advance as well, enclosing or attaching a synopsis of your article.
- If you are thinking of writing a book, contact possible publishers before you do much work. They will be interested in the saleability of your product as much as its inherent quality, and you may need to modify your proposal accordingly. Having a good idea of your potential audience, or market, and of any competing publications, is critical here.

Seeking publication, like research in general, exposes you to the opinions and critique of others, and it is normal to suffer rejection as part of this process, particularly if you pitch your writing to higher-status journals or publishers. The best advice is not to be too disheartened, learn what you can from any feedback or advice you may be given, and press on. There are so many outlets for research-based writing now that you are likely to be able to publish your findings and ideas somewhere, provided you do have something of some interest to say.

Further research

The final option suggested in this section is that of engaging in further research. It is something of an in-joke in research circles that one of the main recommendations of any research project is always that 'further research is needed'. This is not simply a matter of trying to ensure further employment and funding. It is a characteristic of any research project that it almost always generates more questions than answers. Doing research is, therefore, and perhaps primarily, a very good method of determining what needs researching.

It is also a somewhat addictive process for many people. Once you have demonstrated to your own and others' satisfaction that you can do competent research, and that you enjoy and get something from the process, it is very tempting to go on to do more, even if it is not your job. You may now be in a better position to get some funding to expand your research. So, if you want to, do some more research: it's not a sin, at least not a mortal one!

Summary

Having read this chapter, you should:

- appreciate the importance of finishing the research project you are engaged in;
- understand the checking processes you will need to go through in preparing the final draft of your report or thesis;
- be aware of the uses and disadvantages of prefatory material and appendices;
- be forewarned of what might happen during the assessment of your report or thesis;
- know of the options for presenting your results, and for engaging in further research if you wish.

Exercise

11.1 Write a summary of your research project, allowing one sentence each to introduce and contextualize the topic, describe how you carried out the research, and identify the main conclusions and implications (i.e. three sentences in all). Don't write sentences of unwieldy length or structure. Once you have done this, you could do two further things. First, reduce your summary down to a single sentence: this should be useful when people ask you to briefly summarize your research. Second, expand your sentences to provide a fuller summary, but keep it to 200 words or less. This can form the basis for your abstract. Take no more than half an hour in total.

Further reading

In this section we list a limited selection of books, together with an indication of their contents. The selection is in two parts:

• 'How to' guides to the final stages of research, and to what happens next.
• Texts designed to provide a basis for further, and often deeper or more theoretical, reading in different areas of social research.

Guides to the final stages and beyond

Coley, S. M. and Scheinberg, C. A. (2000) *Proposal Writing*, 2nd edition. Thousand Oaks, CA: Sage.
A basic guide to proposal writing, dealing with the context, the different elements of the proposal, and budgetting.

Delamont, S. and Atkinson, P. (2004) *Successful Research Careers: A practical guide*. Maidenhead: Open University Press.
Designed both for those starting a research career and those who advise or support them. Considers getting grants, publishing in journals and writing books, among other topics.

Hughes, C. (ed.) (2003) *Disseminating Qualitative Research in Educational Settings: A critical introduction*. Buckingham: Open University Press.
Six examples of practice are framed within a analysis of historical and contemporary issues, models of dissemination and developing informed practice.

Locke, L. F., Spirduso, W. W. and Silverman, S. J. (2000) *Proposals that Work: A guide for planning dissertations and grant proposals*, 4th edition. Thousand Oaks, CA: Sage.
The three parts cover: writing the proposal (function, content, style, presentation); getting money for research; four examples of specimen proposals.

Murray, R. (2003) *How to Survive your Viva*. Maidenhead: Open University Press.
A practical guide for all of those involved in the viva, which urges planning from the early stages of the research project.

Murray, R. (2005) *Writing for Academic Journals*. Maidenhead: Open University Press.
How to target journals, develop an argument, draft and redraft, and cope with reviewers' feedback.

Punch, K. (2006) *Developing Effective Research Proposals*, 2nd edition. London: Sage.
Considers the context and functions of proposals, and offers guidance on their development.

Tinkler, P. and Jackson, C. (2004) *The Doctoral Examination Process: A handbook for students, examiners and supervisors*. Maidenhead: Open University Press.

Examines the theory and practice of the doctoral examination process in the UK, with guidance for students, supervisors and examiners.

More in-depth reading on social research

Alvesson, M. and Skoldberg, K. (2009) *Reflexive Methodology: New vistas for qualitative research*, 2nd edition. London: Sage.
Reflexivity is presented as an essential part of the research process, enabling field research and interpretations to be placed in perspective. Empiricism, hermeneutics, critical theory, post-structuralism and postmodernism are considered.

Andrews, M., Squire, C. and Tamboukou, M. (eds) (2008) *Doing Narrative Research*. London: Sage.
A comprehensive guide to narrative methods, taking the reader from initial decisions about forms of narrative analysis, through more complex issues of reflexivity, interpretation and the research context.

Atkinson, P., Delamont, S., Coffey, A., Lofland, J. and Lofland, L. (eds) (2007) *Handbook of Ethnography*. London: Sage.
Organized in three sections: the first locates ethnography within its relevant historical and intellectual contexts; the second examines the contribution of ethnography to major fields of substantive research; and the third examines key debates and issues.

Bauer, M. W. and Gaskell, G. (eds) (2000) *Qualitative Researching with Text, Image and Sound*. London: Sage.
The book is organized in four parts: examining different ways of collecting data and different types of data, the main analytic approaches, computer-assisted analysis, and issues of good practice.

Bowen, J. and Petersen, R. (eds) (1999) *Critical Comparisons in Politics and Culture*. Cambridge: Cambridge University Press.
Anthropologists and political scientists debate the problem of comparison, and critique conventional forms of comparative method. Abstract model building and ethnographically based approaches are discussed.

Broussine, M. (2008) *Creative Methods in Organizational Research*. London: Sage.
Chapters consider underlying theories and principles, critical awareness, creative dialogue, drawings and art, stories, poetry, masks and theatre.

Brown, T. and Jones, L. (2001) *Action Research and Postmodernism: Congruence and critique*. Buckingham: Open University Press.
Two teacher educators consider how conventional approaches to action research can be developed through the application of post-structural ideas.

Chamberlayne, P., Bornat, J. and Wengraf, T. (2000) *The Turn to Biographical Methods in Social Science*. London: Routledge.
Examines the historical and philosophical origins of biographical research methods, and shows how such methods are currently useful and popular. Topics discussed include generational change and social upheaval, political influences on memory and identity, and individual and researcher narratives.

Charmaz, K. (2006) *Constructing Grounded Theory: A practical guide through qualitative analysis*. Thousand Oaks, CA: Sage.
Introduces the reader to the craft of using grounded theory in social research, mapping out an alternative vision to that put forward by its founding thinkers, Glaser and Strauss. For Charmaz, grounded theory must move on from its positivist origins and incorporate many of the methods and questions posed by constructivists to become a more nuanced and reflexive practice.

Clough, P. (2002) *Narratives and Fictions in Educational Research*. Buckingham: Open University Press.
Uses five fictional stories to demonstrate the use of narrative in reporting research, discussing how they were created and the role of the author in their creation.

Cohen, M. Z., Kahn, D. L. and Steeves, R. H. (2000) *Hermeneutic Phenomenological Research: A practical guide for nurse researchers*. Thousand Oaks, CA: Sage.
Hermeneutic phenomenology, the study of how people interpret their lives, is presented as ideally suited to nursing research. This book explains how to conduct such a research project, from writing the proposal, through sampling and data collection, to analysis and writing up.

Corbin, J. and Strauss, A. (2008) *Basics of Qualitative Research: Techniques and procedures for developing grounded theory*, 3rd edition. Thousand Oaks, CA: Sage.
Chapters consider the use of memos and diagrams, theoretical sampling, analysing data for concepts and context, and bringing process into the analysis.

Cramer, D. (2003) *Advanced Quantitative Data Analysis*. Maidenhead: Open University Press.
Reasonably accessible explanation of advanced statistical and multivariate techniques, and of common associated software.

Crang, M. and Cook, I. (2007) *Doing Ethnographies*. London: Sage.
An introductory and applied guide to ethnographic methods, focusing on the use of participant observation, interviewing, focus groups and video/photographic work for understanding the lived, everyday world.

Czarniawska, B. (2004) *Narratives in Social Science Research*. London: Sage.
Offers guidelines on the use of narratives in fieldwork and research.

Denzin, N. and Lincoln, Y. (eds) (2003) *The Landscape of Qualitative Research: Theories and issues*, 2nd edition. Thousand Oaks, CA: Sage.
A substantive guide organized in three parts: locating the field, major paradigms and perspectives, the future of qualitative research.

Denzin, N. and Lincoln, Y. (eds) (2003) *Strategies of Qualitative Inquiry*, 2nd edition. Thousand Oaks, CA: Sage.
Considers a wide range of qualitative strategies, from performance ethnography to grounded theory to life history.

Denzin, N. and Lincoln, Y. (eds) (2005) *The Sage Handbook of Qualitative Research*, 3rd edition. Thousand Oaks, CA: Sage.

1210 pages of contributions organized in six sections: locating the field; paradigms and perspectives in contention; strategies of inquiry; methods of collecting and analysing empirical material; the arts and practices of interpretation, evaluation and presentation; the future of qualitative research.

Ekegren, P. (1999) *The Reading of Theoretical Texts*. London: Routledge.
Contributes to methodological debates in the social sciences through an examination of developments in literary criticism, philosophy and critical theory.

Elliott, J. (2005) *Using Narrative in Social Research: Qualitative and quantitative approaches*. London: Sage.
Argues that research data can best be analysed if seen in narrative terms, with guidance on methods and methodologies.

Emmison, M. and Smith, P. (2000) *Researching the Visual: Images, objects, contexts and interactions in social and cultural enquiry*. London: Sage.
Considers the contributions of semiotics, ethnomethodology, symbolic interactionism and material culture studies.

Evans, L. (2002) *Reflective Practice in Educational Research*. London: Continuum.
Focuses on the development of advanced research skills.

Fern, E. (2001) *Advanced Focus Group Research*. Thousand Oaks, CA: Sage.
For those who already have some experience of using this technique.

Giles, D. (2002) *Advanced Research Methods in Psychology*. London: Routledge.
Covers the analysis of variance, regression techniques, questionnaires and scales, qualitative methods and other approaches.

Goodson, I. and Sikes, P. (2001) *Life History Research in Educational Settings: Learning from lives*. Buckingham: Open University Press.
Chapters discuss techniques, epistemological considerations, social context, ethics and power, and dilemmas.

Greig, A. and Taylor, J. (1999) *Doing Research with Children*. London: Sage.
A comprehensive and practical introduction to the issues involved. Three parts cover: the special nature of children in research, and appropriate theories and approaches; reviewing, designing and conducting research with children; and ethical and other issues.

Griffiths, M. (1998) *Educational Research for Social Justice: Getting off the fence*. Buckingham: Open University Press.
A book for those educational researchers motivated by considerations of justice, fairness and equity. Due attention is given to both theoretical frameworks and practical possibilities.

Hack, V. (1997) *Targeting the Powerful: International prospect research*. London: Association for Information Management.
Explains how to conduct in-depth research into a person, company or charitable foundation, and how then to use this information to recommend a line of approach most likely to succeed. Includes a detailed list of books, online suppliers and websites for major countries worldwide.

Hammersley, M. (ed.) (1999) *Researching School Experience: Explorations of teaching and learning*. London: Routledge.

Twelve chapters report on research into, for example, the effects of audit accountability on primary teachers' professionalism, the effects of recent educational reforms, the influences of parenthood on teaching, issues of gender in the classroom and learning about health risks.

Hammersley, M. (2000) *Taking Sides in Social Research*. London: Routledge.
Assesses debates about the inevitability of research being political in its assumptions. Includes a consideration of the contribution of 'founding fathers', such as Mills and Becker, and brings the debate up to the present day.

Hammersley, M. (ed.) (2007) *Educational Research and Evidence-Based Research*. London: Sage.
Combines classic articles with new material to address the problems involved in educational research and the issues surrounding its contribution to policy making and practice.

Have, P. ten (2007) *Doing Conversation Analysis*, 2nd edition. London: Sage.
Aims to introduce the reader to conversation analysis and to provide methodological and practical suggestions for doing conversation analysis research.

Hayes, N. (2000) *Doing Psychological Research: Gathering and analysing data*. Buckingham: Open University Press.
A substantial text, with chapters on such topics as psychometrics, ethnography, conversations and descriptive statistics.

Heath, S., Brooks, R., Cleaver, E. and Ireland, E. (2009) *Researching Young People's Lives*. London: Sage.
An overview of some of the key methodological challenges facing youth researchers and an introduction to the broad repertoire of methods used in youth-oriented research.

Hine, C. (2000) *Virtual Ethnography*. London: Sage.
Includes chapters on the internet as culture and cultural artefact, time, space and technology, authenticity and identity, and reflection.

Holcomb, E. L. (1999) *Getting Excited About Data: How to combine people, passion and proof*. Thousand Oaks, CA: Corwin Press.
Designed for school teachers who want to be able to demonstrate how well their pupils are learning and achieving.

Hollway, W. and Jefferson, T. (2000) *Doing Qualitative Research Differently: Free association, narrative and the interview method*. London: Sage.
Argues for the centrality of narrative and an interpretive method which gives interviewees' free associations precedence over coherence. The use of this approach is then examined, with examples, through the phases of empirical research practice.

Hood, S., Mayall, B. and Oliver, S. (eds) (1999) *Critical Issues in Social Research: Power and prejudice*. Buckingham: Open University Press.
This book addresses the questions: whose interests are served by research? For whom is it undertaken? What research methods are appropriate? How can the researched find a voice in the research process? It considers

research on children, women, black people, elderly people, gay men and the disabled.

House, E. R. and Howe, K. R. (1999) *Values in Evaluation and Social Research*. Thousand Oaks, CA: Sage.
The three sections of this book consider value claims (facts and values, evaluative reasoning), critiques of other views (received, radical constructivist and postmodernist views) and deliberative democratic evaluation.

Hymes, D. (1996) *Ethnography, Linguistics, Narrative Inequality: Towards an understanding of voice*. London: Routledge.
Illustrates the contributions that ethnography and linguistics have made to education, as well as the contribution that education makes to linguistics and anthropology.

Jarvis, P. (1999) *The Practitioner-Researcher: Developing theory from practice*. San Francisco: Jossey-Bass.
This book is organized in five parts, considering the connections between research and practice, the nature of practice, research in practice, practice and theory, and the role of the practitioner-researcher. Designed to help all practitioners for whom research is a tool to help improve practice.

Josselson, R. and Lieblich, A. (eds) (1999) *Making Meaning of Narratives*. Thousand Oaks, CA: Sage.
Following an introductory review chapter, contributors focus on a range of narrative settings. Issues discussed range from the transformation of meanings across generations to the transformational power of stories within organizations.

Layder, D. (1998) *Sociological Practice: Linking theory and social research*. London: Sage.
Considers not just the relations between theory and research, but also practical ways in which research can be theoretically informed and theory can be empirically supported.

Lewis, A. and Lindsay, G. (eds) (1999) *Researching Children's Perspectives*. Buckingham: Open University Press.
Designed for researchers and graduate students in psychology, education, health, social work and law, addressing the issues and practicalities surrounding the obtaining of children's views.

Lieblich, A., Tuval-Mashiach, R. and Zilber, T. (1998) *Narrative Research: Reading, analysis and interpretation*. Thousand Oaks, CA: Sage.
Considers how to read, analyse and interpret life story materials. Four models of reading are presented: holistic-content, holistic-form, categorical-content and categorical-form. Two narratives are then introduced and analysed using these models.

MacLure, M. (2003) *Discourse in Educational and Social Research*. Buckingham: Open University Press.
Practical and provocative, and drawing on a variety of examples of discourses: press articles, life history interviews, parent–teacher consultations, policy debates and ethnographies.

McCulloch, G. and Richardson, W. (2000) *Historical Research in Educational Settings*. Buckingham: Open University Press.
A guide to theory, rationales and problems, as well as to the opportunities for research in the field.
McGivern, Y. (2003) *The Practice of Market and Social Research: An introduction*. Harlow: Prentice Hall.
Examines market research alongside social research in general.
Middlewood, D., Coleman, M. and Lumby, J. (1999) *Practitioner Research in Education*. London: Paul Chapman.
Drawing on the experience of participants in a university educational management programme, the text aims to show how research can make a difference in a wide range of educational contexts in several countries.
Okeley, J. (1996) *Own or Other Culture*. London: Routledge.
Challenges the idea that fieldwork in familiar western settings is easy, or that it discovers what is already 'known'. The subjects examined include British boarding schools, gypsies and feminism.
Ozga, J. (1999) *Policy Research in Educational Settings: Contested terrain*. Buckingham: Open University Press.
Offers guidance on the theoretical and methodological resources available for those with an interest in doing research, and discusses some of the main issues and problems which they may face.
Pink, S. (2006) *Doing Visual Ethnography*, 2nd edition. London: Sage.
Explores the use and potential of photography, video and hypermedia in ethnographic and social research, offering a reflexive approach to the theoretical, methodological, practical and ethical issues of using these media now that they are increasingly being incorporated into field research.
Prichard, C. and Trowler, P. (eds) (2003) *Realizing Qualitative Research into Higher Education*. Aldershot: Ashgate Press.
Ten chapters offer reflections on researching student learning, teaching practices and organization and management.
Prosser, J. (ed.) (1998) *Image-Based Research: A sourcebook for qualitative researchers*. London: Falmer Press.
Eighteen chapters consider the theory, process and practice of image-based research in anthropology, sociology, psychology and education. The examples covered include film, photographs, cartoons, graffiti, maps, drawings, diagrams, signs and symbols.
Rapley, T. (2008) *Doing Conversation, Discourse and Document Analysis*. London: Sage.
Chapters consider studying discourse, generating an archive, ethics and recording data, transcribing, exploring conversations and exploring documents.
Ribbens, J. and Edwards, R. (eds) (1998) *Feminist Dilemmas in Qualitative Research: Public knowledge and private lives*. London: Sage.
The book is organized around the concept of voice, considering the issues involved in speaking, listening, hearing and representing different voices.

Research topics covered include motherhood, sisters, childbirth, mature women students and the self.

Roberts, B. (2002) *Biographical Research*. Buckingham: Open University Press.
A review of the use of life history, oral history, narrative, autobiography, biography and related approaches.

Rose, D. (1998) *Researching Social and Economic Change*. London: Routledge.
An examination of the possibilities and pitfalls of panel studies, as used to analyse social change internationally.

Rose, G. (2006) *Visual Methodologies: An introduction to the interpretation of visual methods*, 2nd edition. London: Sage.
Chapters consider, among other issues, content analysis, semiology, psychoanalysis, visual culture and discourse analysis.

Scarborough, E. and Tanenbaum, E. (eds) (1998) *Research Strategies in the Social Sciences: A guide to new approaches*. Oxford: Oxford University Press.
Focused mainly on quantitative methods. Twelve chapters cover a range of topics from linear structural equation models and categorical data analysis through modelling space and time to game-theoretic models and discourse theory.

Scheurich, J. J. (1997) *Research Method in the Postmodern*. London: Falmer Press.
Considers how postmodernism can be applied to critiquing research approaches and to their reconceptualization. The book goes beyond the philosophical level to show the implications of postmodernism for research practice.

Scott, D. (2000) *Realism and Educational Research: New perspectives and possibilities*. London: Routledge.
Examines the complex issue of power in educational settings, how educational research is being technicized, and how educational researchers are being made accountable for their findings.

Shacklock, G. and Smyth, J. (eds) (1998) *Being Reflexive in Critical Educational and Social Research*. London: Falmer Press.
Thirteen contributions from sixteen authors provide personal, reflexive views of the issues and dilemmas involved in doing educational research. The topics addressed include ethnography, action inquiry, narrative, international development and multiculturalism.

Silverman, D. (2001) *Interpreting Qualitative Data: Methods for analysing talk, text and interaction*, 2nd edition. London: Sage.
Covering the major philosophies of qualitative research, ethnography, symbolic interactions and ethnomethodology, this book focuses on issues of observation, analysis and validity. Uses examples and student exercises.

Smith, L. T. (1999) *Decolonizing Methodologies: Research and indigenous peoples*. London: Zed Press.
This book challenges European epistemology, including emancipatory paradigms. Smith argues that social research methods need decolonizing, and shows how alternative research practices are associated with global indigenous movements.

Stablein, R. and Frost, P. (eds) (2004) *Renewing Research Practice*. Stanford, CA: Stanford Business Books.
Eight researchers in the field of management and organizational studies provide personal accounts of aspects of their research careers, and these are used as the basis for comment and reflection by other researchers.

Todd, Z., Nerlich, B., McKeown, S. and Clarke, D. (eds) (2004) *Mixing Methods in Psychology: The integration of qualitative and quantitative methods in theory and practice*. London: Routledge.
Twelve chapters examine theoretical and historical foundations, the theory and practice of mixing methods, and their place within psychology.

Truman, C., Mertens, D. C. and Humphries, B. (eds) (1999) *Research and Inequality*. London: Routledge.
Examines how issues such as ethnicity, sexuality, disability, gender, ethnicity, health and old age are addressed in research conducted among people who may be the objects of research but who have little control over what is said about them.

Walford, G. (ed.) (1998) *Doing Research About Education*. London: Routledge.
A compilation of accounts of research, including consideration of ethnographic approaches, researching gender and sexuality, longitudinal studies, international projects, directing a research centre, contract cultures and compulsive publishing.

Warren, C. A. B. and Hackney, J. K. (2000) *Gender Issues in Ethnography*, 2nd edition. Thousand Oaks, CA: Sage.
Discusses gender in relation to fieldwork relationships, interviewing and representation.

Webb, E. J., Campbell, D. T., Schwartz, R. D. and Sechrest, L. (2000) *Unobtrusive Measures*, revised edition. Thousand Oaks, CA: Sage.
Reissue of a classic text first published in 1966. Considers the use of physical traces, running records, episodic and private records, simple and contrived observation.

Webster, L. and Mertova, P. (2007) *Using Narrative Inquiry as a Research Method: An introduction to using critical event narrative analysis in research on learning and teaching*. London: Routledge.
Looks at how narrative inquiry can be applied effectively as a means of research in a range of contexts, including flexible, open, distance and workplace learning.

Williams, F., Popay, J. and Oakley, A. (eds) (1998) *Welfare Research: A critical review*. London: UCL Press.
Offers a theoretical and methodological context for research into welfare, and provides examples of research using different concepts (stress, coping, social support and structural inequalities).

Willig, C. (2001) *Introducing Qualitative Research in Psychology: Adventures in theory and method*. Buckingham: Open University Press.
Six distinct approaches are discussed: grounded theory, interpretive

phenomenology, case studies, discursive psychology, Foucauldian discourse analysis, and memory work.

Wodak, R. and Meyer, M. (eds) (2009) *Methods for Critical Discourse Analysis.* London: Sage.

Chapters consider dispositive analysis, the discourse-historical approach, corpus linguistics, and discourse as the recontextualization of social practice.

References

Aldridge, A. and Levine, K. (2001) *Surveying the Social World: Principles and practice in survey research*. Buckingham: Open University Press.

Andrews, J. (2005) Wheeling uphill? Reflections of practical and methodological difficulties encountered in researching the experiences of disabled volunteers. *Disability and Society*, 20(2): 200–12.

Apodaca, P. and Grad, H. (2005) The dimensionality of student ratings of teaching: integration of uni- and multidimensional models. *Studies in Higher Education*, 30(6): 723–48.

Arber, S. and Ginn, J. (1995) Gender differences in the relationship between paid employment and informal care. *Work, Employment and Society*, 9(3): 445–71.

Arbnor, I. and Bjerke, B. (1997) *Methodology for Creating Business Knowledge*. London: Sage.

Atweh, B., Kemmis, S. and Weeks, P. (1998) *Action Research in Practice: Partnerships for social justice in education*. London: Sage.

Bagnoli, A. (2004) Researching identities with multi-method autobiographies. *Sociological Research Online*, 9(2). http://www.socresonline.org.uk/9/2/bagnoli.html.

Barnes, R. (1995) *Successful Study for Degrees*, 2nd edition. London: Routledge.

Berry, R. (2004) *The Research Project: how to write it*, 5th edition. London: Routledge.

Bowling, A. (2002) *Research Methods in Health: Investigating health and health services*, 2nd edition. Buckingham: Open University Press.

Bowman, W. (1992) *'The Ascent of Rum Doodle' and 'The Cruise of the Talking Fish'*. London: Pimlico (first published 1956, 1957 respectively).

Braun, V. and Clarke, V. (2006) Using thematic analysis in psychology. *Qualitative Research in Psychology*, 3: 77–101.

Bruce, C. (1994) Research students' early experiences of the dissertation literature review. *Studies in Higher Education*, 19(2): 217–29.

Bryman, A. (2004) *Social Research Methods*, 2nd edition. Oxford: Oxford University Press.

Burns, R. (2000) *Introduction to Research Methods*. London: Sage.

Butcher, A. (2004) Departures and arrivals: international students returning to the countries of origin. *Asian and Pacific Migration Journal*, 13(3): 275–303.

Calnan, M., Montaner, D. and Horne, R. (2005) How acceptable are innovative healthcare technologies? A survey of public beliefs and attitudes in England and Wales. *Social Science and Medicine*, 60: 1937–48.

Chandra, D. (2004) International migration from Fiji: gender and human development issues. *Asian and Pacific Migration Journal*, 13(2): 179–204.

Chattopadhyay, E. (2005) One foot in each camp: the dual identification of contract workers. *Administrative Science Quarterly*, 50: 68–99.

Cohen, L., Manion, L. and Morrison, K. (2000) *Research Methods in Education*, 5th edition. London: Routledge.

Cohen, L., Manion, L. and Morrison, K. (2007) *Research Methods in Education*, 6th edition. London: Routledge.

Collin, K. and Valleala, U. (2005) Interaction among employees: how does learning take place in the social communities of the workplace and how might such learning be supervised? *Journal of Education and Work*, 18(4): 401–20.

Costello, P. (2003) *Action Research*. London: Continuum.

Crème, P. (2000) The 'personal' in university writing: uses of reflective learning journals. In M. Lea and B. Stierer (eds) *Student Writing in Higher Education: New contexts*. Buckingham: Open University Press, pp. 97–111.

Crème, P. and Lea, M. (1997) *Writing at University: A guide for students*. Buckingham: Open University Press.

Crotty, M. (1998) *The Foundations of Social Research: Meaning and perspective in the research process*. London: Sage.

Davies, H. (2008) Reflexivity in research practice: informed consent with children at school and at home, *Sociological Research Online*, 13(4). http://www.socresonline.org.uk/13/4/5.html (accessed 22 August 2009).

Davis, C. and Salkin, K. (2005) Sisters and friends: dialogue and multivocality in a relational model of sibling disability. *Journal of Contemporary Ethnography*, 34(2): 206–34.

Denzin, N. and Lincoln, Y. (eds) (2005) *Handbook of Qualitative Research*, 3rd edition. Thousand Oaks, CA: Sage.

Dey, I. (1993) *Qualitative Data Analysis: A user-friendly guide for social scientists*. London: Routledge.

Dillon, J. (1990) *The Practice of Questioning*. London: Routledge.

Edwards, A. and Talbot, R. (1999) *The Hard-Pressed Researcher: A research handbook for the caring professions*, 2nd edition. Harlow: Longman.

Fink, A. (2005) *Conducting Research Literature Reviews: From the internet to paper*, 2nd edition. Thousand Oaks, CA: Sage.

Flick, U. (1998) *An Introduction to Qualitative Research*. London: Sage.

Fox, K. (2004) *Watching the English: The hidden rules of English behaviour*. London: Hodder & Stoughton.

Francis, J. (1976) Supervision and examination of higher degree students. *Bulletin of the University of London*, 31: 3–6.

Greenwood, D. and Levin, M. (1998) *Introduction to Action Research: Social research for social change*. Thousand Oaks, CA: Sage.

Griffiths, M. (1998) *Educational Research for Social Justice: Getting off the fence*. Buckingham: Open University Press.

Groenewald, T. (2004) A phenomenological research design illustrated. *International Journal of Qualitative Methods*, 3(1). http://www.ualberta.ca/~iiqm/backissues/3_1/pdf/groenewald.pdf.

Guba, E. and Lincoln, Y. (2005) Paradigmatic controversies, contradictions and emerging confluences. In N. Denzin and Y. Lincoln (eds) *Handbook of Qualitative Research*, 3rd edition. Thousand Oaks, CA: Sage, pp. 191–215.

Hallowell, N., Lawton, J. and Gregory, S. (eds) (2005) *Reflections on Research: The realities of doing research in the social sciences*. Maidenhead: Open University Press.

Hart, C. (1998) *Doing a Literature Review: Releasing the social science research imagination*. London: Sage.

Hart, E. and Bond, M. (1995) *Action Research for Health and Social Care: A guide to practice*. Buckingham: Open University Press.

Hay, I., Bochner, D. and Dungey, C. (2002) *Making the Grade: A guide to successful communication and study*, 2nd edition. Melbourne: Oxford University Press.

Hobbs, D. (1993) Peers, careers and academic fears: writing as fieldwork. In D. Hobbs and T. May (eds) *Interpreting the Field: Accounts of ethnography*. Oxford: Oxford University Press, pp. 45–66.

Holland, J. and Ramazanoglu, C. (1994) Coming to conclusions: power and interpretation in researching young women's sexuality. In M. Maynard and J. Purvis (eds) *Researching Women's Lives From a Feminist Perspective*. London: Taylor & Francis, pp. 125–48.

Hollway, W. and Jefferson, T. (2000) *Doing Qualitative Research Differently: Free association, narrative and the interview method*. London: Sage.

Hughes, C. and Tight, M. (1996) Doughnuts and jam roly poly: sweet metaphors for organisational researchers. *Journal of Further and Higher Education*, 20(1): 51–7.

Kent, G. (2000) Ethical principles. In D. Burton (ed.) *Research Training for Social Scientists*. London: Sage, pp. 61–7.

Kent, J., Williamson, E., Goodenough, T. and Ashcroft, R. (2002) Social science gets the ethics treatment: research governance and ethical review. *Sociological Research Online*, 7(4). http://www.socresonline.org.uk/7/4/williamson.html (accessed 9 March 2005).

Lahteenoja, S. and Pirttila-Backman, A-M. (2005) Cultivation or coddling? University teachers' views on student integration. *Studies in Higher Education*, 30(6): 641–61.

Lancaster University (2005a) *Lancaster University Code of Practice on Postgraduate Research Programmes*. Lancaster: Lancaster University.

Lancaster University (2005b) *Department of Educational Research MA Student Handbook*. Lancaster: Lancaster University Department of Educational Research.

Laws, S., Harper, C. and Marcus, R. (2003) *Research for Development: A practical guide*. London: Sage.

Lee, R. (2000) *Unobtrusive Methods in Social Research*. Buckingham: Open University Press.

Leonard, D. (2001) *A Woman's Guide to Doctoral Studies*. Buckingham: Open University Press.

Letherby, G. (2004) Quoting and counting: an autobiographical response to Oakley. *Sociology*, 38(1): 175–89.

Levin, P. (2005) *Successful Teamwork! For undergraduates and taught postgraduates working on group projects*. Maidenhead: Open University Press.

Lewins, A. and Silver, C. (2009) *Choosing a CAQDAS Package*, 6th edition. http://caqdas. soc.surrey.ac.uk/.

Li, S. (2005) Doing criticism in 'symbiotic niceness': a study of palliative care nurses' talk. *Social Science and Medicine*, 60: 1949–59.

Lipson, J. (1991) The use of self in ethnographic research. In J. Morse (ed.) *Qualitative Nursing Research: A contemporary dialogue*. Newbury Park, CA: Sage, pp. 73–89.

Litosseliti, L. (2003) *Using Focus Groups in Research*. London: Continuum.

Locke, T. (2004) *Critical Discourse Analysis*. London: Continuum.

Mann, C. and Stewart, F. (2000) *Internet Communication and Qualitative Research: A handbook for researching on-line*. London: Sage.

Marshall, C. and Rossman, G. (1999) *Designing Qualitative Research*, 3rd edition. Thousand Oaks, CA: Sage.

Marshall, J. (1995) *Women Managers Moving On: Exploring career and life choices*. London: Routledge.

Mason, J. (1999) *Inheriting Money: Kinship and practical ethics*, Working Paper. Leeds: University of Leeds, Centre for Research on Family, Kinship and Childhood.

Mason, J. (2002) *Qualitative Researching*, 2nd edition. London: Sage.

May, T. (2001) *Social Research: Issues, methods and process*. Buckingham: Open University Press, third edition.

Middleton, S. (1995) Doing feminist educational theory: a postmodernist perspective. *Gender and Education*, 7(1): 87–100.

Mikkelsen, B. (2005) *Methods for Development Work and Research: A new guide for practitioners*, 2nd edition. New Delhi: Sage.

Miles, J. (1994) Defining the research question. In J. Buckeldee and R. McMahon (eds) *The Research Experience in Nursing*. London: Chapman & Hall, pp. 17–29.

Miles, M. and Huberman, A. (eds) (1994) *Qualitative Data Analysis*, 2nd edition. Thousand Oaks, CA: Sage.

Mizrachi, N. and Shuval, J. (2005) Between formal and enacted policy: changing the contours of boundaries. *Social Science and Medicine*, 60: 1649–60.

Morton-Cooper, A. (2000) *Action Research in Health Care*. Oxford: Blackwell.

Munro, A., Holly, L., Rainbird, H. and Leisten, R. (2004) Power at work: reflections on the research process. *International Journal of Social Research Methodology*, 7(4): 289–304.

National Committee of Inquiry into Higher Education (1997) *Higher Education in the Learning Society: Summary report*. London: HMSO.

Nixon, H. (2000) Mediascopes, technoscapes and ideoscapes: educational conundrums for Australian educators. Paper given at British Educational Research Association conference, Cardiff, September.

Oakley, A. (1999) People's way of knowing: gender and methodology. In S. Hood, B. Mayall and S. Oliver (eds) *Critical Issues in Social Research: Power and prejudice*. Buckingham: Open University Press, pp. 154–77.

Papps, F., Walker, M., Trimboli, A. and Trimboli, C. (1995) Parental discipline in Anglo, Greek, Lebanese and Vietnamese cultures. *Journal of Cross-cultural Psychology*, 26(1): 49–64.

Payne, G., Williams, M. and Chamberlain, S. (2004) Methodological pluralism in British sociology. *Sociology*, 38(1): 153–63.

Peacock, W. (1903) *Selected English Essays*. London: Oxford University Press.

Peelo, M. (1994) *Helping Students with Study Problems*. Buckingham: Open University Press.

Phillips, E. M. and Pugh, D. (2005) *How to Get a PhD: A handbook for students and their supervisors*, 4th edition. Maidenhead: Open University Press.

Phizacklea, A. and Wolkowitz, C. (1995) *Homeworking Women*. London: Sage.

Punch, M. (2000) *Developing Effective Research Proposals*. London: Sage.

Punch, M. (2005) *Introduction to Social Research: Quantitative and qualitative approaches*, 2nd edition. London: Sage.

Reed, K. (2007) Bureaucracy and beyond: the impact of ethics and governance procedures on health research in the social sciences, *Sociological Research Online*, 12(5). http://www.socresonline.org.uk/12/5/18.html (accessed 22 August 2009).

Rhodes, C., Nevill, A. and Allan, J. (2004) Valuing and supporting teachers: a survey of teacher satisfaction, dissatisfaction, morale and retention in an English local education authority. *Research in Education*, 71: 67–80.

Richardson, L. (1992) The consequences of poetic representation: writing the other, re-writing the self. In C. Ellis and M. Flaherty (eds) *Investigating Subjectivity: Research on lived experience*. Newbury Park, CA: Sage, pp. 125–40.

Roberts, B. (2002) *Biographical Research*. Buckingham: Open University Press.

Rowley, J., Ray, K., Proud, D., Banwell, L., Spink, S., Thoams, R. and Urquhart, C. (2004)

Using action research to investigate the use of digital information resources in further education. *Journal of Further and Higher Education*, 28(3): 235–46.

Sapsford, R. (1999) *Survey Research*. London: Sage.

Savage, M. (2008) Histories, belongings, communities. *International Journal of Social Research Methodology*, 11(2): 151–62.

Schatzman, L. and Strauss, A. (1973) *Field Research: Strategies for a natural sociology*. Englewood Cliffs, NJ: Prentice-Hall.

Simnett, R. and Wright, A. (2005) The portfolio of knowledge required by industry specialist auditors. *Accounting and Business Research*, 35(1): 87–101.

Strauss, A. (1987) *Qualitative Analysis for Social Scientists*. Cambridge: Cambridge University Press.

Styhre, A., Backman, M. and Borjesson, S. (2005) The gendered machine: concept car development at Volvo Car Corporation. *Gender, Work and Organization*, 12(6): 551–71.

Thapar-Bjorkert, S. and Henry, M. (2004) Reassessing the research relationship: location, position and power in fieldwork accounts. *International Journal of Social Research Methodology*, 7(5): 363–81.

Thomson, A. (1996) *Critical Reasoning: A practical introduction*. London: Routledge.

Tight, M. (2000) Reporting on academic work and life: a year of *The Times Higher Education Supplement*. In M. Tight (ed.) *Academic Work and Life: What it is to be an academic, and how this is changing*. New York: Elsevier Science, pp. 405–40.

Tight, M. (2003) *Researching Higher Education*. Maidenhead: Open University Press.

Tizard, B. and Hughes, M. (1991) Reflections on *Young Children Learning*. In G. Walford (ed.) *Doing Educational Research*. London: Routledge, pp. 19–40.

Torgerson, C. (2003) *Systematic Reviews*. London: Continuum.

Townsend, P. (1996) The struggle for independent statistics on poverty. In R. Levitas and W. Guy (eds) *Interpreting Official Statistics*. London: Routledge, pp. 26–44.

Truman, C. (2003) Ethics and the ruling relations of research production. *Sociological Research Online*, 8(1). http://www.socresonline.org.uk/8/1/truman.html.

Turner, B. (1994) Patterns of crisis behaviour: a qualitative inquiry. In A. Bryman and R. Burgess (eds) *Analysing Qualitative Data*. London: Routledge, pp. 195–215.

Walford, G. (2001) *Doing Qualitative Educational Research: A personal guide to the research process*. London: Continuum.

Walter, T. and Siebert, A. (1993) *Student Success: How to succeed at college and still have time for your friends*, 6th edition. Fort Worth, TX: Harcourt Brace Jovanovich College Publishers.

Ward, J. (2008) Researching drug sellers: an 'experiential' account from 'the field', *Sociological Research Online*, 13(1). http://www.socresonline.org.uk/13/1/14.html (accessed 22 August 2009).

Webb, L., Walker, K. and Bollis, T. (2004) Feminist pedagogy in the teaching of research methods. *International Journal of Social Research Methodology*, 7(5): 415–28.

Wilkinson, D. and Birmingham, P. (2003) *Using Research Instruments: A guide for researchers*. London: RoutledgeFalmer.

Wilson, D. (2004) 'Keeping quiet' or 'going nuts': strategies used by young, black men in custody. *The Howard Journal*, 43(3): 317–30.

Witmer, D., Colman, R. and Katzman, S. (1999) 'From paper-and-pencil to screen-and-keyboard: toward a methodology for survey research on the internet. In S. Jones (ed.) *Doing Internet Research: Critical issues and methods for examining the net*. Thousand Oaks, CA: Sage, pp. 145–61.

Woolf, V. (1995) *Killing the Angel in the House*. Harmondsworth: Penguin (the quote is from a lecture given in 1931).

Yin, R. (2003) *Applications of Case Study Research*, 2nd edition. Thousand Oaks, CA: Sage.

Zuram, D. (n.d.) 'PhD's: what they don't tell you', at http://www.findaphd.com/students/life1.asp (accessed 23 August 2009).

Index